THE WELSH ARSENAL

Dedicated to all those who worked at the factory.
And especially to those who were killed there.

ROF 53

Here, the Almighty God of souls and stars
Has been relegated to the 'Dirty' side
With hedgehogs and moles,
Marsh-mallows and campions,
Cornflowers and the meadow-sweet;

The devil has the 'Cleanway' to himself,
Made clear and smooth,
And polished for his most insolent stride,
To keep him in good humour,
Lest he should loose his temper
And explode,
And bring our coaxing, pleading efforts to defeat.

And so it is throughout the wide and suffering world these feverish days:
God is put aside, as if in some cold-storage,
While men and women toil and mourn, and curse and sweat in pain
Cajoling and harnessing the devil for his handiwork of wreck and ruin,
Of blast and blaze;
The devil kow-towed to, feted, toasted,

That God – so it is whispered – may later come into His own again!

Huw Menai Williams (1887-1961)
INO 387, T&P Section, ROF 53.
Published in *ROF 53 News*

MJ Clubb
with P Tapper

THE WELSH ARSENAL

Gwasg Blaen-y-Wawr

Published by Gwasg Blaen-y-Wawr
116 Merthyr Mawr Road
Bridgend

First published 2007
Reprinted 2009

ISBN 978-0-9557615-0-8
A CIP record for this title is available from
the British Library

Cover design: Simon Hicks

Printed in Plantin by Bell & Bain, Glasgow

Contents

List of Illustrations

ROF 53
(bottom right) Main Admin building; (bottom left) power station cooling tower;
(centre left) Tremains railway station

Introduction

If you climb from the banks of the River Ogwr at Bridgend, up the steep slope of Newcastle Hill, you will reach the remains of an ancient castle built to defend the ford below. From its crumbling stones look north east and see in the distance the still high towers of Coity Castle, which for centuries protected the lands seized by the Norman invader Payn de Turberville. To the south of Coity lie the walls of Ewenny Priory, raised many centuries ago to protect the spiritual life within. Further down the Ewenny River moulders Ogmore Castle, ruined guardian of the passage across the river.

One thing the historian learns: mankind does not change. There is always a need for security to be protected. Within this quadrilateral of defensive structures lies the site of a huge armaments Factory, ROF 53, Wales' Arsenal, constructed nearly seventy years ago, and serviced by tens of thousands of workers labouring in an empire of a thousand buildings. All this gigantic construction and effort was as much a part of a defensive system as ever Newcastle, Ewenny, Coity and Ogmore were.

The story of this Factory is an extraordinary story, or at least the story of thousands of extraordinary lives – thousands of people whose lives were disrupted in a way that the generations that have come after can hardly imagine. Total war tore these people from the familiar to the unknown, displaced them from comfortable, accustomed routine to the alien and frightening. People were sent from London and from Ireland to south Wales, from all the communities of Glamorgan to Bridgend, from their families to a factory, from domestic work to making weapons, from retail shop to workshop. Planners, landowners, engineers, builders, miners, carpenters, railway men, managers, foremen, scientists, chocolate makers, and especially tens of thousands of women, all experienced, suddenly, dramatic changes in the established, ordinary and accepted pattern of their lives.

The individuals who worked in ROF 53 could not have been aware of their total combined contribution, of the many millions of different components produced in the Factory. But what the workforce achieved together in those few exceptional years amounted to a very great deal indeed in the defence of Britain. Some, a very few of the workers, not two dozen, were killed; their total sacrifice is every bit as worthy of remembrance as that of the service men and women whose names are inscribed on war memorials across Britain. The vast majority of employees at the Factory survived. Then, as suddenly as it began, it was ended. Those who worked at ROF 53 went back to the lives they had expected. Except that the experience had changed many for ever. They had a new purpose, even a new identity; no longer shop girl or miner or daughter, but war worker, factory worker.

Gradually over the years the physical remains of the Arsenal have been demolished. Still in some corners of the area you can find evidence of the greatest change ever to overtake what had been a sleepy market town. The Arsenal's administrative building is still here – now the HQ of South Wales Police; the pattern of streets on the Industrial Estate is largely a legacy of ROF 53; a huge blast wall at a still-functioning water pumping station can be seen near Coychurch; one of the great magazine caverns built into the north of Brackla hill is still used as a modern storage facility; South Wales Police sports teams play on what was the burning grounds for defective munitions at Waterton; if you look closely at the side of the main railway line to Cardiff you can just make out the remains of the Tremains platform where thousands of people arrived every day; some houses in Coychurch Road were originally built to house the managers brought down from the Woolwich Arsenal in London; at Island Farm one hut remains of the hostel built for women workers; on the top of Brackla Hill is the reservoir built to service the Factory.

Little enough to remind a new generation of the effort and sacrifice that went on during the war. And yet, as Arthur Askey used to sing about munition workers[1]:

> She's not what you would call a heroine at all.
> I don't suppose you even know her name.
> Though she never boasts of her important post,
> She strikes a blow for Britain, just the same.

Some former workers resent this lack of awareness. Eunice Jones commented,

> We had no recognition whatever. We worked there on explosives: they could have given us a medal or something.

On BBC Radio Wales two employees expressed similar feelings:

> We had no uniform: we had nothing to say where we worked or what we did. I don't even think we had a thank you at the end of it.
>
> There is nothing to say that this was originally built as an ROF factory, and so many people were killed, and so many injured. Other than in people's memories it's nonexistent.

This book is written as a tribute that may remedy this deficiency, by recording the extraordinary achievement of so very many people, men and women, so many years ago; that they will not be forgotten when the last memory fades.

At Last – Recognition

As a result of the initial publication of this book, the members of Bridgend Civic Trust decided in 2009 to erect a monument in Dunraven Place, Bridgend in tribute to all who worked at the Arsenal, and especially those who were killed. At long last: recognition for the contribution and the sacrifices made by the people of Glamorgan and beyond to victory in the Second World War.

Notes

1 In the song 'The Girls who made the Thing-ummy-bobs' by Thompson and Heneker, 1942.

1: A New Woolwich

Bridgend and Berlin

> Bridgend (Pop.9,000), is a pleasant residential and market town situated on the river Ogmore, and having few points of interest in itself. – *Glamorgan,* CJO Evans

On the evening of 30th January 1933, most of the inhabitants of this small and very ordinary Welsh town were at home warming themselves by the fireside. Seven hundred miles to the east things were very different. In Berlin, the capital of Germany, the excited streets were thronged with triumphant uniformed storm troopers, celebrating noisily with torchlight parades the appointment of a new Chancellor, their leader, Adolf Hitler. No one could know then, no one could guess, that as a result of this man's policies the quiet fields and hills near Bridgend would be converted within a very few years into one of the largest armaments factories in the world, covering over 1,000 acres and employing more than 32,000 people from all over the south of Wales and beyond.

What then was the link between those dark events in Berlin and the peaceful meadows of Glamorgan? In accord with the terms of the Treaty of Versailles, signed after the end of the First World

War, German armed forces had been reduced to a minimum. One of Nazism's main aims was to restore Germany's pride and to make her a great power again; inevitably this included rearmament. In 1934 Hitler ordered a rapid expansion of German forces, and the weapons industry needed to supply them. British military leaders advised, and the British Government gradually and reluctantly began to accept, that the United Kingdom also must rearm – either to deter an approaching war, or to meet it if it came.

Dispersal from London

As part of this reappraisal the staff of the War Office began to look at Britain's capacity to produce large amounts of ammunition. At this time the principal armaments factory was the Royal Ordnance Factory (ROF), or Arsenal, at Woolwich on the Thames in south east London[1]. The Defence Requirements Committee decided in 1934[2] that Woolwich was outdated and vulnerable: outdated in that a modern factory had new higher safety requirements, and needed much more space; vulnerable because London was within easy range of Hitler's developing Luftwaffe. This last fear was publicly expressed by Churchill, who

Woolwich Arsenal Central Offices

described the capital as 'the greatest target in the world, a kind of tremendous fat valuable cow tied up to attract the beast of prey,' and predicted 'the crack of bombs exploding in London, with cataracts of masonry, and fire, and smoke.' The War Office was not in the habit of expressing concerns quite so vividly, but the committee under Douglas Hacking[3] did recommend the removal of the ROF's entire manufacturing capacity to less vulnerable places – a decision endorsed by the Cabinet in July 1935. The pessimism of Churchill and of the War Office would be entirely justified. Woolwich was attacked on the very first day of the London Blitz (7th September 1940): on that day there were 300 casualties, the fuze factory and several storehouses were burned down, and the filling factory badly damaged. During the course of the war, as a result of aerial bombardment, a total of 103 workers at the Woolwich Arsenal were killed, and 770 injured.

Meanwhile the ROF had already begun to look for safe and suitable places away from the southeast of England. The chosen site had to be extensive and relatively level, have a reliable water supply, have access to a large pool of labour, and be easily accessible by railway. In south Wales the Great Western Railway Company identified for examination four possible sites adjacent to its lines[4]. Thus it was that on 3rd May 1935 officials from Woolwich stood for the first time among the farms and trees, the hedges and sheep of Glamorgan, and pronounced Bridgend to be the most suitable of the four sites for the construction of an armaments factory in southern Wales.

Reasons Why Not

But other parts of Britain had been examined as well. And the military preferred a site at Euxton, near Chorley in Lancashire, objecting strongly to the Bridgend suggestion for a number of reasons.

In the first place the Air Ministry (apparently preparing to re-fight the Napoleonic wars) pointed out that the area is

> approximately 150 miles from the nearest part of France, and at that distance French bombers would traverse only 50 miles of enemy territory [to reach Bridgend].

In addition southern Wales was within 350 miles of the Low Countries. In other words, Bridgend could be bombed, while Chorley was a more distant and difficult target. Compounding this was the objection, that the site 'could be fairly easily located from the air on account of the closeness of the Severn.' Certainly both Cardiff and Swansea would later see the usefulness to the Luftwaffe of 'Severn's silver flood' as a guide, though the Arsenal at Bridgend was never, in fact, to be attacked by German bombers.

The second objection was that there were serious transport problems. Philip Massey commented at the time in his book *Industrial South Wales*,

> There are vast numbers of Londoners who seem to regard a journey to South Wales as a terrible undertaking. The constant re-iteration that South Wales is inaccessible, whereas Manchester is regarded as close at hand does show a lamentable lack of knowledge.

More seriously the Bridgend plant as envisaged in 1935 would need to rely on a supply of empty shell cases from the Midlands of England, and the unjustified fears were about the rail links between the two. Massey dismissed the concerns with the remark that

> both inside South Wales, and for a longer distance, the railways are capable of handling a volume of traffic vastly greater than at present.

A final objection raised in Cabinet was that the south Wales valleys were liable to flooding. Certainly parts of the proposed site were marshy, especially towards the village of Coychurch, but the comment does seem to represent an appalling lack of knowledge of the area – perhaps typical of the provincialism of many Londoners.

Overall the War Office declared, with perhaps just a hint of exasperation, 'that Chorley has every advantage over the Bridgend site, except that it is not situated in an area which is at present labelled 'Depressed'.' This was an unsubtle suggestion from the Chiefs of Staff that the motive behind the push for a factory in south Wales was political rather than military.

In fact behind the scenes there appears to have been a powerful political factor driving the case for Chorley. This factor had nothing to do with military needs, or vulnerability, or accessibility, or even flooding, but more to good old-fashioned party political advantage. As we have seen, the chair of the committee on the redistribution of ROFs was a Conservative politician, Douglas Hacking. At the time he was Financial Secretary to the War Office, and so was in an advantageous position to influence the deliberations. And significantly, he had been the Member of Parliament for the Chorley division of Lancashire since 1915. Surely it can have been no coincidence that Chorley was eventually chosen – there were not many Conservative MPs in South Wales who would benefit from the choice of Bridgend. No wonder that when he resigned his seat before the Labour landslide of 1945, and was raised to the peerage, he took the title of Baron Hacking of Chorley.

Reasons Why

The word 'Depressed' does tell us why Bridgend had been considered in the first place. These were years of despair and misery in much of Wales[5]. The collapse of the coal and metallurgical industries had put many thousands out of work, and reduced many families to poverty and hunger. At the start of 1935 over 150,000 were unemployed – some 36% of registered workers. And this even though hundreds of thousands of Welsh people had emigrated to English regions to find work – in fact 430,000 left Wales between 1921 and 1949. Much of south Wales had recently been declared a Special (in this context meaning 'Specially Depressed') Area, but the Government's policies had hardly scratched the surface of the economic problems of the principality. It was for these reasons that the commissioner for the Wales Special Area, Sir Malcolm Stewart[6], now urged the Cabinet to set an example by building the new armaments factory in southern Wales.

Certainly a continental war seemed far less immediate than the pressing domestic problems of economic collapse, and the dangers it brought of civil disorder. The Cabinet had been warned on 3rd and 4th February of the intensity of feeling in the south Wales valleys by the demonstrations of 300,000 Welsh people against the Government's policies towards the unemployed. It was no surprise that Ramsey Macdonald (Prime Minister to June

1935), his successor Stanley Baldwin, and the Chancellor of the Exchequer, Neville Chamberlain, all strongly supported the claims of the south of Wales. Such a large industrial undertaking would not only employ large numbers in construction and subsequent production, but it would also stimulate the growth of many local firms, and attract other enterprises into the area to serve the needs of the ROF. All this would in turn reduce the huge pool of the unemployed in the Welsh valley communities – something that the National Government had failed to do by any other means.

Despite the pressing economic and social needs of southern Wales, military – and Conservative party political – priorities prevailed, and planning started for a factory at Chorley, not at Bridgend. But matters on the continent continued to deteriorate. Hitler was beginning to ignore the Treaty of Versailles: conscription was introduced in Germany, and the British Government did not help matters by signing a separate Pact allowing the expansion of Germany's navy. Hitler meanwhile was busy making inflated claims about the progress of his rearmament, claims that were accepted by British intelligence[7]; this in turn made military planners eager to expand the production of munitions. In May Baldwin declared that Britain faced 'a time of emergency': on October 3rd the sense of crisis was intensified when Mussolini sent Italian troops to invade Abyssinia.

For these reasons, and within a very short time, the chiefs of staff increased their demands for weapons. At the insistence of the Robinson Committee (set up to organize the 'Removal of the Filling and Cordite Factories') the Bridgend site was re-examined in October 1935. Enticed by the prospect of a second factory, and so more ammunition, attitudes in London changed. Now the objections mysteriously melted away: arguments were suddenly found in favour of Bridgend:

> It was after all, it transpired, sufficiently far from the coast to be safe, and there were happily no obvious landmarks nearby to guide the bombers in.
>
> The area was level, and there was luckily plenty of land available for purchase; flooding was apparently no longer a problem.

The geological conditions were not unfavourable, and Brackla Hill was ideal for the excavation of the underground magazines[8].

A huge pool of labour existed within a relatively small radius, yet there was fortunately no large urban district in the immediate vicinity to attract bombing.

Transport, it emerged, was no longer a worry: the site was after all conveniently adjacent to the existing mainline railway for ease of bringing in the workforce, for importing shell cases and explosive materials, and for exporting the finished product.

Finally strategic advantages in having more than one factory were discovered – an insurance in case of accidental disaster or enemy action.

Bridgend is Chosen

So the Bridgend site was recommended by the Robinson Committee in December 1935: this was accepted by Woolwich and by the Cabinet in the following weeks.

In November 1935 Baldwin had won a General Election during which he asked the electorate for power to 'remedy the deficiencies which have occurred in our defences' – though he also gave them his word 'that there will be no great armaments' –

Prime Minister Stanley Baldwin

a promise that would prove impossible to keep. The first indication the people of Wales had that a factory was to be built was on 2nd March 1936 when the Prime Minister, no less, declared that a site 'somewhere in south Wales' had been chosen for a second armaments factory. The announcement was made to the House of Commons not during a debate on defence, as might be expected, but in the course of one on the Special Areas. This seems to indicate that that the Bridgend Factory was still regarded by the government as important for economic and political reasons. Baldwin must have felt particular satisfaction in making the decision known personally. He had succeeded in his campaign despite the initial opposition of the forces chiefs, and was able to claim that the government was doing something both for the unemployed of Wales, and for the defence of the realm.

The *Western Mail* of the following morning saw things exactly as Baldwin did. Underneath the banner headline

GOVERNMENT FACTORY FOR SOUTH WALES

and the tantalising

SITE DECIDED UPON BUT NOT REVEALED

came two more headlines which together gave the two main explanations for the announcement

PART OF RE-ARMAMENT PROGRAMME
SCHEME TO ABSORB LARGE AMOUNTS OF LABOUR

Five days after Baldwin's announcement, Hitler's army marched into the Rhineland.

The exact location of the new Government factory could not be kept a secret for long. The *Western Mail* of May 20th revealed excitedly that 'further developments in Bridgend' had been 'current in the Parliamentary Lobby' the previous evening: this was linked with plans already public for the construction of new railway sidings 'north of the by-pass road[9]'. A *Glamorgan Gazette* reporter wrote in the edition of 22nd May that the War Office had purchased the 121 acre Waterton Court Farm from Mr. W. D. Griffiths 'for the purpose of building an ammunition factory'. Thirty other owners of land between Bridgend, Coychurch and Coity had been asked to name their price. Finally, on the morning of 26th May 1936, the *Western Mail* was confident enough to proclaim

BRIDGEND AS "WOOLWICH ARSENAL"
OF THE FUTURE

and to declare that, 'There seems little doubt that the Mid Glamorgan town is destined to play an important part in the new defence programme of this country,' even though 'no information can be obtained at the War Office' confirming any of this, since 'until negotiations for the huge slice of land required are completed nothing will be officially revealed.'[10]

But this was a position that could not be maintained. Later that same day the government's choice was officially confirmed by the Secretary of State for War, Duff Cooper[11], in a Parliamentary answer to George Hicks, the MP for East Woolwich (whose constituents had nearly as much interest in the Government's plans as the people of Glamorgan did). Duff Cooper announced that 'the War Office has under consideration… localities less open to air attack' and that 'two sites have been selected for factories for the operation of filling ammunition with explosives; one at

10

BRIDGEND AS "WOOLWICH ARSENAL" OF THE FUTURE

No Official Statement Until Land Deal is Completed

By OUR OWN CORRESPONDENT

LONDON, Monday.

There is still no official information regarding the scope and character of the Government works to be established in the Bridgend neighbourhood.

There seems little doubt, however, that this Mid-Glamorgan town is destined to play an important part in the new defence programme of this country.

The fact that the War Office is solely responsible for the negotiations lends support to the suggestion that Bridgend is to be the "Woolwich Arsenal" of the future.

No information, however, can be obtained at the War Office. They say that until negotiations for the huge slice of land required are completed nothing will be officially revealed.

PEMBROKE DOCK'S DISMAY

Placing of New Armament Works

By A CORRESPONDENT

Rumours that the new arsenal is to be built at Bridgend have caused dismay at Pembroke Dock.

From time to time since the Government's armaments expansion proposals were announced Pembroke Dock and its environs have been mentioned as a probable centre of armament activity, but it seems as if the optimism of the inhabitants and civic leaders has been sadly misplaced.

TRANSFER OF LABOUR

What is the Government going to do for Pembroke Dock? The town was thrown on the industrial scrap-heap by the Government's action in 1926 in [illegible]

14

NATURE OF GOVERNMENT WORKS AT BRIDGEND

Factory for Filling Ammunition With Explosives

FROM OUR OWN CORRESPONDENT

LONDON, Tuesday.

Speedy confirmation was forthcoming in the House of Commons today of the exclusive announcement in this morning's *Western Mail & South Wales News* that part of Woolwich Arsenal was to be transferred to Bridgend.

In a written answer to the following question by Mr. E. G. Hicks, Socialist M.P. for East Woolwich:—

To ask the Secretary of State for War whether he is in a position to state what localities have been selected as sites for the new ordnance factories on removal from Woolwich Arsenal.

Mr. Duff Cooper stated:

The War Office have had under consideration the provision in localities less open to air attack of certain of the factory activities now carried on at Woolwich Arsenal and Waltham Abbey.

Two sites have been selected for factories for the operation of filling ammunition with explosives, one at Chorley, in Lancashire, and one at Bridgend, in South Wales.

A third site in Scotland is under consideration for a factory for the manufacture of explosives, but it is not possible at present to state the precise locality, as inquiries have not yet been completed.

Reports in the *Western Mail*, May 26 and 27, 1936

Chorley in Lancashire, and one at Bridgend, in South Wales.'

The announcement was greeted with huge excitement by that rare breed, Welsh Conservative MPs.[12] Their joy was entirely in the anticipation of economic improvement and increased employment, rather than in the strengthening of Britain's forces. Reginald Clarry, MP for Newport, rejoiced that the new work would 'do a great deal to relieve unemployment in Wales...and give a definite fillip to the steel industry, and indirectly to the coal industry.' Temple Morris, MP for Cardiff East, enthused that 'it should lead to great developments and bring new hope and employment to many people in Glamorgan.' More precisely he promised that 'it offers infinite possibilities of developing the Bridgend and Porthcawl areas.'

Opposition

But the news that an armaments factory was to be built at Bridgend was not received in Wales with universal or uncomplicated joy. For example, Pembroke Dock, a town 'thrown on the industrial scrap-heap by the Government' in 1926 through the closure of the naval dockyards, experienced despair and dismay as civic leaders had nurtured hopes that the factory would be built there.

There was opposition, too, in Maesteg. In 1934, when the building of war-related establishments in the area had first been suggested, Arthur Edwards, a local councillor, had expressed his opposition to such developments in dramatic language[13]. He claimed that the unemployed of Maesteg would not want to be 'employed in manufacturing deadly armaments.' He went on to affirm that 'people would rather starve than work at making armaments to kill others.' Despite Edwards' denunciation on behalf of his people, subsequent employment patterns seem to show that it was unlikely that many of his electors would in fact prefer destitution to working in the Arsenal.

Ambivalence towards the news was clearly shown in the comments of Ted Williams, the local Labour MP: 'While I welcome employment for a distressed area like my constituency, it is difficult to feel elated over the nature of the industry that is to provide employment'. Williams expressed his dilemma perfectly thus:

> South Wales has been clamouring for something to be done for the area. Of course that makes it difficult to complain that the government does not give us exactly what we want.

The Welsh Nationalist Party had no such inhibitions; it had always campaigned fiercely against the building of any military establishments in Wales. In May the *Echo*'s cartoonist JC Walker lampooned Plaid Cymru's opposition. He caricatured their leader, Saunders Lewis[14], as a hot-head needing to be dipped in a 'Horse-sense Trough' of cold water for trying to obstruct the chances of work; meanwhile Dame Wales welcomed the Government's plans for the jobs that they would bring to 'that sane lad of mine,' the unemployed of Wales. In September three members of Plaid, including Lewis[15], showed that they were prepared to back their words of opposition to government plans with action, and they set fire to a building at a new RAF training base at Penyberth near Pwllheli in Llyn.

At the same time, in association with the Welsh Churches in Cardiff, the party appealed to Glamorgan County Council to oppose the War Office's plans for Bridgend, on the grounds that the project showed the 'callous indifference of the government' to the needs of the area, and that the factory would 'do great harm to the locality, destroying beauty and charm.' The County Council agreed to debate Plaid's stand[16], and several Councillors attacked the plan for the new Arsenal. Councillor the Rev. David M Jones (Cwmaber, Caerphilly), representing the pacifist lobby, called it 'one of the maddest things ever undertaken.' He urged the Government to 'set their energies on the establishment of peace in the world, instead of spending money on armaments.'

The communist Councillor Lewis Jones[17] (Tonypandy), with an eye to the interests of his voters, was particularly incensed that the project was planned for a green field site, and near Bridgend. Obviously he wanted the factory to be built in an industrial area – presumably in the Rhondda – though where the large level area of land would be found there is a mystery. He declared: 'If munitions works were to be erected, it should be in the industrial areas at

SOUTH WALES ECHO AND EXPRESS, MONDAY, MAY 25, 1936.

CARTOON BY J. C. WALKER

WHAT DAME WALES SAYS

DAME WALES: You go ahead, sir, and give that sane lad of mine a job while I coo off this hot-head.

(The Welsh Nationalist Party is opposing the Government scheme to build air bases etc., in Wales.)

present declined', and not 'in the beautiful Vale of Glamorgan.' When the vote was taken at the end of the debate, the socialist-dominated Council carried the motion to oppose the Government's plan.

Great Expectations

Thus after years of demanding government action to provide work, the County Council objected to this sudden promise of jobs because the Factory was to make weapons, and because it was to be built in an area of beauty and agricultural value. The environmentally conscious twenty-first century might have some sympathy with the concerns of the councillors; not surprisingly the council vote provoked fury in Bridgend itself.

Already in May 1936 the *Glamorgan Gazette* had eagerly predicted that the proposed Factory would 'bring more trade to the town and so provide an indirect means of relieving unemployment'. In September the *Western Mail* reported the opinion of an indignant Bridgend shopkeeper that the County Council 'should be the last to prevent the establishment of the new works'; anticipating lower rates, he claimed that new jobs would reduce the number of the unemployed, and that this would reduce the County's Rate – which was 'breaking the backs of every tradesman.' Indeed at that time 40% of the county rate was charged for Public Assistance to help the unemployed. (6s. 6d out of a total rate of 16s. 9d in the £) And local landowners, eager for a profitable sale, were quick to claim that the land earmarked could not be called valuable because 90% was used for grazing.

The Town Council debated the issue on 22nd September. Councillor Banner began by deploring 'the conditions which compel the making of armaments' but affirmed that 'as things are in the world today it is necessary, and it is our duty to support it.' He complained that 'a wave of public opinion …unfavourable to the factory coming to Bridgend' had been created, and suggested that the Bridgend Council 'should express our satisfaction at the works coming.' He raised the issue of the county rate and complained that of the increase of 5½d just announced, 4¾d was for Public Assistance. Like the indignant shopkeeper, he believed that the Council had

> no right to oppose anything which will tend to promote more work in the area.

Councillor Williams invoked fair play when he pronounced that

> the government has been pressed to put factories in our area, and I think it is very bad form that this opposition should come so late in the day.

Councillor Oates referred to the concerns that had been expressed about the loveliness of the area when he declared that 'beauty will not fill empty stomachs.' He went further and showed himself apparently prepared to enter into a Faustian contract: 'if Old Nick himself established a factory, I would support that.'

Councillor Field referred to the 'aimless, hopeless' lines of the unemployed when he declared that the County Councillors 'talk

of beauty spots, but it was no beauty spot to see the men standing about on Station Hill.'

Finally the Chairman contemptuously dismissed the County Council vote opposing the Factory with: 'the resolution is too ridiculous to be taken much notice of.' Unsurprisingly, the meeting closed with the passing of a motion

> expressing appreciation on behalf of the people of Bridgend of the works coming to the town.

The last comment on the County Council came in another *Echo* cartoon by JC Walker – which might not be seen as very 'correct' today. The drawing was headed 'WRONG BODY INSIDE,' and is recognisably set on the road outside the walls of the Angleton Hospital at Penyfai. Bridgend was the location of several large 'mental asylums' and Walker suggested in the cartoon that the existing inmates, driven 'nuts' by heavy rates, were the Bridgend Ratepayers; these he proposed should be joined inside the asylum by the obviously mad members of Glamorgan County Council, who had voted against the Arsenal.

In fact, of course, the County Council was powerless to prevent the Imperial Government building the Factory. And expectations in the area were high. According to the *Western Mail*, Bridgend business people had experienced 'unbounded joy,' and were looking forward to more prosperous times. A local auctioneer breathlessly claimed to have had as many as six inquiries from English industrial firms. Owners of quarries in the Ewenny area anticipated a huge demand for hardcore to provide a firm foundation for the Factory. The *Gazette* perceptively predicted that 'the whole trend of the social and industrial life of Bridgend and the Vale of Glamorgan will be to a great extent changed within the next few years.' The newspaper contrasted the current situation, in which depression was indicated by 'the small numbers visiting the town from the valleys,' with a future of work for thousands of munitions workers from the local area; a time was promised when the streets of Bridgend, if not quite paved with gold, or flowing with milk and honey, would again be 'filled to capacity on Saturday nights' – an indication, apparently, of returning prosperity. And social stratification showed in the hopes of the golf clubs at Porthcawl, Southerndown and Kenfig that the officials of the Woolwich Arsenal who would be coming to Wales to run the new enterprise would join, increasing their membership – and funds.

Hope Deferred

Despite all this acrimonious debate, neither hopes nor fears were to be fulfilled for a long time, since apart from the surveying of the site and the sinking of trial bore holes very little work began till October 1937 – nearly two years after the initial announcement. Why this lengthy delay?

In the first place there was no real sense of urgency from the government. The purpose of rearmament at that time was not to wage war, but to act as a deterrent to Hitler, and so to ensure the peace of Europe. To that end announcements of plans were perhaps as effective as actual buildings on the ground. As the historian of British war production, M.M. Postan, wrote,

> the early stages of rearmament were dominated by the need for a deterrent display – a front line strength impressive on paper, but not necessarily backed by sufficient establishments.

And of course Chamberlain, who became Prime Minister in May 1937, believed that negotiation with Hitler over Germany's 'legitimate' grievances would prevent hostilities. He had the support of most people: no sensible Briton wanted a rerun of the carnage of the First World War.

Secondly, armaments factories are expensive and have to be paid for, and politicians then as now were in no hurry to court unpopularity by having to increase taxation. Chamberlain summarised this dilemma nicely in February 1938, when he said:

> A gigantic scheme of rearmament is essential to the maintenance of peace: I have never ceased to deplore what seems to me a shameless waste of money.

The general attitude in Downing Street seemed to be to hope that the need for expensive rearmament would go away, and so the wretched thing in south Wales might never be built.

The third delaying agent was the Treasury, which, as usual, saw its role as guardian of the public purse as more important than the interests of the nation. Current economic theory blamed government extravagance in part for the depression. Thus as late as 1938 Sir John Simon, the Chancellor of the Exchequer was objecting to expenditure on rearmament on the grounds that it would undermine the UK's ability to finance a long war: even on the first day of the war Simon could say that the country was spending more on armaments than it could afford! Accordingly, in October 1936 the Treasury sanctioned the building of Chorley, but refused to approve expenditure at Bridgend on the grounds that the plans were not specific enough. In the icy bureaucratese of Whitehall the Treasury dismissed the War Office with: 'the matter is not ripe for presentation to the Chancellor.'

The War Office itself did not help to expedite matters; detailed planning was made difficult by delays and uncertainties over the exact size and role of Bridgend. In February 1936, 450 acres had been deemed sufficient: this was doubled to 900 in May, and to 1,040 by August. These planning changes were in turn a factor of the time taken by the different branches of the armed services to decide what weapons they needed: then Woolwich had to work out what would be produced at Chorley – all this before Bridgend's role and capacity could be determined. There was, then, according to William Hornby, in the official history of Second World War factories, a limited knowledge of the most suitable structures for a modern filling factory. Woolwich was far too old to be a guide, and the experience of the First World War was of limited use because of the many subsequent developments in weapons and components, the much greater variety of ammunition to fill, the many different compositions that had been developed, and the introduction of new regulations governing the spacing of munitions buildings and other safety aspects. The latest government standards were important factors affecting the eventual cost of the construction, and the considerable length of time taken to complete the Factory at Bridgend.

Plans are Laid

Planning serious and detailed enough to satisfy the Treasury began at Woolwich by the end of 1936, and went on for most of the following year. This work was under the overall control of Sir Francis Carnegie, the Chief Superintendent, but was actually carried out by the Chief Mechanical Engineer and the skilled technical staff of the Engineering Department (Filling) at Woolwich. The engineer in charge of the design of the site and its buildings was Percy Masters[18].

Meanwhile, at Bridgend, the Office of Works' Chief Surveyor, S.E.Scammell, and his staff began the task of surveying the land purchased for the Factory. One unintended consequence of this process was the identification of two important archaeological sites to the north of Brackla Hill, and therefore on the site intended for the magazines. Scammell informed the authorities at the National Museum in Cardiff, and in April and August 1937 both these cairns were excavated before the bulldozers could move in[19]. The burial mounds appeared to contain Bronze Age internments dating from between 1600 and 1300 BC. Both had stone burial chambers at their centre, and both chambers had urns containing the remains of cremations. One of these cremations had used coal brought to the site from an outcrop over a mile away – the first evidence of the use of coal in Wales. Also found were flint tools, a bronze pin, and grains of wheat and barley: the first scientific record of Bronze Age food grains in southern Britain. There was proof of activity during the Roman period as well, including a Romano-British pot. The cairns cannot be visited today: both were casualties of war – destroyed in the building of the Arsenal.

By the beginning of 1937 staff at Woolwich had the experience of planning the sister establishment at Chorley, plus a more certain knowledge of what would be required in Glamorgan. The Arsenal was to be constructed at two main sites. The main Factory was to be built to the east of Bridgend – north of the Bridgend-Coychurch road, and south of the main railway line; a site often referred to as Waterton. The second site was to the north east of Bridgend – south of Heol West Plas (the road to the village of Coity). There huge storage chambers were to be driven into Brackla Hill from the north. This area was usually referred to as the Brackla site. At this time the work was expected to cost £4,650,000, and the Factory to eventually employ 15,000 mainly male workers.

Decisions had finally been arrived at as to what would be produced. Bridgend was to be primarily a weapons component-filling Factory. In other words it was to make the various often very small and very dangerous parts of larger ammunition (e.g. the fuzes and the primers), plus the filling of breech loading cartridges with cordite, and the manufacture of pyrotechnics. It was not to make large fixed ammunition, or to deal in high explosive. The components prepared at Bridgend would then be sent on to other ROFs (such as Glascoed[20] in Gwent and at Hereford) for finishing.

Progress remained slow. On 1st January 1937 the *Gazette* reported that 'It is understood that contracts are to be signed shortly.' But the *Gazette*'s New Year optimism was unfounded. The first contracts were not to be signed until September. In fact by April only 35% of the drawings were completed, despite the fact that most of the factory buildings were to be identical in type and size to those at Chorley. Nevertheless, in March 1937 the government announced that £1,150,000 had been allocated to the building of a munitions factory at Bridgend for the financial year starting in April[21].

In April 1937 Germany's Luftwaffe attacked the Basque town of Guernica, providing devastating evidence of the effectiveness of aerial bombing. Cinemas showed newsreel film of the results; pictures of the terrible destruction, and of the bodies of young children and adults laid out in the streets of the town struck terror into the hearts of the British people. One consequence was that defence chiefs were forced to rethink their calculations on the needs for anti-aircraft ammunition, and the increased demand had then to be factored into the proposed production at Bridgend.

In the Budget of April 1937 the difficult matter of financing the weapons programme was finally tackled: despite his reservations the Chancellor raised Income Tax by 3d, to 5s 6d in the Pound[22], a new 'National Defence Contribution' tax of 5% was imposed on profits, and arrangements were made for hugely increased government borrowing.

The complex process of planning Bridgend continued through to the summer months of 1937. The designers now had to take into account the Factory Act of that year which laid down standards for conditions in factories affecting such features as temperature, light, sanitary conveniences, washing facilities, personal clothing storage, and the safe fencing of machinery.

In June the War Office finally presented the scheme to the Treasury, asking for the release of £4,650,000. In July the Treasury approved most of the work, but true to form insisted on various savings, including the postponement of some parts of the Factory till a future theoretical 'Emergency' i.e. until the actual start of hostilities. These changes were incorporated into a final plan costed at £4,633,000 in September 1937. The timetable set out was to finish the construction of the various buildings by December 1939, with occupation and start of production in March 1940 – a relaxed approach partly dictated by the expectation that Glascoed would not be ready to receive Bridgend products till September 1940[23]. At last, after two years in the planning, the construction of ROF 53 could begin in earnest.

A New Woolwich

Notes

1 The only two other Royal Ordnance factories in operation at the time were both to the north of London: the Royal Small Arms factory at Enfield, and the Royal Gunpowder factory at nearby Waltham Abbey.

2 After the war a Fellow of Peterhouse College, Cambridge, Dennis Mack Smith, was asked to summarise (in an unpublished typescript – CAB 102/625) the various negotiations and decisions that brought 22 of the new ROFs into existence. Mack Smith was born in 1920, and from 1941-1942 worked in the Cabinet Office. He later became the principal historian on Italian matters writing in English.

3 Douglas Hewitt Hacking MP. Prominent Conservative politician: born Clayton le Moors, Lancashire 1884, died 1950.

4 One of the other sites examined for a filling factory was Pembrey.

5 For a discussion of the Depression in Wales, see KO Morgan's *Wales1880-1980* Ch 8

6 Sir Malcolm Stewart 1872 – 1951: industrialist (bricks and cement). Knighted 1937.

7 Not the last time that British intelligence was to overestimate a potential enemy's capacity!

8 Though this judgement was later to be shown to be at least partially flawed.

9 This was the new road from Bridgend to Coychurch that 'by-passed' the old Coychurch Road.

10 Negotiating the purchase of the land could not have been easy: the Brackla site alone was held by twenty one different landowners, including Lord Ogmore, the Dunraven Estate, Glamorgan County Council and St. David's College, Lampeter.

11 Alfred Duff Cooper; 1890 – 1954: Conservative politician.

12 Just 6 out of 34 Welsh seats were won by Conservatives in the 1935 election.

13 *Gazette*, August 1934

14 Saunders Lewis 1893–1985: Academic, Author and Politician – founder of Plaid Cymru.

15 The others were Lewis Valentine and D.J. Williams.

16 *Western Mail* 18.9.36

17 Lewis Jones: 1897–1939: miners' leader, and author (the novels *Cwmardy*, and *We Live*).

18 Percy Earnest Masters. Born Plumpstead 1886. Educated at Bloomfield Road Secondary School, Plumpstead. Joined Woolwich Arsenal 1901.

19 *The Times* 1.4.38

20 Glascoed was originally designed to produce weapons for the Navy, and so initially took components from Bridgend produced in the sections dedicated to manufacturing for the Admiralty.

21 *Gazette* 5.3.37

22 Income tax was to be increased to 7s 6d in 1939.

23 In the event Glascoed (constructed by two firms, Nutthall and John Morgan) was ready to receive in May 1940 – soon after the Bridgend plant itself started production.

2: Building the Arsenal

The work of constructing the Factory was divided up into a number of contracts, and bids were invited from local and British companies. In the event most of the work was done by three firms: Robert McAlpine & Sons; Gee, Walker and Slater; Lindsay Parkinson & Co. South Wales firms were not considered large enough or experienced enough to win any of the major contracts[1].

Railway Preparations

Some preparation for a new railway system had already begun. The GWR had started to get ready for the extra rail traffic that the Arsenal would generate; as early as May 1937 the *Gazette* mentioned that about 200 men 'have already been engaged in connection with the GWR sidings portion of the undertaking.' The tracks were needed to receive and marshal the construction materials and equipment that would come in by rail to build the Factory – and of course eventually these rails would be used to bring in the explosive material, and the empty components, and to export the finished product. There were two main sites for sidings.

The first was immediately south of the main south Wales line about one mile east of the Bridgend station, and directly to the north of the Factory site. Here also the GWR built two signal boxes – Tremains East and Tremains West – to control the sidings.

These sidings and signal boxes were brought into use on 19th May 1938 at a cost to the War Office of nearly £85,000.

The second site for railway work was off the old Barry Railway line which ran from the Vale around the north of Bridgend to Coity sidings on Coity road: a junction was constructed with a line leading on to the Arsenal site to the north of Brackla Hill.[2]

Building the Magazines

This new line with the associated sidings formed part of the first contract for the project. But the major part of this first contract was for the excavation and construction of seven huge caverns under Brackla Hill – the magazines for the storage of explosives. The contract was won by McAlpine at £525,141 15s. 11d, a figure agreed on September 15th 1937. The designer of the tunnels was Harold Temple-Richards[3], who had gained considerable experience of tunnelling while working on the extension of the London Underground system's Northern Line in the 1920s. For Brackla he first had to design the project[4] without cast iron lining, as all the pig iron available in Britain was directed towards the making of armaments, ships, guns and tanks; instead the tunnels were supported with engineering brick-arch roofs. In October bulk excavation of the magazines began, and so at last

Brigadier Harold Temple-Richards

physical work had actually started on the Bridgend ROF – nearly two years after the Cabinet decision to build, and just under two years before the start of the Second World War.

The magazine contract was let out first, partly because the dangerous explosives would have to be bought in and stored before any munitions could be made, but mainly because of the magnitude of the task. The amount of steel McAlpine expected to use gives some idea of the work involved:

366 tons of steel reinforcements
266 tons of constructional steelwork
211 tons of steel rails

The enormous quantities of concrete and mortar needed required a huge nearby supply of sand. Luckily this was available a few miles to the south of Bridgend. Ogmore Down, up above the valley of the River Ogmore is largely sandy heath land, and at Pant Mari Flanders is an ancient sand pit, used for centuries by the people of St. Brides Major for sand to clean the brick or stone floors of their dwellings. The twentieth century had a rather larger appetite for sand. Excavators dug down 30 feet and thousands of tons were taken away to Waterton and Brackla.[5]

Huge amounts of water were also wanted, both during the construction, and subsequently, when the Factory was fully functioning (at least two million gallons a day). Water for the town of Bridgend came from the Schwyll spring near Ogmore Castle. This produced five million gallons a day, and a new pumping station had been built in 1932. However, various options were considered so that the Factory would not have to pay for its water. The first borehole on site was drilled in September 1937, to a depth of 400 feet. Water was found, but consumption by the Arsenal had a catastrophic effect on the wells of local farmers. Mr. Wautier of the Grange, Coychurch would complain in June 1940 that his well's depth had fallen from 12 feet to 3 feet, 10 inches. Not unnaturally he worried about water for his family's domestic needs, for his cattle to drink, and for cooling milk. He had to bring in 240 gallons every day from the water works. J. Jones of Heol West Plas in Coity would see the pond that he used to water his cattle disappear: the ROF had to construct a special water supply to his farm. Water for the Arsenal itself would eventually be stored in a covered reservoir on the top of Brackla Hill, above the magazines, with another near the main Administration building in Cowbridge Road.

At first the other materials needed had to be brought in by lorry from railheads some miles away, but once the internal lines had been laid, railway engines were able to bring building requirements right up to the scene of operations: McAlpine brought nine of the company's own saddle-tank steam engines to shunt wagons on the site[6]. To ensure speedy construction, and to overcome the shortage of specialist labour as much mechanisation as possible was used. Conveyer belts took the excavated material out from the tunnels into railway wagons, and concrete was pumped in from as far as 900 feet away.

McAlpine soon came across serious problems which the original surveys of the ground seem to have missed. Brackla Hill is made of a rock called Blue Wenlock Shale. The strata on the west of the site was sound for tunnelling; good hard alternating beds of

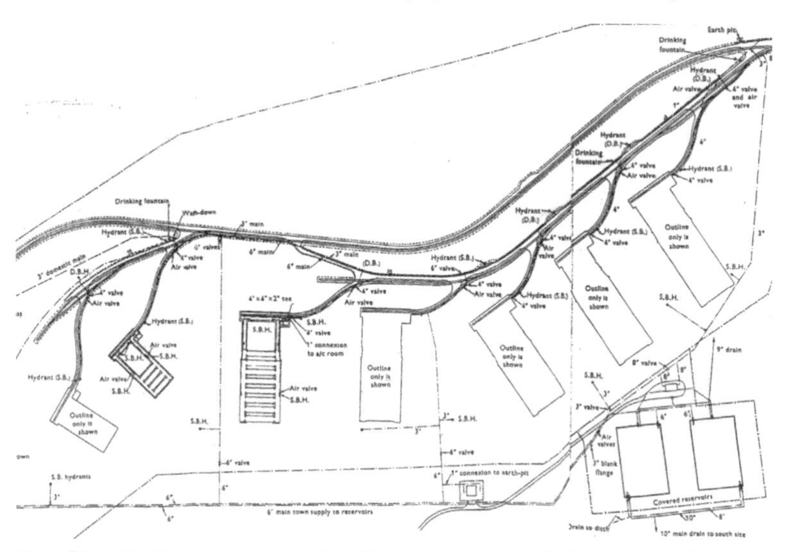

Plan of Brackla Magazines: two smaller HE magazines to the left; five larger cordite magazines to the right

limestone and shale. Thus there were no problems in constructing the two High Explosive Magazines. But further east the rock deteriorated to a shaley material, so soft that it could be picked out with the fingers. The absence of the limestone bands meant that as tunnelling went on, the ground above simply collapsed. If nothing were done, the Magazines would be left unprotected. Initial attempts to use more concrete failed: the eventual solution (approved in December 1938) was to use cast iron lining in the Cordite Magazines, at the enormous extra cost of £100,000 – the Treasury's fury at this unexpected expense can only be imagined!

Labouring on the tunnels was hard work. Jim Westrop spent three years on the job, and recalled working 'with Irish navvies, who moved 5cwt girders with their bare hands.' He lost several fingers in an accident on the site. Jack Loveday also worked in the Magazines: 'there was a lot of machinery there, and a lot of pick and shovel.' He also had a nasty experience:

> they had overhead pipes up on gantries taking the concrete from outside into the tunnels. They were dismantling this one night when one slipped off the gantry, straight onto my foot – broke every bone in my foot!

Jack remembered workers coming down from the valleys, the effects of the depression obvious; 'when they came down first you could see that they were underfed, they were on Poverty Street.' But most of the workers were not from the valleys. As Jack said 'on the tunnels 75% of the workers were Irish.' Jack had fond memories of these workers:

> There was good and bad there. I remember them cooking breakfast, bacon and eggs, over a fire on their shovels. They used to go to the pubs and the Milk Bar on Dunraven Place in Bridgend – the Milk Bar was open till 10.30 at night. And every one of them went to the Catholic Church in Ewenny Road on Sunday morning.

Trouble with Workers

The question of where the workers building the Arsenal came from caused a great deal of local anger. When the original plan was made public, the *Glamorgan Gazette* had confidently declared that the workers would be 'drawn principally from the immediate neighbourhoods.' The first hint of problems came in the November of 1936. An anonymous 'Prominent Bridgend Resident' had visited West Farm, which formed part of the land bought for the construction of the Arsenal. He noticed work going on there, and he spoke to one of the men – who immediately gave himself away by speaking with a Lancastrian accent. 'We have been brought down from Manchester', the worker confessed, 'to sink trail holes for the new munitions works.' The shocked PBR alerted the *Western Mail*, which asked; 'Have Manchester men prior claims over Welshmen to be employed at the new ammunition works?' Bridgend Councillor D.E. Davies pronounced it shameful. He told the *Western Mail* reporter that he could hardly conceive of such a thing when there were so many unemployed in Bridgend and the Valleys.

The controversy did not really explode for another year. In the autumn of 1937 both Bridgend and Penybont Councils, and the local MP, Ted Williams, protested not only about the importing of labour from outside the Mid-Glamorgan area, but also about the way in which local people were treated. According to Councillor I.D. Davies, lorry loads of men from other parts of the south of Wales (such as Ebbw Vale) were signing on at the Bridgend Labour Exchange, thus qualifying for local work. Even worse, according to Mr S. Schofield, the Chairman, local men were being sacked, and replaced by outside men: 'ten Bridgend men were given notice to finish, and ten outside men were put on the same night.' This paranoia has disturbing echoes of 21st century tabloid panic about migrants coming into Britain in hoards, and taking people's jobs. McAlpine's answers to these accusations were, that of 37 labourers then employed, 31 were local men; other work was skilled, and had to be done by skilled men, and these had to be brought in by the firm, since the expertise needed were not available locally.

But the Penybont Council had more serious and upsetting allegations about the treatment of local men seeking work on the Arsenal site. Councillor Len Betty of Aberkenfig complained that

> twelve men were told to report to the armaments factory. The men went to Bridgend, paying their own bus fares, and dressed

up as best they could – but when they got to Bridgend, they were looked up and down just as if it were a horse or cow that was being examined. Men have been asked to show their hands.

Councillor Phil Squires of Coytrahen supported Councillor Betty:

Last week they had 84 men there from the Penybont district, and only one man was appointed. I don't see that it is necessary for them to drag men down and examine them as if they were examining a horse – and then appoint only one.

Perhaps the sensitivity of local opinion is understandable in the context of the high unemployment and endemic poverty of the area. Councillor Betty's words tell us a great deal: 'Dressed up as best they could,' and 'paying their own bus fares' speaks of anxious and desperate men doing the best they could within constrained means and under intolerable circumstances. No wonder the editorial writer in the *Gazette* commented

the great majority of these men, discouraged by periods of enforced idleness, are desperate for work, and the least thing one would expect is that they should be treated with courtesy and consideration.

The Penybont Council sent a letter of protest to the Ministry of Labour. The response explained that an official from McAlpine had come to the Bridgend Employment Exchange to select potential workers. He had interviewed 50 Bridgend men, of whom 39 had been selected: 12 men from Aberkenfig had been seen, of whom 6 had been chosen. None of those selected had been refused work on site. This reply did not satisfy the councillors. Phil Squires alleged that 'the men employed have to work 12 hours a day, yet they will not take on more.' Eustace Brown continued to complain that 'the method of interviewing the men is most objectionable'. Another letter of complaint was despatched to London.

The then Tory *Western Mail* gave a far more positive spin on the impact of the building on local employment. According to its reporter in March 1938:

The new works have absorbed practically all the available unem-

> ployed labour in the town, and also drawn on a considerable proportion of unemployed in the adjoining valleys.

Nothing to complain about, then.

But the problem of 'foreign' labour continued to fester locally, and resurfaced in the press in February 1939. Again it was Ted Williams, the local MP who raised the issue, and so strong were feelings in his constituency that he tabled a question in Parliament: 'Is the Minister of Labour [Ernest Brown] aware of the grave feelings of unrest at Bridgend over the importation of Irish and foreign labour, while local labour is available?' According to the *Gazette*, Ted Williams and local workers were complaining about Irish and Cypriot workers, as well as men from Scotland, Liverpool and London.

The local trade unions were at the forefront of the protests. George Powell was secretary of the Bridgend Trades and Labour Council. He told a *Gazette* reporter that the BTLC

> had no intention of discriminating against any particular nationality so long as the 'foreigners' did not affect local men.

But he went on to raise the spectre of spies and terrorists by suggesting that the foreigners could 'give information to potential enemies and create sabotage.'

Answers provided by the contractors to the concerns raised included the defence that 'Cyprus was in the British Empire, and the men could be termed as Britons', and that most of these 'foreigners' were skilled joiners and carpenters. But such arguments were to no avail: the contractors surrendered to the political pressures on them, and the Italians and Cypriots were dismissed.

According to the parliamentary answer to Ted Williams, 200 of the Irishmen employed had been resident in Great Britain for over two years, and of the remaining 200 on site all but 20 had been here for longer than several months. As far as local employment was concerned, the Minister's comment was that 75% of the men employed had been recruited from within a radius of 20 miles of the site. If this was the case, then it appears that there was no real substance to local fears.

The positive effect of the construction of the Arsenal on local employment is shown by some figures listed in the *Gazette*[7]:

Date	Unemployed at Bridgend Office	Employed at Arsenal
Nov 1936	1149	0
Nov 1937	870	259
Nov 1938	571	3600

Thus at a time of rapid expansion of the labour force the number of unemployed registered at the Bridgend office had fallen by over 50% in two years. It would seem that after all the Arsenal was absorbing numbers of the unemployed from the local area. And if the answer to Ted Williams' question in the Commons is to be believed, then most of the men from places other than Bridgend did come from within the county of Glamorgan; from the area between Swansea in the west, Cardiff to the east and the Rhondda to the north.

This second table gives some idea of the contractor's labour and skill requirements, and also shows the numbers coming from Unemployment Offices other than that at Bridgend.

Workers found jobs at the Arsenal by Unemployment Offices June – November 1938

SKILL	From Bridgend	From Elsewhere	TOTALS
Carpenters	42	558	600
Bricklayers	60	390	450
Painters	0	20	20
Navvies	15	215	230
Builder's Labourers	1	79	80
Mechanical Drivers	32	68	100
TOTALS	**180**	**1300**	**1480**

Housing The Workers

Statistics show that very many of the workers building the Arsenal were coming from outside the immediate area. This meant that they had to have somewhere to live near to their place of work. The good citizens of the town were obviously determined to make the best of this situation. In 1939 a headline in the *Gazette* pronounced 'EXPLOITATION' OF ARSENAL WORKERS above a report on a local council meeting. It was Councillor Fred Williams of Aberkenfig who leapt to the defence of Arsenal workers by denouncing people in Bridgend for 'charging as much as 30s. a week for lodge, and giving practically nothing in return.' The Council had before it an application for a license for a single caravan to be put in a field in Coychurch, but the councillors obviously had a vision of the countryside being covered with moveable dwellings because of the rapacity of Bridgend landlords. 'Unless something is done we shall find a small township being set up at Bridgend as a result of the establishment of the Arsenal', warned Councillor Williams. 'We don't want a second Portobello' agreed Councillor Baker, referring to unauthorised dwellings placed on common land along the banks of the Ogmore River near Portobello House between Ogmore Castle and Ogmore-by-Sea; 'people might put up a cheap type of van, and get substantial rentals for accommodating workers.' Unsurprisingly the application was refused.

The *Western Mail* had a different perspective on the housing problem: a reporter pointed out that it was not only outsiders who were affected by rising charges: 'Our townspeople are suffering because rentals are tending to increase.' The demand for living accommodation stimulated other developments. According to the *Western Mail* in March 1938, there had been 'a boom in the building trade, hundreds of houses having been erected in the district within recent months.' Houses were being advertised in the *Gazette*. People could buy a 'distinctive villa on a healthy and select site' for £560 on the Westfield Estate, or a house on the Brewery Field Estate for a mere £465.

Building the Main Factory

The huge extent of the works became better known publicly in the spring of 1938. As the headlines in the *South Wales Echo* of March 3rd revealed:

£4,500,000 TO BE SPENT ON BRIDGEND FACTORY

HUGE ORDNANCE PLANS

The *Western Mail* of the following day was even more fulsome, declaring that 'the announcement has caused jubilation.' At the same time the government announced that a further £1,105,000 had been allocated for expenditure at Bridgend in the financial year commencing in April. Ten days later Hitler annexed Austria. Not much cause for jubilation about that.

Meanwhile work began on the main Factory site between Bridgend and Coychurch. The first contract here was to clear the trees and hedges, level the fields, drain marshland, and culvert the stream (Nant Pont-y-Sanau), which flowed north-south across the site. The huge amount of stone needed as hard core to give a solid base for the foundations of the Factory buildings and roads came by lorry from the quarries near Ewenny. Some idea of the quantities of stone required comes from the comment by John Williams, a driver for a quarry firm, that he 'worked on those trips back and fore to the Arsenal for about 12 months.' Next the contractors were required to put in the perimeter fencing, roads, reservoirs and water mains plus the site rail lines to individual buildings.

Before these lines were laid the building materials had to be brought in from the nearest railheads by road, using GWR 4-ton and 5-ton lorries, and Fordson tractors and trailers. An indication of the amount of effort required is given in a booklet about the railways published just after the war (*It Can Now Be Revealed*). According to the anonymous author[8]

> During the three years of construction, cranes at the three nearest railway depots performed 20,000 separate lifts. At one little goods shed alone... the inward flow amounted to no less than 496,018 tons.

As the permanent lines were laid they could be used to haul building materials: the firm of Lindsay Parkinson had four aged steam engines[9] for this purpose. That company also laid 2ft-gauge temporary tracks around the site, and purchased ten brand new two-and-a-half ton diesel engines[10] to transport supplies to the various construction locations.

Continued opposition to the building of an ordnance factory, plus an accurate description of the work being done, is seen in a poem written at that time by Elliot Crawshay-Williams[11]:

Where, now, is sanctuary?
O peaceful Vale, ruin has rushed upon
Your quietude; your beauty is all gone,
Outraged and slain, lamented not,
And soon to be forgot.
Where, late, a cow's tail switched a fly away,
Grim monsters crawl and burrow
By night, by day.
O'er field and furrow
Teeming and trim and map-like there arise
Inhuman structures of one hideous size,
And square mile on square mile
Man's maquillations Nature's face defile;
This that anon man fellow-man may slay.[12]

But poetic denunciation could not hold up the inexorable progress of the construction work. The second main Factory contract was for erecting the first tranche of buildings (about 300) designed to house the various operations which would take place on the Arsenal, plus the power and heating plants.[13] The sections included in this contract were Smoke, Cordite, Pellet and Fuze along with storage for filled shells. The two lowest tenders for this work were from Gee, Walker and Slater, and Holland and Hannen, and the contract was awarded to the former for £1,100,618 on 27th May 1938. The *Gazette*, reporting on this announcement predicted that the works would be finished in 18 months, and that it would eventually employ 700 workmen. It seems the true size of the operation was still being withheld from the public. Unlike the Germans the British were underplaying their plans for war. By June 2,120 men were employed in total on the various contracts.

One of these workers was the young Stan Martin of Maesteg. He got a job as a labourer, 'wheeling a barrow at 1s.3d an hour.' He was 'earning £3 a week, more if I worked Saturday afternoon.' This was a very good wage for a youngster: so good he 'thought it was Christmas!' His task was to service skilled bricklayers. He was 'one of forty wheelbarrow men,' who were 'tending what seemed like hundreds of brickies.' The work was hard; 'we were wheeling the mortar from a giant mixer to the buildings where the brickies were – we were like a string of ants going all day, except for a 30 minute break for lunch.' Later on Stan got 'a semi-skilled job, digging trenches and laying earthenware pipes' before joining the armed forces.

In September 1938 Chamberlain flew to Munich, and brought back his piece of paper signed by Herr Hitler, and promising 'Peace for our time.' Time to build factories to produce armaments for the inevitable conflict had been gained – at the expense of the Czechs, who had to surrender the Sudetenland to Germany. The Munich crisis caused the Government to relax normal contract procedure at Chorley to finish that factory in the minimum possible time. It was suggested that the same should be done at Bridgend to try to complete by September 1939: the idea was rejected. However the armed forces increased their requirements greatly, and a 2-pounder shell programme was added to Bridgend at an additional cost of £75,400.

In fact far from the work being completed before time, the contract fell behind its targets. First of all there was an industrial dispute. In September 1938, The *Gazette* reported that 100 bricklayers employed by Gee, Walker and Slater were on strike. Obviously workers were not imbued solely with a desire to toil in the National Interest without what they considered to be proper recompense. The men were seeking an extra 1½d per hour. Apparently the authorities expected trouble; after all south Wales had experienced serious violence during industrial disputes in the past. According to the *Gazette* 'a large contingent of police were drafted in as a safeguard against possible disturbance'. However most other labourers employed on the site continued to work as normal, and the incident seems to have passed off without trouble. The total labour force by November was 3,600.

The second cause of delay was far more serious. The weather in the autumn of 1938 was dreadful[14], and conditions on the Arsenal became almost impossible. David Power was working there at the time. He recalled

> it was marshy land. The big earth-moving contractor put their massive machines in, and they just disappeared overnight – swallowed up by the bog.

This might seem like an impossible exaggeration, but in the National Achive at Kew is a letter from the union representing the men complaining about the conditions of work, and seeking extra payments; one paragraph is worth quoting in full:

> Is it a normal building job where caterpillar tractors disappear in the mud, or where men are in danger of being drowned in mud? He would be a bold man who would say so. To get to their places of work, the men have to wade through a sea of mud.

The firm concerned was actually a sub-contractor, Bernard Sunley of Middlesex. They complained that their huge mechanical scrapers could not be used; their employees were having to go back to the methods of a hundred years before, and use shovel and barrow. As a result tasks that should have taken several hours were taking several days. The first main site contract was supposed to be finished by January 1939, but the working conditions ensured that it was only 85% complete in March; in an attempt to 'hurry it on' the main contractor took over direct control of operations from Sunley, which was eventually bankrupted.

There was a desperate need to hurry up the work. On March 15th the last semblance of legitimacy disappeared from Hitler's activities, when the Czech lands were occupied by the German army. A fortnight later Chamberlain promised to defend Poland if it were to be attacked, and announced the doubling of the size of the Territorial Army. In April conscription was introduced for men under 21 years old. Events were tumbling rapidly towards war.

Meanwhile the contract for the remainder of the planned buildings on the main site had been signed in February 1939. This contract included the Initiator and Pyrotechnic sections, the Textile workshops, and the main Administrative building.

By April 4,600 men were working on the two sites; but new causes of delay arose. There were eventually to be around a thousand buildings on the Arsenal. That would require huge quantities of bricks (about 30 million) and wood; and in the summer of 1939 there was a sudden severe shortage of bricklayers and carpenters. This was because the dramatically expanding Army had to be accommodated in new hutted militia camps, and carpenters and bricklayers were needed to construct them. According to CM

Kohan, writing in the official history of construction and buildings in the Second World War,

> the repercussions of the scramble for skilled labour were widespread and disturbing. The almost frantic speed and energy with which the camp programme had been tackled, the sudden demand for labour, and the special inducements offered had begun to draw off in large numbers the men

needed for factory construction. The firms which had won the contracts for the camps were prepared to offer extraordinary inducements, since the cost of this fell on the government, and not on the contractors. Often these incentives included subsistence allowances and unlimited overtime including Sunday working. Advertisements in the press guaranteed 90 or 100 hours work in seven days. Workers could earn as much as £8 a week. Kohan remarks that

> this bidding for labour upset the orderly completion of other urgent contracts. At Bridgend men were being drawn off to work on a militia camp fifty miles away.

The Ministry of Works recruited skilled labour for the Bridgend Factory from where it could. On the promise of a job there Jim Barnes, a young carpenter of Wigan, married his sweetheart on 2nd September and travelled down from Lancashire to digs in Porthcawl the following day.

Meanwhile the estimated completion date had fallen back by 5 months to August 1940. In July the use of 'full emergency powers' was considered; apparently if these powers were used the Factory could be completed by December 1939. The idea was rejected on the ground that the cost of overtime and night working was 'undesirable.' With the forces of evil gathering across the English Channel, it is good to know that concerns about excessive overtime payments were occupying the thoughts of the Treasury. At the end of July work was delayed further by a strike of 200 carpenters and bricklayers (perhaps motivated by comparisons with workers at the militia camps) demanding from Lindsay Parkinson & Co a daily subsistence payment of 3s.6d a day towards their lodgings. The next day another 200 men came out in solidarity, and a meeting was held at the Bridgend Rugby Club's ground at the Brewery Field. The dispute was settled in a few days. And there was some progress to celebrate; in August, Smoke was the first section to be completed – just 14 weeks late.

The Coming of War

In June 1939 the National Eisteddfod for the following year was proclaimed at the Gorsedd stones in Newbridge Fields. But there was to be no Bridgend Eisteddfod in 1940: it would not be possible in that year to give an affirmative answer to the traditional question 'A oes heddwch?'[15].

The last Bank Holiday of peace was celebrated on 7th August with a Coychurch-Arsenal Grand Carnival Sports event on the Coychurch village cricket field. As well as Jazz Band and St. John's Ambulance competitions, there was a 'special sports section for Men engaged on Royal Ordnance Factory, Waterton and Brackla,' including an 8-a-side Tug-of-War. Other events included a Treasure Hunt, Clock Golf, Comic Golf, Hoopla and Skittles as well as Air Rifle shooting – perhaps foreshadowing shooting of a more deadly kind. A prize for everyone was promised. A Carnival queen (Lillian Roberts of Coytrahen) was crowned, and the

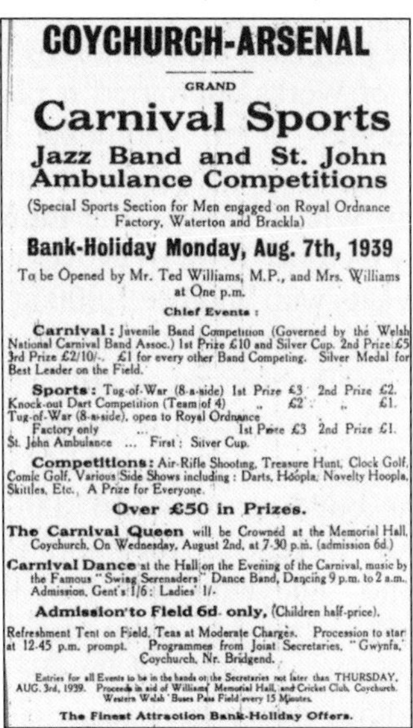

COYCHURCH-ARSENAL

GRAND

Carnival Sports

Jazz Band and St. John Ambulance Competitions

(Special Sports Section for Men engaged on Royal Ordnance Factory, Waterton and Brackla)

Bank-Holiday Monday, Aug. 7th, 1939

To be Opened by Mr. Ted Williams, M.P., and Mrs. Williams at One p.m.

Chief Events:

Carnival: Juvenile Band Competition (Governed by the Welsh National Carnival Band Assoc.) 1st Prize £10 and Silver Cup. 2nd Prize £5 3rd Prize £2/10/-. £1 for every other Band Competing. Silver Medal for Best Leader on the Field.

Sports: Tug-of-War (8-a-side) 1st Prize £3 2nd Prize £2.
Knock-out Dart Competition (Team of 4) „ £2 „ £1.
Tug-of-War (8-a-side), open to Royal Ordnance Factory only ... 1st Prize £3 2nd Prize £1.
St. John Ambulance ... First: Silver Cup.

Competitions: Air-Rifle Shooting, Treasure Hunt, Clock Golf, Comic Golf, Various Side Shows including: Darts, Hoopla, Novelty Hoopla, Skittles, Etc., A Prize for Everyone.

Over £50 in Prizes.

The Carnival Queen will be Crowned at the Memorial Hall, Coychurch, On Wednesday, August 2nd, at 7-30 p.m. (admission 6d.)

Carnival Dance at the Hall on the Evening of the Carnival, music by the Famous "Swing Serenaders" Dance Band, Dancing 9 p.m. to 2 a.m., Admission, Gent's 1/6: Ladies' 1/-

Admission to Field 6d. only, (Children half-price).

Refreshment Tent on Field, Teas at Moderate Charges. Procession to start at 12-45 p.m. prompt. Programmes from Joint Secretaries, "Gwynfa," Coychurch, Nr. Bridgend.

Entries for all Events to be in the hands of the Secretaries not later than THURSDAY, AUG. 3rd, 1939. Proceeds in aid of Williams' Memorial Hall, and Cricket Club, Coychurch. Western Welsh Buses Pass Field every 15 Minutes.

The Finest Attraction Bank-Holiday Offers.

'Famous Swing Serenaders Dance Band' would provide the music at the carnival Dance – 'Dancing 9pm to 2am.' There is an affecting charm in the thought of these innocent activities defiant in the face of the tremendous forces that would so soon be unleashed on Europe.

The Nazi-Soviet pact of August 23rd cleared the way for Hitler to act. The arrival the following day at Bridgend of 100 soldiers of the Royal Engineers to guard the incomplete Factory intensified the sense of crisis. On 1st September German troops invaded Poland: two days later Britain declared war on Germany.

The future theoretical 'Emergency' had finally become awful reality. Suddenly the completion of the Bridgend Ordnance Factory became an overriding priority. One day after the outbreak of war the acceleration of work 'was officially accorded priority before all other Government Department requirements whatever' because of the danger of imminent aerial attack on the vulnerable Arsenal at Woolwich. The strict grasp of the Treasury was finally broken, and another £225,000 was allocated to the completion of the Factory. Even this was considered insufficient: a memorandum from Ernest Brown, the Minister of Labour on 30th September commented on the slowness of the project because of the shortage of skilled labour, and remarked that the proposed completion by June 1940 might be too late. The Office of Works submitted a plan to complete the Factory within 5 months at an additional cost of £425,000. Progress was being made; according to an entry in the diary of Police Superintendent William May,[16] the tunnel magazines were practically finished by October 16th. By November 6,800 men were working on the main site, with another 1,000 at Brackla.

War concentrated the minds of the planners. The success of removing ordnance production away from the south and east would now be put to the test. But just in case the bombers of the Luftwaffe did find their way to Bridgend, £35,000 was allocated for camouflaging the buildings, and £67,000 for the establishment of Passive Air Defence. And additional capacity was proposed at Bridgend. The land that had been purchased at Brackla extended to 500 acres. The main reason for purchasing so much more than was actually needed for the magazines and its associated railway sidings was to keep unwelcome attention away, but a side effect was that there was ample room for the construction of more buildings there. The Treasury had already approved the expenditure of £84,500 on a fuze powder factory on Brackla. A Ministry of Supply memorandum dated December 1939 explained that because the production of 40mm High Explosive shells would rise to 500,000 per month by the following June, increased filling capacity was needed. This would be provided in temporary buildings at Brackla at a cost of £146,000.

In January 1940 another MoS memorandum proposed the erection of temporary buildings at Brackla for the 2inch and 3inch High Explosive shells. The estimated cost was £1,500,000. In March a contract was agreed with McAlpine for the construction of a factory at Brackla to produce High Explosive and Pellets to be completed by September. Groups A and S would be based there in what was named Filling Factory No.11.

The construction of this factory was treated with great urgency. In May McAlpine was asked to put into operation a 60-hour week, and to work double shifts. Work also went on in the hours of darkness, which caused some problems, because the special lighting that had to be used was very visible, and might have been a target for the Luftwaffe. The extra expense of these measures was £30,000, including provision for the cost of that essential part of the British workman's day, an extra quarter of an hour tea interval! By May all men under 28 had been conscripted, and the difficulty of getting good quality workers at this juncture of the war is shown by McAlpine's complaint that many of the men employed on building Filling Factory No.11 'are dilutees [the unskilled] and old men.' In the end there were three sections on the Brackla site, together making up Factory No. 11, but all under the control of the superintendent at the main site. Group A was built just south of Heol West Plas; the Fuze Powder section, Group F, was built immediately south of the village of Coity, and the Group S buildings were placed in the extreme south east of the site.

Perhaps not surprisingly, the first few months of the war while the Factory was still incomplete was a time of greatly increased tension. Already on 26th August Superintendent William May had noted in his war diary that he had 'conferred with Major Edwards of Searchlight Company Royal Engineers on the possibility of sabotage and other treasonable or subversive activities' at the Arsenal. Then, on the night of 17th November there was a shooting incident involving three young sentries who fired off several rounds of ball ammunition at a non-existent enemy. May commented sympathetically in his diary that they 'were probably scared out of their wits.'[17] On the 9th January May received a message from Ministry of Supply headquarters warning that: 'Sabotage is suspected by a foreign power – want you to take necessary precautions. Make sure that the police and military are extra vigilant.' These fears seem to have been unfounded, since there is no evidence of sabotage during the life of the Factory.

Deaths during Construction

As far as we know five workmen were killed as a result of accidents during the building of the Arsenal. Since this was one of the greatest engineering projects ever to take place in Wales, it is perhaps no surprise that people were killed in the course of the construction; what is perhaps surprising is that so few workers lost their lives in the time before the Factory started production.

This is a list of the known fatalities during the building of the Arsenal:

Date of Death	Name	Age	Living in	Cause of Death
11/7/39	Thomas Meredith	19	Coed Ely	Crushed by skip
18/8/39	Joshua Edwards	57	Cymmer Porth	Sunstroke
8/10/39	William S Haines	25	Port Talbot	Fell while painting
1/3/40	Archibald F Chilcott	37	Tondu	Electrocuted
27/1/41	Stanley D Campbell	21	Pencoed	Railway accident

The first fatality that we have been able to find was that of Thomas Meredith of Coed Ely – a young man just 19 years old. He was working outside the great ammunition store chambers on the Brackla site. A skip containing concrete was running on temporary rails into the tunnels when, for reasons which are not clear, it tipped over onto its side. Thomas was unfortunate enough to be beside the skip, and he was crushed beneath it.

The second fatality was that of Joshua Edwards of Trebanog Road, Porth. He was also labouring on the northern site. He was digging with pick and shovel on an August day which was described as very hot. He suddenly collapsed, and was taken to the Bridgend Hospital, but attempts to revive him were unsuccessful. The verdict of the inquest was that he died of 'heart failure due to sunstroke while at work.'

William Haines, of Port Talbot, an unmarried man of 25 was employed as a painter by Whittles of Nottingham. He was painting the ceiling of a store building, and was working from a plank supported by a trestle at one end and a ladder at the other. It seems that the ladder gave way, taking the plank and William the twelve feet to the ground: the painter suffered fatal injuries.

Archibald Chilcott from Tondu was a fitter working for the Lamden Sheet Metal Company. This firm had been contracted to provide the air conditioning plant which was to provide fresh air in the Munitions stores under Brackla Hill. No one saw what happened, but perhaps Archibald tripped and caught hold of a coil of live electrical cable left looped up by workers from the South Wales Power Company. Death was caused by 'respiratory paralysis due to an electric shock.' The verdict of the coroner was accidental death.

Stanley Campbell of Hendre Road, Pencoed was not an Arsenal worker: he was employed by the railway company as a 're-layer' with a track repair gang. On 27th January 1941 he was working on the track near Tremains Platform. A witness at the inquest described what happened. It seems that Stanley was walking besides the track carrying a sleeper, when a train coming from Cardiff struck the timber, which was split into two pieces. Stanley disappeared from sight for an instant, and then his body whirled into the air and was thrown about 30 yards.

Despite these sacrifices, most of the work of construction of the munitions Factory was completed during 1940. The end of the project was marked with a presentation to Gee, Walker & Slater's site engineer, Stirling Rogers. He was given a solid silver tray with coffee set. According to the *Western Mail* of 2nd June1992, the tray alone was valued at £1,500 – what price can be put on the Bridgend Royal Ordnance Factory? In April 1941 the cost of constructing the magazines and the main Factory was calculated at £6,790,000[18]; Filling Factory no.11 cost £1,500,000. Thus the total to that time was approximately £8,290,000.

During the lifetime of the Factory there was further spending on improvements and extensions. By the end of December 1942 the total expenditure up to that point was put at £9,279,643. The estimate produced at the end of the War in June 1945 of the total capital cost of building the Bridgend ROF was £9,700,000.[19]

Stirling Rogers: site engineer

Notes

1 The contract documents are held in WORKS 26 files at Kew

2 An indication of how important the railway was considered to be for the success of the Factory was the modernisation of two existing signal boxes at Coity Junction and Cowbridge Road: £102 was spent converting the boxes from oil to electricity.

3 Brigadier Harold Beecham Temple-Richards, 1889–1969: Senior Civil Engineer of HM Office of Works (Defence Architects' Department). 1910: BSc in Engineering, University of London. 1914 -1918: Royal Engineers (founded their School of Heavy Bridging). 1939 – 1945: after working on the Brackla Magazines built the storage tunnels for the National Gallery treasures in slate quarries at Manod, Blaenau Ffestiniog; was involved in the planning and building of 'Mulberry' harbours for D-Day.

4 Temple-Richards' own description of the project is in *Symposium of Wartime Engineering Projects* (ICE)

5 The great hole created was filled in the 1950s with the rubble from Arsenal buildings as the former munitions factory was demolished.

6 These were all 0-6-0 steam engines of various ages, and made by Hudswell, Clarke & Co. of Leeds.

7 The following 2 tables are based on figures in the *Gazette*, December 1938.

8 Probably George Dow.

9 One veteran dating from 1883.

10 Built by Motor Rail Ltd of Simplex Works, Bedford: 28hp 0-4-0 locomotives with Dorman motors.

11 Elliot Crawshay-Williams: 1879 – 1962: Liberal politician (MP for Leicester), and writer of poetry, novels, plays, film scripts and travel books. Lived at Coed-y-Mwstwr.

12 'Munition Works, Vale of Glamorgan,' in *No one wants Poetry* (The Welsh Outlook Press, 1938).

13 Later the construction of sewerage tanks was added to this contract at a cost of £1750.

14 October saw winds of over 100mph off Milford Haven, a Dutch coaster driven onto the shore at Kenfig, 3 inches of rain in 24 hours at Ystalyfera, and two people drowned in the swollen River Rhondda.

15 'Is there Peace?' – a necessary condition for the Eisteddfod to take place. The National Eisteddfod finally took place in Bridgend in 1948, when there was peace – of a sort.

16 William C May, superintendent in charge of C division, Glamorgan Constabulary, and based in Bridgend. He kept a diary during the war which has proved to be a useful source of information.

17 In March 1940 there was another shooting incident involving a sentry. While on patrol Tom Bevan, the Senior Warden, heard a rifle shot, and found two stokers from the Boiler House attending to the wounded soldier, Private Jenner of the 15th Welch Regiment. Laconically Bevan commented in his report that the wounded man 'was taken away in a lorry.'

18 This was around £900,000 more than the Treasury had approved: the difference had to be justified in great detail – even down to the extra cost of using lead-free paint instead of bitumastic paint on the boundary fences (£1,100)

19 A slightly lower figure of £9,580,000 is given in Hornby's book *Factories and Plant*, published in 1958.

Top: Flooded excavations, October 1938
Bottom: Dumper in mud, October 1938

Top: Steam-roller compacting hard-core
Bottom: Sunley's digger

Top: Working in Brackla Magazine Tunnel, March 1939
Bottom: Interior of reservoir, March 1939

Top: Workers in electrical cabling trench, May 1939
Bottom: Steel framework of Boiler House, July 1939

Top: Filled components store (7A12), July 1939. Note men finishing earthworks
Bottom: Completed pellet building (2c5) with earth traverse, September 1939

Top: Shunting engine in Factory sidings, November 1939. Group 3 in background
Bottom: Avenue D looking west from Street 5, November 1939

3: An Empire of Ammunition

The Bridgend Arsenal had taken three years to build at the enormous cost of over £9 million pounds. It was a project that could properly take its place in the history of major construction projects in Wales along with Offa's Dyke, Edward I's castles, the canals and railways of the nineteenth century, and the great steelworks of the twentieth. According to Postan, the official historian of British war production, it was built and equipped to a standard that some critics of the total cost described as 'palatial.' What had the nation got for its money?[1]

The Buildings

The Arsenal occupied over 1,000 acres of land on two main sites each surrounded by a formidable wire link mesh, barbed wire-topped fence; it was made up of in excess of 900 separate buildings. Something in the region of 12 million bricks, 10,000 tons of constructional steel, 500,000 yards of steel reinforcing and 15,000 steel window frames had been used to construct the Arsenal's many structures. The total floor space of the Factory was at least 1,630,000 square feet.[2]

The Arsenal had a huge variety of services and buildings, including many miles of railway lines and sidings plus locomotive sheds, its own main-line railway station, a bus park, internal bus service, vehicular garage, special pedestrian clean ways and vehicle routes, power stations and boiler house, miles of steam piping, a borehole, reservoirs and sewage storage tanks, engineering shops, a textile factory, laundry, a printing works, canteens, surgeries, first aid and cleansing centres, laboratories, clocking in and security buildings, police stations, fire stations, air raid shelters, anti-aircraft defences, a searchlight depot and pill boxes as well as shifting houses, ablution blocks, underground magazines and other storage accommodation for explosives, components and filled ammunition, plus the hundreds of process workshops. Outside the Factory, but within its orbit, were a number of houses for key staff, and four separate settlements built to accommodate workers. This whole Empire of Munitions was governed from the main Administration Building on Cowbridge Road.

Within the site there were few large buildings. The experience of the First Word War, plus government regulation meant that for safety reasons it was impossible to concentrate production in single large blocks, except for the few workshops where explosive materials were not processed, such as textiles and engineering shops. The Bridgend Factory was planned as a 'manufactory' in which the bulk of the work was carried out by large numbers of manual workers using their hands, small hand tools, or small-scale machinery. The employment of large-scale machinery was made impossible by the layout of the Factory. Most buildings in the groups were relatively small; the most common structures were essentially long rectangular single storey blocks, which could be adapted to different or changing processes as required. Workshops for the manufacture of fuzes were 80ft by 30ft: workshops for cordite filling of any calibre were 60ft by 30ft. These buildings were designed to offer the least resistance to explosion, were separated by a sensible distance, and some were surrounded by earth mounds to protect adjacent buildings from any accidental blast. Despite the multitude of function, many buildings were of identical design to each other, and to the buildings at Chorley, and they incorporated standard components such as doors, steel frame windows and roof trusses: it was almost building by numbers.

Wayne Cocroft gives an unflattering description of the structures in a filling factory in his book, *Dangerous Energy*:

> The nature of the activity in filling factories ensured that their buildings were more substantial than many others built for wartime... they were utilitarian, designed for speedy and economic erection using relatively unskilled labour with maximum economy in the use of building materials. Their drabness was compounded by a coating of camouflage paint, and the battleship grey or brown paint of the door- and window-frames. Interiors were a little brighter, generally painted in cream gloss and furnished with utility-quality furniture.

At one time over 32,000 people were employed in the Arsenal; it was one of the very largest industrial undertakings in Britain. Yet according to Hornby it proved to be by far the most economic of all the ROFs built before and during the war. Not only was it cheaper than other filling factories for its size, but also it came nearer than any other to its optimum labour strength i.e. it was able to recruit and employ the number of workers for which it was designed – an achievement that proved impossible for all other large scale ordnance factories. Thus the cost per worker employed of building the Bridgend Factory was the lowest in Britain, as this chart printed in Hornby's book shows.

Relative cost of some RO Filling Factories

ROF	Total Cost (£millions)	Cost £per worker
Bridgend	9.58	334
Kirkby	8.63	436
Aycliffe	6.64	455
Chorley	13.14	487
Glascoed	6.30	514
Risley	13.39	610
Thorpe Arch	5.95	672
Swynnerton	13.60	680

Services

Electricity was provided to the Arsenal by its own coal-fired power station built in the extreme northwest of the Waterton site, next to the main railway line. Adjacent to the power station was its coal storage yard and distinctive cooling tower. As an insurance, another power station was planned to the northeast of the main Factory, but this was never built. Each power station was designed to produce 5 megawatts. There were seven substations, which transformed the power down to a 400/230-volt, three phase supply to the buildings. The system formed a ring circuit: if any part of the circuit were broken (through bombing or explosion) the rest of the ring could continue to function. 300 miles of cabling carried electrical power across the site.

The Power Station was also used to produce heating: steam was carried across the whole site in an elaborate system of over 30 miles of above-ground pipes. These were lagged with asbestos covered with black felt, and wrapped in chicken wire. Jack Loveday remembered the steam pipes well: 'Oh Hell aye, they were hot to touch!' The pipes were supported on concrete stanchions, and in places reared up into grand arches over the roads in order to allow the passage of vehicles. The power and heating production area was designated Group OY.

Water was pumped up from a borehole (drilled to nearly 400 feet) at the Coychurch end of the site. This borehole was capable of producing 450,000 gallons a day. There were two reservoirs – one on the top of Brackla Hill which held 3,000,000 gallons, and the other near the main Administration building. There were two water supplies to ROF 53 – one for everyday use, and a separate high-pressure supply for fire fighting. The Factory was provided with cast iron, red-painted distinctive American-style hydrants. Altogether there were 20 miles of water mains.

The sewage produced by the Arsenal was channelled into holding tanks not far from the administrative building, then pumped to 'lunar tanks' on the estuary of the River Ogwr. At low tide the valves were opened, and the sewage discharged untreated directly into the sea. There were 64 miles of drainage pipes on the site.

There was a grid system of 58 miles of roads linking the various groups and buildings of the Factory. To make it easier to find the way around the enormous area and the many structures of the Waterton site, there was a logical numbering system of identifying these roads:

> Roads running west to east were named Avenue A West and East to Avenue E.
>
> Roads running north to south were named Street No. 1 to Street No. 8.

Distances inside the Arsenal were considerable, so, according to Teresa Barnett utility buses with wooden slatted seats took employees from the gates to the workshops. Other travellers had more comfortable transport. R. Redwood reported that

> There was quite a lot of transport all over the Arsenal, dashing about the avenues and all going about their business. Of course they had their own vans. There was a huge Transport Department to carry people around; visitors and VIPs around the Arsenal. Mr Barber was Transport Manager.

The railway was vital to the Arsenal, bringing in supplies and taking away completed weapons components. Adjacent to the main line were 10 exchange sidings, measuring a total length of 3 miles, and able to hold 600 railway wagons at one time. It was in these sidings that munitions trains were made up for collection and subsequent transport to their destination by the locomotives of the GWR.

The buildings of the Arsenal were served by 24 miles of railway track built to the standard gauge to avoid the need for transhipment. All the transit sheds were fitted with raised platforms, so that wagons could be directly unloaded and loaded without the need for lifting. Fireman Redwood described the railway system thus:

> There were lines running all through the Factory, and sidings branching off the main lines into the stores. Every part of the Factory was served by the railway. Not only that, they had proper little engines, proper little Puffing Billys. And they used to draw

> the trucks out to form the freight trains. You had the railway running at the side of the road. What they did, they had the Puffing Billys there, they used to back in a truck and the men would load it up. And then they would come and connect all these up to make a freight train. There were trucks being trundled along all over the place. They had railwaymen there shunting and hitching up.

There was a maximum of ten shunting locomotives working at the Bridgend Arsenal during the war[3]. Nine of these were 0-4-0 diesel locomotives with mid-body cabs built by John Fowler of Leeds; they were fitted with a 150hp Fowler 4C engine, and weighed in at 29 tons. The odd one out was one steam shunter 0-4-0, built by Peckett & Sons of Bristol, and presumably used to shunt coal wagons from the main line to the power station: it could hardly work in areas with explosives because of the sparks it produced. All the engines were brand-new, except No 9 which worked originally at ROF Elstow in Bedfordshire before coming to Bridgend in October 1943. Two of the locomotives were based on the Brackla site, and the remainder worked on the Waterton site.

Shunting Engine No. 4, with its driver Albert Meadows

The Groups

The Factory was a highly complex organisation because of the development since the First World War of many new types of fuzes, detonators and other ammunition components, as well as the multitude of recently developed explosive compositions needed to detonate them. To manage all this, the site was divided up into individual production sections, or Groups. These operated as self contained units which each dealt exclusively with one type of weapon part, or other activity. Workers rarely moved from one group to another. The arrangement of the groups and buildings had to be planned to take into account the import and storage of explosive powders and weapons parts, their movement about the site to the relevant workshops, the manufacturing or filling of components, and finally their storage and export from the Factory to other ROFs for assembly and finishing. Typically buildings on one side of each group were occupied by offices and changing rooms, magazines[4] on a second side contained partly completed components, buildings on a third edge stored empty components, and sheds[5] to hold completed items awaiting transport out of the group were built on the fourth side. In the centre of the group was the business area – the process workshops. Each group was serviced by railway lines along which empty components were brought in, and completed parts were taken away.

As we have seen, the Arsenal had two sites, each of about 500 acres.

The Northern Site - Brackla

The Northern site (to the north of Brackla Hill, and south of Heol West Plas and Coity village) contained seven huge magazines, tunnelled deep under Brackla Hill. These magazines comprised Group 8 of the Factory. They were familiarly known as 'the 8xs,' after their identification number. The two smaller magazines to the west were designed to hold 40 tons each of High Explosive[6], while the five larger magazines to the east were built to hold 200 tons each of Cordite[7].

Essentially the bulk magazines were storage chambers, about 40 – 50 feet below the ground. Brackla Hill itself, rising to 287 feet above sea level, thus gave some protection from bombing, and also insulation from the effects of an accidental explosion. Leading to the magazines were open cuttings along which a railway engine could push several trucks. These lines lead to the reception areas which looked rather like an underground tube station with a single railway line coming to a dead-end, and a platform for unloading and loading the precious and deadly cargo (see photos p. 316, 317). From the platform, at right angles, two 300 feet long passages (about 120 feet apart) disappeared under the hill. Branching off the passages were entrances to the series of concrete chambers where the explosives were stored.

As well as the magazines, and the associated railway lines and sidings, there were three sub-factories on the Brackla site which were added to the original plans during 1939 and 1940.

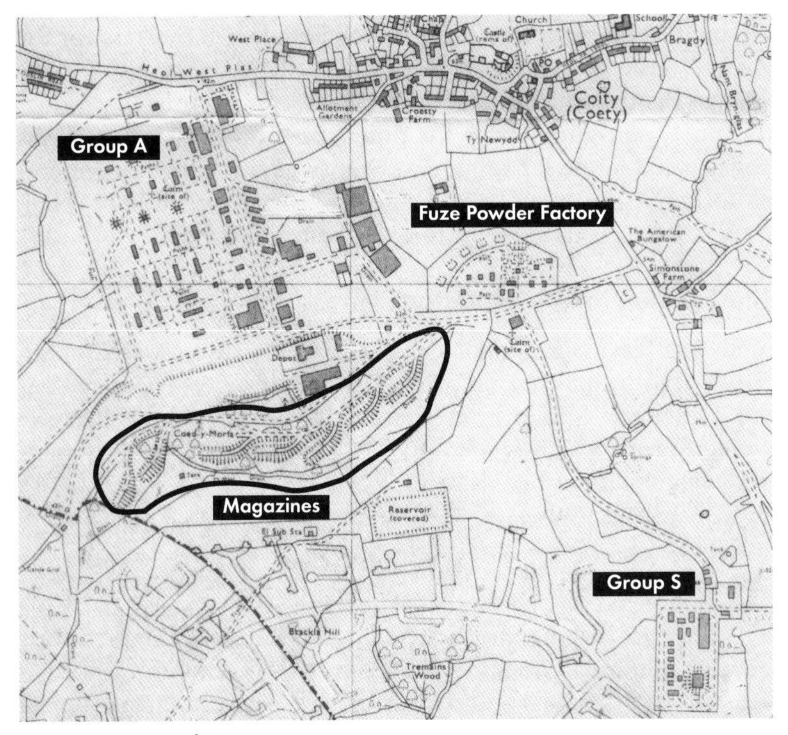

Brackla Factories and Magazines

Brackla Group A Factory

The largest of these sub-factories was Group A, which was placed between Heol West Plas and the Magazines. It was probably built to fill High Explosive 2-inch and 3-inch mortars for the Army. To the east of Group A, and directly to the south of Coity village was the small Fuze Powder Factory, presumably producing fine grain gunpowder for time fuzes. Finally Group S was constructed in the far south east of the site, near the present crematorium; this may have been for filling the 40mm High Explosive shells used for Bofors[8] anti-aircraft guns.

The Southern Site – Waterton

This was the main part of the Factory, and also covered about 500 acres. In the extreme southwest of the site was Group OA, the Ordnance Administration area. It was from here that the whole Arsenal was managed. In 1947 the two storey main building would be described as being:

> very soundly constructed, of steel framing encased in reinforced concrete, and outer walls of brickwork, faced with very attractive rustic bricks.'

The design was not completely utilitarian. The lead hopper heads on the rainwater system were each regally embossed with a crown. Over the door of the main block was a magnificent representation of the cypher of the King, George VI. Inside, the

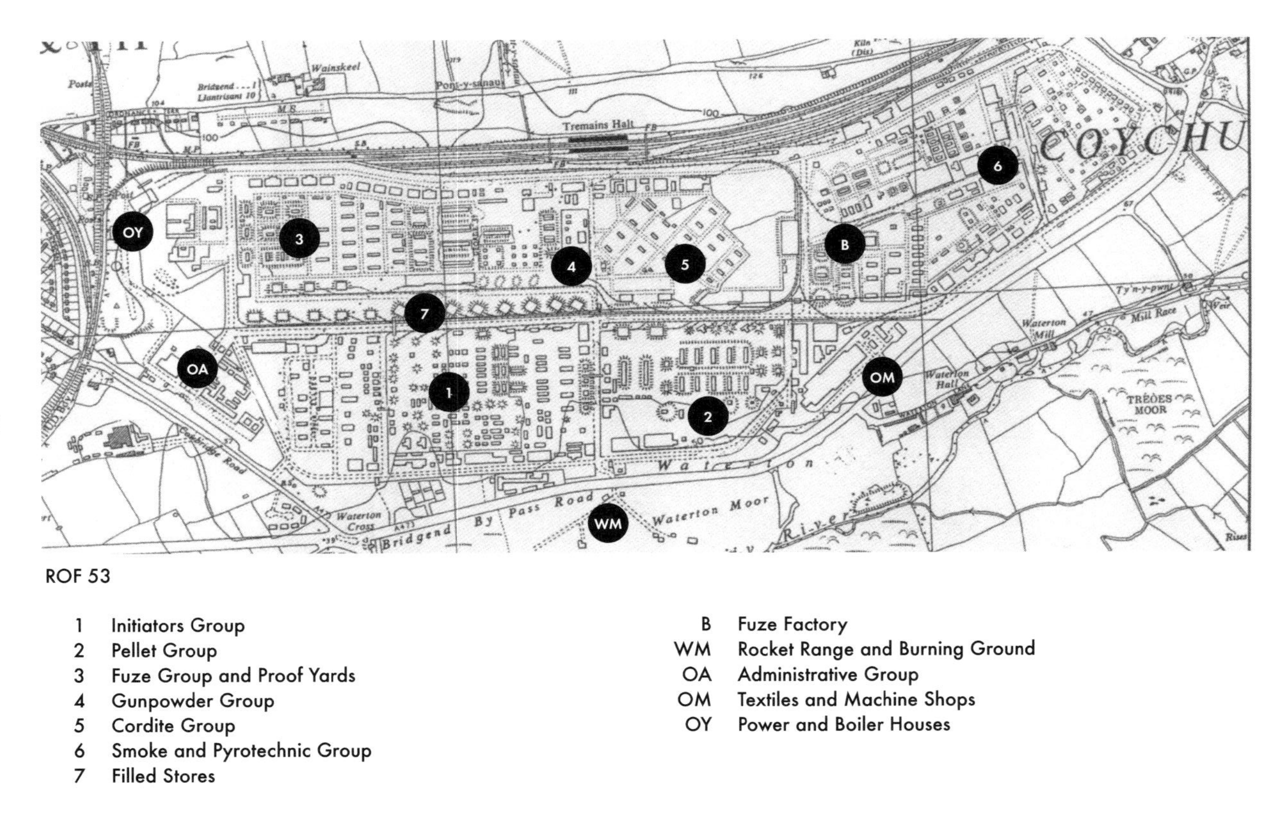

ROF 53

1 Initiators Group
2 Pellet Group
3 Fuze Group and Proof Yards
4 Gunpowder Group
5 Cordite Group
6 Smoke and Pyrotechnic Group
7 Filled Stores

B Fuze Factory
WM Rocket Range and Burning Ground
OA Administrative Group
OM Textiles and Machine Shops
OY Power and Boiler Houses

The Welsh Arsenal

Main Adminstrative Building

Royal Rainwater Goods

Superintendent and his management team worked with an army of clerks on planning, management, administration and pay.

There were a number of departments based in the Administration building: the main telephone switchboard with 12 telephonists on each shift; the Registry with its Typing Pool dealt with all incoming correspondence and files; the Progress and Planning Department controlled the actual manufacture of ammunition; the Labour Department managed the workforce and its welfare; the Wages Branch was responsible for calculating remuneration and paying the staff; the Stores Department supervised the import and storage of raw materials, and the storage and export of finished ammunition. Mair Davies worked there: she recalled 'My job was in the stores office, keeping account of goods received and booked out, charging them to the Army or Navy.' There was a Public Relations Office with its own Photography Department and Printing Works. Also based in Administration was the War Department Constabulary, responsible for the security of the Arsenal, and the offices of the Munitions Inspectorate of the three services.

Other buildings in the group included a surgery, a first-aid and cleansing centre, a fire station, laboratories, a canteen and restaurant, and garages. Here too was one of the main entrances to the Arsenal. The buildings that made up the main administrative offices of the Arsenal are still in use today as the headquarters of the South Wales Police Force.

Directly to the east of the main Administrative building was Group 1, the Initiator Group where Detonators were manufactured for, among others, 20mm cannon shells as used by Spitfire fighters, and 40mm and 20 pounder anti-aircraft shells. The Initiators, or Detonators were the primary trigger for explosive devices. Roy Davies of Bridgend gives one impression of what it was like to work there:

> Initiators was more dangerous – that's where the dets were made up. I was with other boys there; a lot of them were from Maesteg and from the Garw Valley. We were on the machines pressing detonators. There were brass plates, quarter of an inch thick, about 20 moulds on a plate, with the detonators inside, and you were pressing the powder in using water pressure. The machine had

> special thick glass, and we'd watch them through the glass. We had a little egg timer thing – you had to leave the plates for two or three minutes for the dets to settle in the machine, but it would still go off BANG !! You'd be deaf, then, you couldn't hear a thing. It would buckle the plate; you'd have to put a new plate in. Then you'd do four or five more – you'd do another half-hour. Then, BANG, it'd go off again. It would damage the punches, and the overlooker would have to get the engineer.

Richard Rees, an ex-collier and Arsenal worker explained the need for strict regulations and extreme care in Group 1 in an article in the *Empire News* in 1957:

> Workers knew only too well when they started a shift that it might be their last – ended violently by the treacherous fulminate of mercury, a harmless-looking light brown powder, and lead azide, which looked rather like castor sugar. This was the stuff that had to be pressed into the shining detonators at pressures of up to 15,000lb per square inch. We called them Tweedledum and Tweedledee.

East of the Initiator Group, but still in the southern half of the site was the Pellet Group, Group 2, where yellow powder was fitted into circular pellets. The yellow powder was a Composition Explosive (CE), usually Tetryl. The pellets were used as a secondary trigger in the ignition process.

To the east of the Pellet Group was another main entrance where buses would deliver workers to the Factory at the start of each shift. Next to the entrance was the Textiles section. This was where girls of 16 and 17 worked – they were not allowed to come into contact with explosives until they reached the age of 18. In the Textiles building factory clothing, including clean-side overalls and headgear, was manufactured and repaired. The operatives worked at cutting tables, sat at rows of sewing machines, or pressed completed articles. Betty Nettle recalled that when she started:

> Half of us had never seen a sewing machine in our lives, but we soon learned. We made trousers, jackets, waistcoats and caps for men out of a thick material. For the women we made white coats and caps, and belts with the colour of the shift. We also repaired shoes.

As well as clothing, specialist material items were made in Textiles, including parachutes, packing material, washers, spacers, discs, cambric strips for priming, exploder bags and cordite charge bags. Another part of the shop produced goods made of cardboard and paper, such as corrugated packing. Betty Nettle described the work:

> we made boxes and tubes out of sheets of material and glue. There were lots of machines for cutting out shapes, and huge guillotines to cut the card for pasting. The men who worked these thought they were chocolate!

The laundry washed garments on an industrial scale. It handled over 100,000 items per week, with a dry weight of over 20 tons. One of the problems that had to be dealt with in the laundry was the cleaning of used garments impregnated with explosive materials. For example TNT has a melting point of 83 degrees Centigrade: to get rid of the chemical from the material the woollen overalls had to be washed at that temperature. But of course this heat causes woollen fabric to shrink. A special press was used to reduce shrinkage, but it took considerable skill to maintain the shape of the garments.

Underneath the textiles rooms was the biggest canteen on the Arsenal. Here meals were prepared in the kitchen: there was a vegetable preparation room, and a bakery that produced bread, cakes, buns and doughnuts. Textiles canteen also prepared the food to be served in the smaller satellite canteens in the different groups. At the far end opposite the buffet counter was a stage for entertainments. There was a separate dining room with waitress service for people of higher rank. Rowena Harris, who worked in the canteen, did not approve of this separation:

> Well, that didn't help pulling together; we didn't think it should have been there to be honest. We didn't see why they couldn't have their dinner like anybody else.

Rowena catalogued activity in the canteen:

> When we started in the morning, the first thing we did was make hundreds and hundreds of toasts. They'd all have a cup of tea and toast. Mind, we didn't let people buy up a whole loaf – they would have one or two pieces of toast. You could have a dinner for a

> shilling or something. The cigarettes we could sell one at a time because the people came out of the danger area and had a cup of tea. They only had time for one cigarette and then had to go back into the danger area. When we sold tea, we had to measure the sugar and each person was allowed just about the size of my nail. Of course, we had to do all the cleaning and those urns, they shone, it was real hard work. We used to wash the walls down from time to time. And a lot of people when they had finished work, they come to the canteen before going to their buses and buy cakes and sandwiches, because you couldn't get them outside the Arsenal because of the rationing: this food wasn't on ration.

Next to textiles was the Machine Shops area, where were based the various engineers, mechanics, plumbers, electricians and carpenters that designed, manufactured, serviced and repaired machinery and systems across the site. The shops contained lathes, drilling machines, overhead travelling cranes, a forge, machines for welding and sheet metal work as well as all the equipment needed for the woodwork shop. Here also was a garage and a locomotive shed where motor vehicles and railway engines were serviced and repaired. This was the headquarters for the Arsenal's fleet of some 20 cars (driven by chauffeuses) used to transport important people around the Factory, or to other locations. These service areas together comprised Group OM.

North of the Textiles area was a section known as Group B. This was where the different types of fuzes were manufactured, and originally had a separate factory number – 41. However to all intents and purposes, Factory 41 was a part of Factory 53.

Nearest to the village of Coychurch, in the northeast of the site was the Smoke and Pyrotechnic Group, Group 6. This section filled a variety of non-explosive stores: smoke shells – used to screen attacking troops; flares – designed to indicate targets to aircraft; signal shells – producing different colours for communication; thunder flashes – used in training to simulate the battle experience. In addition tracer rounds were filled here. A fireman at the Arsenal, Redwood described what happened when one of the smoke bombs went off by accident:

> we had an alarm, and we tore out with the engine, and when we got there one of these canisters had leaked and gone off, and the

Building 6D4 in Pyro, taken in the 1980s

> whole place was full of an oily black smoke. And what they were afraid of was, there were thousands of these stored ready to be taken away, so we had to get them out and we had to use breathing apparatus. We got the crate out that was holding the smoke bomb that had started off.

Returning west across the northern half of the site, to the south of the main south Wales railway line, the Cordite Group, Group 5 is next. Cordite was mainly used as a propellant to deliver the explosive to the target: the Cordite was packed into bags, cartridges or cylinders.

The next section directly to the west of the Cordite Group was the Gunpowder Group, Group 4. Fine-grained gunpowder was used in time fuzes for priming shells. Joan Hunt described what it was like to work there: 'I ended up working in the 'Black Shop.' The gunpowder got everywhere, so it was like working in a pit.'

Between Group 7 and the railway line to the north was Group 3. This was the Fuze Group, where a huge variety of fuzes were filled, including time and percussion fuzes. According to Redwood:

> Bridgend had the honour well, if you can call it an honour, of making the fuze for the blockbuster[9], Blue Peter, I think they called it. It was a very big fuze, and quite a lot of intricate work with it. Bridgend had the contract, and they were the blockbusters that they used to drop on Germany – Cologne and places like that: they caused tremendous havoc.

Also In Group 3 were the Proof Yards where completed stores were tested. Here a random but calculated selection of munitions were fired to check that the inspection of processes was satisfactory, that the ammunition could be stored and transported safely, and that the items would perform as required on the battlefield. In his 1949 history of Royal Ordnance Factories, Ian Hay describes an example of the testing process:

> Half a dozen fuzes were set to detonate in a given time – 11 seconds. Each was then placed in device resembling the breech of a gun, and the 'gun' was fired by a smart blow from a heavy hammer…The igniting spark, travelling along the powder train within the fuze, reached the detonator, and exploded it. In every case the time recorded was within less than one-tenth of a second of the 11 seconds, and so the rest of the batch was passed.

Not all workshops in the different groups were used for production. A great deal of research went on in various places about the site. Myra Jenkins enjoyed doing this type of work:

> I went into the experimental section. I liked what they were doing there. There was not that rush that I'd had in the other workshops, it wasn't as busy. It wasn't so humdrum, much more interesting. You had various types of things to inspect. Anything new that was brought in would be tried out by them before it was put into production. Most of the staff working in experimental were College girls, Oxford, and they were very nice. They were charming people, they would do all the experimental work and we would do the inspections.

To the south of Group 3 and Group 4 was Group 7, the line of reinforced and earth-covered stores, where completed ammunition was kept before being sent out. These buildings were built along the line of the current main avenue, Kingsway, through the industrial estate. Teresa Barnett describes them as 'like giant molehills, but flat topped.' She remembers tall daisies swaying on the top of these mounds in May and June each year.

On the other side of the Bridgend–Coychurch road was 'Watertown Moor'. This area was part of the Arsenal's land and was given the designation of Group WM – which presumably stood for Watertown Moor. Here was the Burning Ground and

Rocket Range, which were linked to the main Factory by a tunnel under the road. Faulty, contaminated or redundant explosive materials were destroyed there by burning, using an electric system of ignition to avoid explosions. Redundant TNT, for example, was allowed to solidify, broken up into small pieces, and then ignited in steel trays where it burnt in a roaring bonfire of hot red flames and dense black smoke.[10] Because of the blackout destruction took place in daylight. An article in the *ROF 53 News* for November 1942 gives a fanciful description of what would have been seen if incineration had taken place at night:

> Green and red flares; great roaring, leaping yellow flames of cordite; huge clouds from Smoke composition and, occasionally, Star Shell parachutes floating across the sky-line.

But, according to the writer, during the day

> to see anything of the show you must be near at hand when it hisses warningly at you and occasionally detonates violently.

The article goes on to appeal to workers in other sections to ensure that material sent for destruction was as safe as possible:

> Every care has to be taken to prevent the increase of dangerous hazards. Burning Ground staff have something more to bother about than tending fires in the wind, cold and rain. These men must always be on the alert, and improperly dispatched consignments from the factory may spell real danger to these men where none should exist. Carelessness on the part of persons is unforgivable when dealing with explosive waste.

Rather testily the writer reminds his readers that

> General Safety Directions are not provided as an additional annoyance to the staff, but to safeguard yours and the other man's life.

The Burning Ground was used as a training area for the Factory Fire Brigade. Fireman Redwood described a session:

> The Chief's favourite trick was, he'd trigger off one of these alarms and get the Fire Brigade out and he'd be waiting at this point which he triggered off, and then he'd direct us to the Burning Ground. There was a river down there and he put us through a series of drill and it was two or three o'clock in the morning, and we'd came back from there all our hose was soaking wet and we had two or three

> hours work scrubbing up the hoses and putting them out to dry on the big tower and he would go back home to bed rubbing his hands and we were absolutely done up!

Every one of the buildings in the Factory, including toilets and air raid shelters, was given a unique number. This consisted of three parts: the group number, followed by the letter indicating a series of buildings in a sub-group, followed by a number of the building within that sub group. Thus the canteen in the Initiator Group, Group 1 was numbered 1J1, and a workshop in the Pellet Group, Group 2, was numbered 2B6. On the northern site, the magazines under Brackla Hill were numbered successively 8X1 to 8X7.

The Arsenal was designed and built to what were the very latest and highest standards. Chamberlain's 1937 Factory Act had been introduced during the design period of the Arsenal, and crown factories had not been exempted; planners had had to take those regulations into account in their work. The Act set down new requirements for cleanliness, temperature, ventilation, lighting, sanitary conveniences, washing facilities, changing rooms, and the safety of machinery. In any case the overwhelming importance of safety impelled the architects to design to high specifications. In addition properly equipped facilities for the workers such as surgeries, and subsidised canteens were provided to encourage satisfied workers and so high production.

Such good provision had not previously been a part of the south Wales industrial experience. Pre-war working conditions in the many existing pits and metallurgical works of Glamorgan had been poor; they were noisy, dirty and dangerous places, lacking many basic and civilising facilities. The ruling elite had considered even the concept of the provision of pithead baths to be dangerously revolutionary. Many factories (producing motor cars or electrical goods) with modern facilities had been built in Britain in the 1930s, but these were largely confined to the prosperous areas of the south east of England, around conurbations such as Oxford and London; they were outside the consciousness of those who had not moved to England in search of work. There can be little doubt that the experience of so many, from such a wide area of southern Wales, of such good working and welfare conditions in the Bridgend Arsenal raised the post-war expectations of Welsh unions and workers for better standards in other places of employment – especially as the coal, steel and transport industries were nationalised by the Labour Government in the later 1940s.

Housing

Scattered around the boundary of the main Factory site were houses that were allocated to important staff working at the Arsenal. A number of these were dwellings that predated the Factory; presumably they were compulsory requisitioned from their original owners. Near Coychurch were Frondeg and Maesgwyn; south of Group 1 was Priory View: adjacent to the Main Administration building was Afan Court: to the north, on the old Coychurch road was Picton Court plus seven smaller existing houses, and five newly built (known collectively as Ordnance Terrace). These quarters on Coychurch Road enjoyed their own footbridge over the main railway line giving access to the Factory. Nearby, and opposite the then Wainskill Farm[11] two grand new houses named Woolwich House and Ordnance House were built for senior management. There seem to have been

'Woolwich House' – built for senior management on Coychurch Road

twenty-four houses for top managerial staff, and about twenty houses for key workers, Collectively these staff dwellings were given the group title of OQ (ordnance quarters).

The management at the Arsenal was able to demand and adapt other houses if the need arose. In June1941 Bridgend Council received a letter from the management at the ROF asking that houses in Bridgend be commandeered 'for key men employed at the Factory.' Councillors tried to protect the interests of their constituents, and expressed concern about the 'special financial difficulties in which owners of properties in Parcau Road would be placed if such premises were requisitioned.' But the local authority was powerless, and a number of properties were occupied: for example, numbers 7 and 11 Merthyr Mawr Road were appropriated and converted into flats for transferred war workers at a cost of £418. Hope Chapel's Manse was also used for Arsenal workers – the owners were paid £1 per week in compensation. Not every landlord submitted graciously to the needs of the national crisis: On 29th December 1941 Superintendent May of the Glamorgan Police notes in his Diary that Ivor Price, a local bookmaker, was resisting the occupation of the house named Pencastell that he owned in West Road, Bridgend, and which had been requisitioned by the War Department for a Royal Ordnance Factory worker: policemen had to enforce the seizure.

Two housing estates were built to house the families of

Bryntirion Estate

employees who had been brought from the Woolwich Arsenal or other employment in London to work at ROF 53: one at Bryntirion, to the west of Bridgend, and the other at Abergarw to the north of the town.

The Bryntirion estate was built alongside the road between Bridgend and Laleston: the architects were Colcutt & Hamp of Chesham. About 180 temporary bungalows were constructed there. After the war the original houses were replaced by more permanent structures, but the location is easily identified today because the names of the roads on the original estate survive: Broad Oak Way, Chestnut Way, Elm Crescent, Ton Glas, Coed Helyg, Bryn Glas.

The Abergarw estate was situated between Bryncethin and Brynmenyn, on the banks of the River Ogmore. One new resident commented that 'it was as if a magic carpet had transported a collection of people from London to this quiet corner of the Glamorgan countryside.' Not all the incomers were appreciative

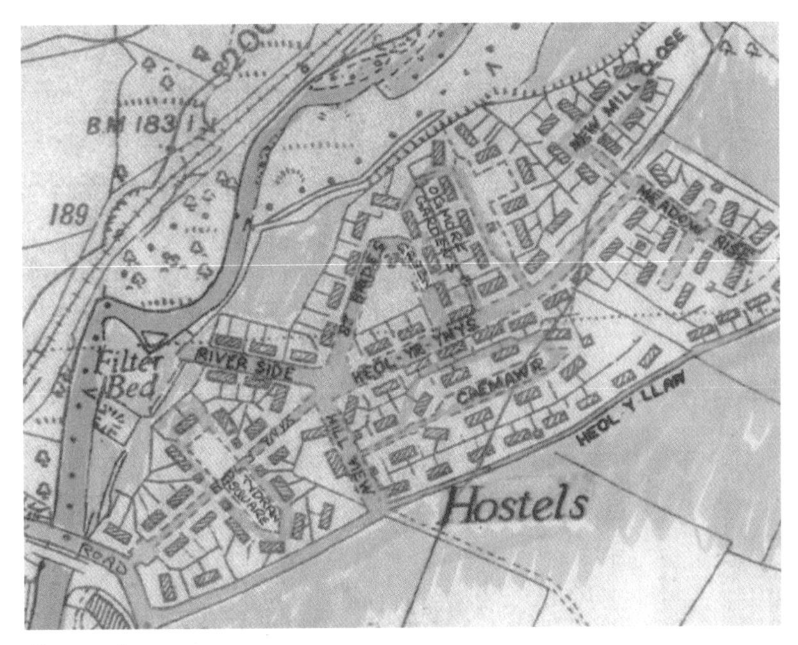

Abergarw Estate

of their new surroundings. One Londoner, a Mr Stidolph, characterised the area as 'nothing but cows and grass!' which seems to undervalue the sheep and horses that also foraged on the nearby commons. The estate was commonly known as 'the Hostels,' but in fact it consisted of some 200 semi-detached bungalows, set along eight roads and cul-de-sacs, and around grassy areas such as Tydraw Square. Some of the dwellings were made of wood, some of brick: some had two bedrooms, some three.

Many of the inhabitants of the new estates were delighted to secure one of the houses, as they had been living in digs before. Typical of the newcomers from London were the Lazell and White families. Ted Lazell had been brought to south Wales to run the printing works at the Arsenal, and for eighteen months he, his wife and two sons had lived in rooms in Porthcawl; they were allocated a house in the spring of 1942. Even more pleased to arrive at Abergarw were the White family which included five daughters. For a time they were separated, with the two eldest girls placed unhappily in Abertillery; later the seven of them were living in just two rooms in Pencoed, with the cooking done on a Calor gas ring on the landing.

People who lived at Abergarw remember that a marvellous society was created there. According to Vera White, 'friendships were forged then which have lasted to this day.' David Lazell believed that 'it was a unique community, isolated by the necessities of wartime.' Very many of the inhabitants enthusiastically give their non-working time and talents to provide activities for the estate. Led by Harry White, a Tenants Association was formed, and a community centre was built on St Bride's Green out of a wooden frame and asbestos panels. It was officially opened on 17th April 1943 by the local MP, Ted Williams. The hall enabled a huge variety of functions to take place – Guides, Scouts, Whist drives, old-fashioned dancing, fancy dress parades, concerts like the Friday Social (admission 3d including glass of cordial) and the Saturday Special (admission 9d)[12] plus the annual Pantomime. The estate had other facilities, including air raid shelters, an allotments association store, library and a day nursery. The bungalows had a design life of ten years, but were still in use in the 60s. Today the area, like the Arsenal itself, is an estate of factories. A hugely entertaining description of life on the Abergarw estate can be found in David Lazell's autobiography, *The Bridgend Biffy.*

Two huge Hostels were built to accommodate single workers in dormitory-type accommodation at Island Farm[13] and at Pencoed.

The Superintendents

The Lord of this Empire was the Superintendent. There seem to have been two senior managers of the Arsenal. The first Superintendent was Reg Edmonds. He had been chosen from amongst the senior staff at Woolwich to get the Bridgend Factory started. Edmonds was born on 5th March 1895, in Sundorne

Reg Edmonds (in the centre) with Bennett, former Prime Minister of Canada

Road, Charlton, no more than two miles from the Woolwich Arsenal. Christened Reginald Joseph, he was the son of Josiah and Annie Edmonds[14], both themselves born in south London. Reginald must have inherited his interest in technical skills from his father, who, according to Reg's birth certificate, was a mechanical engineer. Presumably Edmonds must have joined the staff of the nearby Woolwich Arsenal soon after leaving school, and worked his way up to a senior position by the outbreak of Second World War.

By December 1939, aged 44, Edmonds was in charge of ROF 53, and managed it during its difficult early days. According to the telephone directory for 1941, he was living in Picton Court in Coychurch Road, one of the houses requisitioned for the Factory. Sometime during 1941 he left the Factory, and became the Assistant Director of Filling Factories for the Western Region (comprising Bridgend, Glascoed and Hereford). From 1947 to 1950 he was the Superintendent of ROF Glascoed, which continued to operate after the war.

His replacement at Bridgend, Len Corbett, came from an entirely different environment – chocolate. Corbett's story is a truly remarkable one. He was born in Bristol on May 12th 1897, and christened Leonard James. His father – James Corbett – came from Rotherham in Yorkshire, and worked as a railway clerk. His mother was a Bristol girl, Emma Mary (nee Vowles). Corbett went to school in Bristol, first to Sefton Park and then to Fairfield Secondary School.

As soon as he was 18, in 1915, Corbett joined the Army Service Corps. The ASC was the vast organization that transported supplies such as food, equipment and ammunition to the front in Belgium and France. In the Great War the vast majority of this tonnage was brought from England by sea and then transported to where it was needed, using horsed and motor vehicles, railways and waterways. The ASC performed prodigious feats of logistics and so contributed significantly to the eventual victory. Corbett's father worked for the railways – so did Corbett join the ASC because of that background? Perhaps he had got a job with the railways when he left school. Certainly the experience of being part of a huge organization dealing in among other things the efficient movement of armaments would be useful to Corbett at Bridgend.

After the war Corbett returned to Bristol and worked for the largest employer in Bristol, Fry's, the chocolate manufacturers, based then in Union Street. In 1921 Fry's decided to move to a new site, Somerdale, at Keynsham. Presumably Corbett was involved in organising the factory move, which was not completed till 1935. The Somerdale factory employed 5000 people. If Corbett was a manager at Somerdale, then he would have gained valuable experience at managing a large workforce.

In line with their Quaker beliefs, the owners (the Fry and Cadbury families) were interested in the welfare of their workers. The directors tried to encourage the spirit of "Happiness in Industry": medical services, pension schemes and other welfare provisions were made available to employees. Playing fields and facilities for social activities such as amateur dramatics, music and photography were an integral part of the Somerdale plans. There was a vegetable garden providing supplies for the subsidised works canteen. Again, experience of this ethos would have been invaluable to Corbett at Bridgend – perhaps he was brought to the Arsenal partly because of his experience at organizing the provision of services and leisure time organizations to improve morale and hence production.

During this period, Corbett proved to be an exceptionally talented sportsman. He was good enough to play cricket for Gloucestershire in nine county championship matches. A right-hand bat, he scored 373 runs at an average of 21, and with a highest score of 55.

But his greatest ability was in rugby. He played in the centre for his home town, Bristol, over 200 times, scoring 98 tries and 27 drop goals. He went on to win 16 caps for England between 1921 to 1927 including one match against the New Zealand tourists. He played four times against Wales, and was always on the winning side[15]. In 1924 he was selected for the Lions tour of South Africa but he did not go, as his employers would not release him. His leadership qualities were shown when he was chosen to be captain of England for all four games in 1927.

On his first selection for England, Corbett received in the post a six inch square of cream flannel with the red rose of England. The player had to provide the rest of the kit. His family were too poor to buy a new white jersey, so his mother sewed the badge onto one of his father's woollen vests. Unsurprisingly he commented that 'I actually wore that for my international debut, feeling rather self conscious.'[16]

As a player, Corbett was certainly innovative. The Cotham Park (Bristol) RFC website declares that he 'was accredited with selling the first dummy in the game.' Another source proclaims him 'the inventor of the back flip.' In the game against Wales in 1923 he caused a sensation by passing the ball between his legs to his wing, Smallwood, who promptly dropped the winning goal.

According to WJT Collins (in *Rugby Recollections* in 1948)

> Corbett was a very clever runner, a beautiful drop kick, and his touch finding revealed the judgement of a master. Brains, brains, brains! He made as good use of his gifts as any English centre in my time. In some matches his individual genius and captaincy turned the scale in England's favour.

Len Corbett

HJ Henley in *The Game Goes On* (1936) draws a picture of Corbett as a man who could cope with pressure – another attribute that would be essential in managing the Arsenal:

> Has there ever been a cooler player than Corbett? His sang-froid made his presence a joy. He would drop a goal with the nonchalance of a man lighting a cigarette. Nothing affected his air of icy detachment. In addition, his attitude of mind seemed to be reflected in his appearance. Just as nothing could affect his tranquillity, so nothing could ruffle his hair, or disarrange his raiment. His sleek brown head never had a lock astray. It suggested the ballroom rather than a football field. And although so busy a player inevitably got very muddy on a wet day, he never looked bedraggled as other men do.

Another aspect of his character is revealed by an incident after a Pontypool–Bristol game. A player in the Bristol team recalled that after the match the players went to a local hotel for a meal, and found that there was a screen down the room, separating the two teams. Corbett was furious, and insisted that the screen was removed. After that, 'The players had a marvelous evening mixing together.'[17]

In the early months of the war Corbett was involved in the organization of four rugby matches designed to raise money for the Forces Welfare Fund to enable it to provide sports equipment for the armed services. He raised teams representing the West of England, and an Internationals XV.

Some time in 1941, at the age of 44, Corbett was appointed Superintendent of the Arsenal. It may seem surprising that a manager from a chocolate factory should take over control of an armaments factory. In fact it was common government practice to take people with management skills in another area to direct armaments factories. The ordnance factory at Elstow in Bedfordshire was entirely supervised by experienced managers loaned to the Ministry of Supply by the firm of J Lyons & Co – perhaps better known for homely matters such as ice cream, hotels, tea shops, 'Nippies' and Swiss Rolls, rather than for the production of weapons of destruction.

In 1942 Lewis Silkin, the chairman of the eleventh report of the Select Committee on National Expenditure expressed his astonishment at two matters concerning ROF superintendents. The first was that they were paid so little. The salary at that time was £1,500 pa: according to Silkin 'a man responsible for the organization of more than 25,000 workers is worth £5,000 a year.' Silkin was fulsome in his praise of ROF superintendents: 'It is to their credit that in spite of this low remuneration, they are doing excellent work.' The second aspect was their lack of independence. Apparently superintendents could not even appoint a shop manager without getting approval from Woolwich. As Silkin said, 'A superintendent should be king in his own castle...and that is not the position today.'[18]

When the Arsenal closed, Corbett was the obvious choice to oversee a smooth transfer to peaceful production as the manager of the new industrial estate on the Waterton site. On 1st October 1947 he became General Manager of the Wales and Monmouthshire Industrial Estates Company, controlling industrial estates and factories from Trefforest in the south to Wrexham and Anglesey in the north. In March 1956 he was appointed a director of the company. Geoffrey Percival in the official history of industrial estates in Wales describes Corbett as 'a man of great force of character.' He retired as General Manager in May 1962, and as a director in 1967, having served the industries of Wales in war and peace for over twenty-five years.

Len Corbett was eventually awarded the OBE. He died on January 26th 1983 aged 85 in the hamlet of Horner on Exmoor, near Porlock. A fireman at the Arsenal gave an epitaph that would no doubt have pleased Corbett: 'He was very fair too, he was a very fair man.'

Corbett in 1960 with Portrait of the Superintendent as a Young Man

Notes

1 Much of the information on the layout of the main site at Waterton comes from a large scale map of the factory drawn in July 1939 and held at Kew (AVIA22/2513)

2 This figure, from 'South Wales Outline Plan,' published in 1949, related to space available for private firms to rent, and may have excluded the area retained by the Royal Navy after the war. The magazines and other storage areas were probably also omitted from this calculation.

3 For details of each engine see appendix A

4 Explosive expense magazines.

5 Filled ammunition stores.

6 High Explosive – probably TNT (Tri-nitro-toluene). Used as the main filling, and to be detonated at or near the target.

7 Cordite – Nitro-glycerine and nitro-cellulose made in the form of cords or sticks. Used as the main propellant to send missiles towards the target.

8 Named after the Swedish company which developed the original version. At El Alamein Bofors guns were used to fire tracer horizontally to mark safe paths for units through German minefields.

9 Blockbuster – a bomb which was powerful enough to flatten a block in a town or city. The largest conventional bombs used by the RAF, varying from 4,000 lb to 12,000 lb. The bomb casings were thin to allow a maximum weight of explosive – basically a dustbin full of explosive.

10 Caused by the presence of carbon released by the action of air on toluene.

11 The 'Haywain' public house today.

12 Starring local groups such as the Western Revellers, the Kenbar Gleemen, and Ken Murray's Concert Party.

13 The story of the hostels is explained in Chapter 6.

14 Annie was born Sarah Ann Elizabeth Marvin.

15 1923 Twickenham 7-3 : 1924 Swansea 17-9 – the first English victory in Wales for 11 years, and the first at Swansea for 29 years: 1925 Twickenham 12-6 – although Corbett did not score, the Daily Mail commented that 'Many men since England first played Wales have done much to win a game for their side, but none can have taken a bigger part in a victory than Corbett played at Twickenham.' : 1927 Twickenham 11-9 – Corbett scored a try and kicked a goal from a mark.

16 Chris Ducker, *Rugby Bristol Fashion.*

17 Chris Ducker, *Rugby Bristol Fashion.*

18 House of Commons debate, August 1942

4: 'Pour Out the Munitions'

The Woolwich Connection

Thoughts now turned towards staffing the Factory and starting production. No one in south Wales had any expertise in the management of such a vast and complex works: the Superintendent and his senior staff would have to come from Woolwich. No one in south Wales had any expertise in the intricate processes of filling components: a nucleus of those process workers able to teach the raw recruits of Glamorgan would have to come from Woolwich and the other established ROFs. We do not know how many men actually came from London to Wales, but we can assume that the figure was similar to that of those transferred to the sister plant at Chorley. The management at Woolwich decided that 472 'Pivotal' staff from Superintendent to Overlooker would go to Lancashire, and a further 190 process workers would be needed to start production and train the workforce. We can therefore surmise that between 600 and 700 staff from Woolwich would have been needed to start up the Bridgend Factory.

Certainly a large group of Woolwich workers arrived in Glamorgan in October 1940 – presumably as trainers. That month the clerk to Maesteg Urban District Council reported that: 'About 400 workers from Woolwich Arsenal had been transferred to the Bridgend Arsenal.' Obviously there were problems in finding enough landladies to look after all these incomers, as the clerk had been asked to 'endeavour to find accommodation for them.' He had sought the aid of formidable allies to deal with the problem. As he reported to the councillors, 'local ladies organizations had been and were canvassing to see what could be done.'

Actually, apart from the possibility of German bombing on London, many of the workers at Woolwich had little incentive to move voluntarily from the capital to what for most of them would have seemed a remote and in some ways a strange place. At that time the pay in the Royal Arsenal varied from £2 19s.8d. to £4 14s.7d. for a 47 hour week. The pay on offer outside London – and therefore at Bridgend – was considerably less. Even enticing relocation allowances of from £5 to £20 could not persuade some. Harry Fletcher was working at the time as an engineer at Woolwich. Notices were put up inviting volunteers to move to Bridgend. Harry recalls,

> I went to look at the notice. The rate of pay was half what I was getting at the time, so I thought – no thanks, not with those wages – and I had in mind that it was only temporary while the war was on.

Harry stayed in London for the duration of hostilities.[1] Those who did move would have found life very different in some ways. David Lazell's father came to southern Wales a little later, but all the transferred staff must have experienced some of the emotions described by David:

> Many of the workers had arrived at short notice, and there was an inevitable culture shock for anyone who had been in Putney High Street, London, one Thursday, and at a bus stop in Brynmenyn a week later!

Nevertheless by December a small nucleus of 28 led by the first Superintendent, Reg Edmonds, had arrived at Bridgend from Woolwich. Obviously construction was still in progress, and completed buildings had to be fitted out with services and equipment, including the machinery associated with the many processes that would take place in the Arsenal. Gee,Walker & Slater came up with an ingenious idea to expedite completion. They needed a way to transport equipment and materials to finish off buildings, but the clearways that provided access were too constricted to accommodate the usual lorries. Someone discovered that the width (or track) of Austin 7[2] motor cars was narrow enough (at just 40 inches) to fit the clearways, and light enough, (at 794 pounds) not to damage the special newly-laid surface. A small fleet was bought, and adapted to carry equipment and materials to and from the multitude of workshops about the site.

A snapshot of the situation at the beginning of 1940 is revealed in a report written on 12th January to a Dr Bridge – presumably at Woolwich. In it the author says that he had visited the Arsenal four days before, and that it had 'not yet started any form of production,' but that it was 'intended that work should start in February.' In the event this proved optimistic – though not by much. In the same month in a speech at Manchester, the Prime Minister, Churchill, tried to inspire the people of Britain to dedicate themselves to the effort and sacrifices needed to achieve victory.

> Come then, let us to the task... to the battle, to the toil – each to our part, each to our station. Fill the armies, rule the air, pour out the munitions…There is not a week, not a day, nor an hour to lose.

The people of south Wales would soon have the opportunity to respond to his urgent appeal.

Production begins.

There were just 312 employees at Bridgend by March 1940, but tentative and limited production actually did finally start early that month. Dr. Bridge's correspondent wrote to him again to report on a further visit to Bridgend on 15th March:

> They have started within the last fortnight some process work in a very small way on the day shift, employing at present males only…The work consists of filling gunpowder into cartridge cases, and fitting (but not making or filling) the fulminate of mercury cap; some forty workers were so employed in excellent working surroundings…We traversed much of the extensive area

> of the factory, visiting canteens, bathhouses, changing rooms etc. There is nothing really doing yet.

But there would be – and not before time: the situation of the country would soon be desperate. In May, Germany invaded and occupied Holland, Belgium and northern France. Dunkirk may have saved much of the BEF, but the rescued soldiers had abandoned the equipment and ammunition of nearly 10 divisions on the Continent. According to Postan, in June 1940 Britain was

> standing not only alone, but also unarmed. The whole of the supplies available at home on the morrow of Dunkirk was barely sufficient to equip 2 divisions.[3]

Most of the 1,500,000 soldiers in the Army had no weapons at all – training took place in a world of make believe. It would be some two to three years before sufficient weapons had been stockpiled to enable British forces to take on an offensive role. It was to play a vital part in producing those armaments that Bridgend ROF had been built. Now was the time to produce the goods.

The management of staff in the first months was complicated. Bridgend was of course dependent on a consistent inflow of weapon components and explosives from other factories, and in the early part of the war many of these other workplaces, like Bridgend, were in the process of being built, equipped and staffed. Thus ROF 53 had to wait until Pembrey started to produce the explosives TNT and Tetryl, until Marchwiel (near Wrexham) and the Royal Naval Propellant Factory at Caerwent began to manufacture cordite, and until Theale (plus many other, private, factories) started to produce the fuzes and other components that were to be filled at Bridgend.[4] In addition much of the Factory was a construction site for most of 1940. For these reasons it was difficult at first to ensure that all staff were gainfully employed. The overall impression given at this time is that systems and machinery were being tested, in preparation for the huge influx of untrained labour that was soon to pour into the Factory. Writing in the Factory magazine *ROF 53 News* in November 1942, Billy Hughes, a worker at Bridgend, remembered that

> during the time that labour was being recruited for the factory in the early days, the position seemed very confused and it looked as if production would never start.

Recruiting the workforce.

As Hornby commented in *Factories and Plant*,

> the problem of recruiting the large labour force required [by the filling factories] constituted a major operation, and to do this in a short period was even more difficult.

The process had begun at Bridgend in January 1940, when 350 women were interviewed for positions at the Factory. The numbers of workers employed at the Arsenal grew with extraordinary speed during 1940 and 1941: well over a thousand people were processed every month. In April 1940 there were just 700 male workers – including the original nucleus brought in from Woolwich – and 250 females recruited locally, making a workforce numbering less than a thousand. Within two months there were 1,471 males and 2,071 females, a total of 3,542; by the end of 1940 the number of operatives employed at the Factory had passed 10,000. In December 1940 the workforce at the sister plant of Chorley, which had started production a year before, was considerably larger than ROF 53, at 17,800 – but Bridgend would soon catch up and surpass the Lancashire plant[5].

Numbers employed at the Bridgend Arsenal: September 1939 – December 1940

Date		Male	Female	Total
1939	Sept-Dec			28
1940	March			312
	April	700	250	950
	May	1200	1150	2350
	June	1471	2071	3542
	Sept	2064	3884	5948
	Oct	2418	4946	7364
	Nov	2835	6005	8840
	Dec	3327	6810	10137

It must be remembered that the number of applicants processed was far greater that the number of workers listed as employed, for two reasons. First of all many applicants were judged to be unsuitable for a variety of factors, and so not given jobs at the Factory: secondly many of those appointed were either dismissed, or decided for themselves that factory work was not for them[6]. The recruitment, medical examination, allocation and training of such huge numbers in such a brief time is little short of remarkable, and a tribute to the organizing capacity and sheer hard work of the management team and the process workers from Woolwich, and of the new recruits.

One of the reasons for the successful recruitment of men for the Factory was the continuing high rate of unemployment in Glamorgan. As we have seen, one of the factors securing the location of the Arsenal in southern Wales was that this was a 'Depressed' area of exceptionally high unemployment. The construction of the Factory had provided several thousand temporary jobs, but overall the National Government's effort in the 1930s to reduce the numbers of the workless in Wales had been tentative, and pitifully under-funded. Kenneth Morgan in his *Wales 1880 – 1980* criticised the official relief programme as 'ill-conceived and half-hearted.' He went on to write that

> relative to other, more thriving parts of Britain, the Welsh coalfield actually fell back...With its continuing high unemployment in the coal, steel and tinplate industries, it showed far fewer signs of recovery than did [areas with] a more diversified industrial base.

Even in 1939, and despite massive emigration, the official jobless figure for southern Wales stood at well over 100,000: in contrast, the total number of jobs created in new factories in the whole of south Wales amounted to a derisory 3,043. All this ensured that there was no shortage of applicants for positions at the Factory. As Hornby pointed out in the official history of the War

> it was significant that the Bridgend factory, located in south Wales, where unemployment persisted even in 1940, had the least difficulty [of all the filling factories] in recruiting labour.

The vast majority of those registered as unemployed were men. By May 1940 all eligible males under the age of 28 (the younger, and therefore fitter and healthier) had been swept up with conscription for the armed forces. The men that remained available for employment at the Arsenal were inevitably older, and potentially less fit. In addition, very many of the applicants had been out of work for years. This presented problems. New recruits had to undergo a strict medical examination, managed at Bridgend by a local GP, Baird Milne. The standard set for this test by Woolwich was the same as that used in peacetime, and was not dissimilar to the level required for entry to the army. In fact the examination was much more stringent than that used to process workers for privately owned weapons factories. The result was that a large number of potential workers were rejected. At Chorley a high percentage of the male interviewees were not appointed, and we can presume that there were similar problems at Bridgend[7]. Interestingly the percentage of women recruits who failed the test was less than half that of men – presumably because the women were younger and healthier. MacNalty (in the official report on health and medical services during the war) gives figures for rejects at one ROF as 35% of males and 14% of females. In June 1940 the Director-General of Ordnance Factories himself expressed concern about the rate of rejection:

> We are being hampered in our efforts to increase our number of employees through the operation of our requiring all candidates to undergo a thorough medical examination.

In August 1940 the medical standards were marginally lowered; medical officers were told to use their common sense and not to reject all but the fittest. Officials were further asked to take account of the needs of the actual job to be done by each applicant.

The issue caused frustration and anger locally, and revealed a prejudice against women obtaining jobs while men remained unemployed. That autumn the Maesteg Council expressed concern at the difficulties which men without work were experiencing in obtaining positions at the Arsenal. In October councillors were eager to assist in 'obtaining employment at the Arsenal for men who were not fit enough for manual labour, but who could do work at present carried out by women.' It was resolved to contact the Factory's management to try to influence employment policy. Presumably little satisfaction was obtained, since in November the councillors appealed directly to the Minister of Labour with a more precise and forceful resolution:

> Owing to the very high figure of unemployment in this area... all vacancies at the Factory should be filled by men and not women

It is not surprising that this intervention by the Maesteg Council could not affect policy when we consider that the Ministry's own Welfare Board was unable to effect any change. As late as May 1941 the Board complained about the medical examination as an obstacle to the recruitment of labour, and went on to request 'that the present arrangement should be very considerably modified.' Despite this appeal no changes were authorised. There is a suspicion that civil servants were refusing to change in order to avoid paying compensation if workers unfit in some way were appointed, and subsequently suffered injury or illness. Obviously fear of a compensation culture is not a new thing. By mid-1942 just over 3,000 ex-coalminers had managed to pass the examinations, and most of those were classed as fit for light work only.

Training

Very few of the recruits to Bridgend – men or women – came from a factory background[8]. An article in the *Western Mail* in 1935 had predicted the problem: – 'How can Welsh girls be expected to take kindly to factory conditions when nothing in the traditions of their home or social life has prepared them for this kind of work?' In November 1941 Superintendent Corbett complained that the Arsenal management had 'to deal with people who were not industrially-minded'. Billy Hughes, writing in the Factory magazine, in 1942 agreed:

> We people of Wales have never been factory-minded. At the commencement of work here we looked with amazement at the different components as they were brought before us on the bench to be assembled into the real thing.

Inevitably there were major problems of adjustment to the different ways of operating in a munitions factory. Numbers of those given jobs were soon found to be unsuitable, often because they flouted Factory rules. Hay quotes one manager as complaining that some of the newly employed were 'only too prone to use a hammer vigorously on components filled with explosives, or to use a stick of TNT as chalk.' For a period at Chorley almost as many men were being dismissed as were started.

The new entry at Bridgend had never before so much as filled a banger for Guy Fawkes night, and it was only too clear that they would have to be schooled in the ways of an ordnance factory. What formal instruction was provided? Recruiting adverts in the local press implied that the level of skill required was not very high, and so not much training would be necessary. An article in the *South Wales Echo* in 1940 suggested rather casually that working in munitions factories was 'A straightforward job, easily picked up.' A 1941 advert in the *Glamorgan Advertiser* explained that 'No previous experience is necessary.' Later that year the management declared that: 'Any housewife who can bake a cake can do the work required.' Yet, as Billy Hughes suggested, when the new employees started work they would be faced with an alien situation, unfamiliar processes, and an entirely new language of terms and initials. In the early days recruits were often placed first into the incoming component warehouses where they could work alongside Woolwich veterans, and so become accustomed to the essential discipline and to sensible ways of working. Billy Hughes was to pay fulsome tribute to these Woolwich trainers:

> our friends from other factories with great patience and tact instructed us in the operation. Gradually there grew a bond between the staff [from Woolwich], and the operator willing to cooperate.[9]

Former workers are unable to recall a great deal of tuition. Betty Cartlidge was put in Dets: according to her, 'We had no training – they just showed us what to do, and we got on with it.' Joan Chuckley agrees with this description: 'We had no training. They took you up to the section and that was it.' One of Mari Williams' interviewees (quoted in her book *The Forgotten Army*) remembers that 'We did a little course, what we had to do, and how careful we had to be.' Later she was required to show new workers the task, but the guidance 'wasn't very long, because we didn't know much ourselves.' Two CIA examiners, Myra Jenkins and Sally Loveday recollect having had little training for their work. The truth was that many of the jobs in the Factory were straightforward and repetitive, and not much preparation was needed. Peggy Inman (in the official history of *Labour in the Munitions Industry*) notes that 'In many operations in the filling factories recruits could be trained in a day,' though she goes on to comment that other tasks required up to a fortnight's instruction. The official line was that enough instruction was provided. Hay commented that the 'delicate and intricate work' done in the ROFs could 'only have been performed by highly trained workers,' and went on to describe the information given at a factory training school: 'The course had of necessity to be brief, but it served its valuable purpose in imparting certain fundamental rules.' At first the course was usually of just half a day's duration; the new recruits suffered a series of lectures, and were issued with sheets on the dos and don'ts of a munitions workshop. From the spring of 1941 the course was extended to a day,

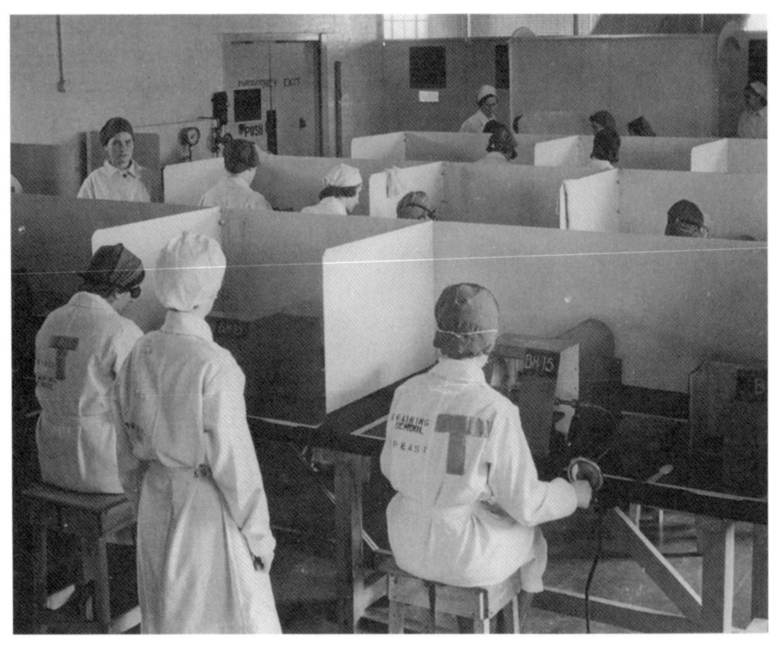

Training Department, B East

and included attempts to inspire the workers with the importance of their work. Two photographs have survived which show women in the training department of ROF Bridgend – one wearing an overall clearly marked 'Training school' and a very large letter T – presumably standing for Trainee. The actual task that each operative would perform seems to have been explained in the relevant workshop, and on the job. How effective was the training provided at the Factory? The safety record of Bridgend was reasonably good[10], so it would seem that the introductory training provided at ROF 53 was at least sufficient for the tasks in hand.

'She's the Girl That Makes the Thing'

As more buildings were fitted out with machinery, and as supplies began to pour into the Arsenal, more and more staff were needed in the administration offices, and in the completed workshops. Despite the opposition expressed by the Maesteg Council, the vast majority of this workforce was to be female, and it is obvious from the table above that increasingly most of the new recruits were women. The January letter to Dr Bridge reported that it was planned at that time that 70% of the total labour force would be women. Already by December 1940 there were twice as many female as male employees in the Arsenal; by the end of 1941 73% of the workforce was female.

It had always been envisaged that once war began, the bulk of the employees in filling factories would be women. In the first place there would be insufficient males available because of the demands of the fighting forces. And secondly there was a common perception that women had smaller fingers and so were more dextrous, and would be better able to work with the small components processed at factories like Bridgend. Inman affirmed that 'The ROFs preferred to employ women workers in many occupations,' and that 'particularly intelligent and deft fingered women were needed in fuze and initiator sections.' Hay confirms this stereotyping by reporting that 'women workers, one is everywhere informed, were capable of far greater concentration than their male colleagues.' Even the Minister of Labour claimed in 1941 that the work available at Bridgend needed 'nimbleness and dexterity,' and so was 'particularly suitable for women.'

On the face of it there were many potential problems which might have made working at ROF 53 unattractive to the women of south Wales. These disincentives included: fear of the unknown, of unfamiliar processes and of strange substances; the huge size of the Factory; the lack of a tradition of female working outside the home; the perception that factory workers were somehow 'common'; disease, accidents and explosions; discipline and regulation; the possibility of unwanted attention from the Luftwaffe; the considerable distances to be travelled to work; night-time shifts; long hours; repetitive work; disruption of domestic responsibilities. In October 1943 the *Aberdare Leader* gave an impression of how the Factory was perceived by outsiders:

> ROF – these three letters... have come to hold rather contrasting meanings for the people of coalmining, conservative, non-conformist south Wales. ROF is hazy in its form and significance, a place quite often mentioned in the police-courts when workers are fined for absenteeism or pilfering...a place associated with unfamiliar sounding industrial terms...an indefinable place of obscure functions.

But despite all this, initially there does not seem to have been a problem in attracting recruits. The local newspaper, the *Glamorgan Gazette*, had no specific advertisements seeking staff for munitions factories till January 1941. Presumably before then all that was required was word of mouth, and radio exhortation[11]. However, according to Mari Williams in *A Forgotten Army*, there was a 'severe shortage of labour at Bridgend ROF' in 1941, which led to a 'big recruiting drive in the area.' The main strategy was to tap a 'large reservoir of unoccupied women [i.e. housewives and young women not in paid employment].'

Stella Old remembers one recruiting device used to demystify the work done in the munitions industry, and so to entice women into the Factory – a live tableau in the main display window of London House[12] 'Four or five munitions girls sat in the window doing their usual job, but using only dummy components.' This may not have given an altogether accurate picture of life in the Factory, for as Stella remarked, 'It was much cleaner than their

Munition Workers

Women (Married or Single)

Urgently Required

for Munition Work.

Age 18 to 50.

Apply nearest Employment Exchange.

usual work.'

The earliest newspaper appeal to women that we have seen, published in the *Gazette* in January 1941, was simple to the extent of being brusque. It comprised a plain, un-illustrated panel, and the text was devoid of any encouragement or incentive. 'Munition Workers' it proclaimed, and then more specifically, 'Women (Married or Single) Urgently Required.' Next it explained 'For Munition Work,' in case readers had not noticed the words 'Munition Workers' at the top of the advert. Further clarification of the target age followed; 'Age 18 to 50', before a peremptory instruction to 'Apply nearest Employment Exchange.' This could hardly be described as a masterpiece of enticing copywriting, and subsequent public notices were far more sophisticated.

A series was published by the Ministry of Labour and printed in successive weekly editions of the *Glamorgan Advertiser* during July 1941. The first one has little text, and is dominated by a drawing of a smiling female worker waving a banner, and encouraging patriotic Welsh women readers to 'Fall in under Wales's War Work Flag,' with a personal promise: 'There's an urgent war job waiting for you.' The advert went on to direct potential workers to

the local office of the Ministry of Labour, 'who will gladly help.' So here is a different tone entirely from the *Gazette* offering, and a much more welcoming appeal.

Subsequent adverts printed in the *Advertiser* are also illustrated, but provide more information. The second shows women busy in a factory above the caption 'South Wales Girls on War Work.' The text starts with another appeal to patriotism. 'The young men are at their posts in the Fighting Services,' it declares; 'Thousands of young women are supporting them in Auxiliary Services.' It's your turn next is the implication of the following sentence: 'Now comes the call to women in all walks of life, who are not yet engaged in any work of National Importance.' The text refers to institutions like the Bridgend Arsenal – 'Vast factories, built and equipped since war began, are now ready to produce to their utmost capacity.' The advert goes on to point out to those fearful that they do not have the necessary expertise that 'no previous experience is necessary.' Women worried that they live 'beyond daily travelling distance' are promised 'excellent hostel accommodation.'

The third appeal in the newspaper displays two women chatting over a garden fence above the caption: 'Let's show 'em what South

Wales can do.' Presumably by headlining an every-day situation, the implication is that the appeal is to ordinary housewives. The text confesses that the country is desperate for female workers; 'The Ministry of Labour wants thousands of women for vital work in local war industries.'

The final announcement in the *Glamorgan Advertiser* was illustrated with a drawing of two women with shopping bags watching a third. The caption is: 'Where IS Mrs. Jones going?' The answer, unsurprisingly, is 'she's off to make munitions.' In this panel the writer appeals to a number of factors. It's the right thing to do; people like Mrs. Jones 'know their duty.' There is a personal advantage for loved ones: she is 'bringing nearer the day when her soldier-husband comes back home.' There is an appeal to feelings of self-worth and of being part of something huge: 'You'll be happier' and the job will be 'of real importance…in the Great Munitions army.' Finally, and for the first time in the series, there is an appeal to greed, as the potential recruit is assured that she will be 'very likely more prosperous' – presumably because of the generous wages on offer at the Bridgend Arsenal.

Of course many women were attracted by the relatively generous wages[13], but they came into the Factory for all sorts of reasons and from all sorts of situations – domestic service, laundry workers, shop assistants, barmaids, waitresses, cooks, seamstresses, milliners, agricultural workers, clerks and typists, and other casual and part-time jobs – and from running homes[14]. Megan Jones of Pencoed remembers:

> I wasn't going to stay in a chemist shop... So off I went to become a clerical assistant, first class, at the Ordnance Factory.

Margaret Plummer was working in a laundry in Swansea for 10s. a week. When her mother prevented her from applying to join the ATS, Margaret said 'Well, I'll go and make the ammunition for the men' – so she went to work at the Factory at Bridgend.

Joan Hunt of Pontypridd was working in a factory on the Trefforest Trading Estate, sewing nurses uniforms, but she decided to transfer to the Bridgend Arsenal because 'it was the best paid job.' Sixteen year-old Betty Reynolds of Stormy Down was a nursemaid in Laleston on 7s.6d. a week:

> I saw my sister, who was working in Pyro [the Pyrotechnics section], had a bit of freedom, so I decided to go down the Arsenal myself.

Betty Edwards of Caerau was in service in Paddington on 18s. a week; she came home when the war broke out. She relates,

> My friends and I said 'let's try the Arsenal.' Well, everyone was going down there. My father and my younger brother worked there as well.

Myra Jenkins was working as a shop girl for Stradlings the grocers in Bridgend. She summed up the situation thus:

> It seemed that everybody wanted to go down the Arsenal. It was an avalanche. They were earning good money down there. And we felt we were doing our little bit for the war.

It was not possible for all new entrants to get the position they wanted. When Lucy Hughes turned 17 she went down to the recruitment office and asked for a job in Admin – but none were available. In fact,

> The clerk laughed like a drain: even a qualified typist couldn't get

> a job in the office: I was told to go into textiles.

Mixing so many people from diverse backgrounds caused a few cultural shocks. Myra Jenkins of Bridgend was embarrassed by the swearing of some fellow-workers:

> You met some very odd types down on the Arsenal, especially girls from the Rhondda, Oh dear me! And the language! I wasn't used to it. My brothers were never allowed to swear at home, in those days you weren't allowed. And they never did, even though they were in the forces. There was a Cockney down there, he was a key man: he was one of them that had come down from Woolwich. He was an awful tease, but he was very fatherly, and he could see who was embarrassed. He used to say to me, "Don't take any notice of them, you'll get used to it, love." Eventually I did get used to it.

Roy Davies of Bridgend was disturbed to find people speaking in a language which he could not understand: he recalled that on his first day at the Arsenal,

> There were a lot of girls around me from West Wales; from Carmarthen, from Swansea, some from the Rhondda valley, and they were all talking in Welsh. They were all looking at me and talking, so I thought, I'm not sticking here. So I walked off, and the overlooker said to me, "Where do you think you're going?" I said, "I'm not staying with them. They're all talking Welsh." And she said, "Well, what are they saying?" and I said, "I don't know, they're talking Welsh, but they're looking at me, so they must be talking about me." Remember, I was the only boy among the whole section and I was only 17. Anyway, I thought I'd better go back. And in the end, I got on all right with them. I got used to them.

Whatever the difficulties for management, and the attractions or social problems for employees, the numbers processed and employed at the Bridgend Arsenal climbed relentlessly during 1941. The table shows that the biggest monthly increase was between March and April that year when the number of men employed went up by 2,000 and that of women by over 5,000. One probable explanation for the huge increase of these months was the introduction in March of compulsory registration for women. At the same time the government applied the Essential Work Order to filling factories like Bridgend. This directive applied to men and women alike, and its purpose was to reduce the number of people giving up work at the Factory for their own reasons by forcing them to notify the national service officer of their intention. This official had the power to refuse permission for the worker to leave the Factory, and in this way the government began to stem the wastage of operatives from munitions factories, including Bridgend.

By the end of the year there were more than 32,000 employees on the books of ROF 53, now probably the largest Factory of any kind in Britain.

Numbers employed at the Bridgend Arsenal: January 1941 – November 1941

Date	Male	Female	Total
Jan	3999	7374	11373
Feb	4614	8559	13173
March	5225	10613	15838
April	7283	15913	23196
May	7642	16432	24074
June	8265	17569	25834
July	8338	18792	27130
Aug	8384	19943	28327
Nov	8581	23465	32046

The Conscription of Women

To ensure a constant stream of new recruits for war work in Britain as a whole, the Government started the process of the conscription of women during 1941. William Beveridge[15] had researched the potential supply of labour for the war effort, and he reported that not only were the demands of war industries bound to rise, but that the demands of the armed forces threatened to produce a 'famine of men.' In January the Minister of Labour, Earnest Bevin, declared that 'the reservoir so far as men are concerned is practically dry.' The implication was that only the unemployable amongst males – the old, the infirm and the recalcitrant – were still available. On the other hand there was a perception in the civil service that women were not coming forward in sufficient numbers. Penny Summerfield in *Women Workers in the Second World War* satirises the image held in Whitehall of females not offering themselves for war work thus:

> A stubborn woman, idly painting her nails in a station kiosk on a deserted platform, in front of shelves sparsely filled with bars of chocolate and packets of cigarettes.

This is not an image that would have been recognized in south Wales.

Nevertheless in March 1941 under the Registration of Employment Order all women aged 18-45 who were already in paid or unpaid employment were requested to visit their local Employment Exchange, and register. They could then be allocated to war work, and if they refused, they could be directed under force of law – though Bevin was very reluctant to use compulsion unless it was absolutely necessary. In any case there were many exemptions, including mothers with children younger than 14, and those caring for others. The process was very slow to produce results. By August 1941 over two million women had registered in Britain, but only 90,000 had been allocated to munitions or the forces. In the Bridgend context it does seem possible that part of the explanation for the considerable increase in the number of employees in April 1941 was the fact that many local women who had to attend the employment exchange to register had decided to apply to their local factory in order to avoid being directed elsewhere. Other factors may have included the Ministry of Labour recruiting drive.

In December 1941 the National Service Number 2 Act initiated the compulsory call up of all single women, starting with those aged 20. The system was tightened in February 1942 by the Employment of Women Order under which all women aged 20-30 could be employed through Employment Exchanges only, so that they could be directed to essential work. Over the following months the Orders were applied more vigorously by cutting down on women with non-specific domestic responsibility and in the end only those women with children living at home were excluded from compulsion – and those were encouraged to take up part time work. An example of this is the situation of Teresa Barnett: she had a nine year-old daughter, so when she went down to the Office in Adare Street, Bridgend she was given part-time work at ROF 53 because of her family situation.

Peggy Thomas of Coity had a daughter born in 1941; her husband was in the forces, so she went to work as a telephonist on the day shift only.

In its search for labour the tentacles of the Arsenal reached the remotest parts of Wales. Gwen Lloyd was 28, and lived at Borth in Cardiganshire. The furthest that she had ventured before was the six miles into Aberystwyth. Called up in 1942 as a consequence of the Employment of Women Order, she hoped to be sent to the firing range then under construction at nearby Ynyslas. But she was mobile, and she found herself on the long train journey across Wales to a hostel at Bridgend. In the event she adapted well to the sudden change – partly because, as she said 60 years later in a tribute to her colleagues, 'south Walians are so friendly.'

In 1943 the upper limit for registration was raised to 50, causing some to dub it the conscription of grandmothers!

The Housewives Brigade

In the autumn of 1941, in their desperation to recruit workers, the Factory management came up with an innovative idea which the *Glamorgan Advertiser* described as 'the opportunity the housewife has been waiting for to have a "crack" at Hitler and his thugs.' Women who were not liable for registration under National Service (mainly those with children under 14 at home) were invited to volunteer for a 'Housewives Brigade.' This group of workers would enjoy restricted hours; just 4½ hours each weekday, and no shifts. They could work either in the morning, from 9.00 to 1.30, or in the afternoon, from 1.30 to 6.00. The volunteers would work in separate designated workshops, and not be expected to mix with the rest of the workers. The pay was to be

1s. an hour (22s.6d. a week) and the plan applied only to those women who lived within walking or cycling distance of the Factory. The idea was that women could work in the Arsenal, but also do the shopping and run their homes. As usual emphasis was put on how easy the work was. A public meeting to explain the scheme was held at the Embassy cinema in Bridgend at 2.30 on November 10th. The *Western Mail* reported that the promoters of the scheme hoped that 'their experiment will be followed by similar schemes in other factories. The combination of convenience, money and patriotism attracted around 400 women to sign up for the Housewives Brigade at Bridgend.

Infants to War

One way in which mothers could be brought into work at the Arsenal was by the provision of nurseries for their young children aged between two and five. There was an ambivalent attitude towards the provision of such facilities in south Wales – many supported a traditional view that it was the job of mothers to look after their own children in their own homes. But not every one believed this: the authorities in Bridgend were certainly keen that the facility should be provided in the town. A letter to the local council from Mrs E Rouse of the Bridgend Labour Party claimed that a survcy of a third of the town showed that there were 80 mothers on war work and that these women had 169 children who could be placed in a local nursery. At a Bridgend Council meeting in November 1941 (just after the formation of the Housewives Brigade at the Arsenal) the Chairman pointed out that the government was trying to bring married women into the workforce, and that there 'were plenty of women who would do such work if someone would care for their children. Wartime nurseries were necessary for the town,' he declared. Councillor Oakes urged haste: 'We want this thing now,' he insisted, 'Some of these women are already at work, and you will not have the spirit in these women of offering to work unless they can have a place where the children can be looked after.' Two nurseries were built in Bridgend at a cost of £1483. In June 1943 the *Gazette* reported that the one at Cowbridge Road had an average attendance of 19 children per day, and that at Caevatry 21[16]: figures that would suggest that Mrs Rouse's survey had been optimistic in its predictions.

Other local councils also promoted the provision of nurseries in their areas. In December 1940 members of the Ogmore and Garw Council expressed concern for the welfare of the children of mothers working at Bridgend. One councillor warned:

> A number of the mothers in the area were now engaged at the ROF, and young children were, in consequence, left in the charge of older children or aged persons, with unsatisfactory results in some cases.

By October 1941 the Council was able to boast that there were three nurseries in the two valleys. One was established at Pontycymer, and a second at Cae Du Park in Ogmore Vale. A third, 'for evacuated children and those whose mothers were on war work,' was open in Nantymoel by the time of the Royal visit to the Arsenal that December. According to the *Western Mail*, both monarchs contributed to the war effort: George by proffering advice to the infants on the making of sand pies, while Elizabeth 'knelt on the floor and built a castle with bricks.'

By the following March the Penybont Rural District Council was able to post a notice in the *Glamorgan Advertiser* to the effect that four nursery centres were open in its area. The notice emphasised the purpose of the nurseries:

> Mothers with young children who wish to help in the war effort should make a point of visiting the nearest nursery to see how it can help them.

These nurseries were located at Aberkenfig Memorial Hall, Kenfig Hill YWCA, the Malt House, Wick, and the Recreation Ground, Pencoed. The cost of the latter was £850, but that had been paid by the industrialist Rolfe Stein. A nursery was later opened on the Abergarw housing estate, and the Wick nursery was closed. An advert for staff for the Pencoed nursery reveals that the warden in charge was paid £120 pa, her assistant £52 pa, and a cook/cleaner 25s. a week. Undoubtedly the care and play equipment provided at these nurseries was of a high standard – and often included a meal, milk, cod-liver oil and orange juice.

But were the nurseries a success in catering for workers at the

Abergarw Nursery

Arsenal? The Abergarw nursery had opened in November 1942, yet already by the following February councillors were concerned at the low numbers of children using the facility. In March the warden was asked to resign, but matters do not seem to have improved much. Throughout the autumn of 1943 members of the council were concerned about the low attendances at the nurseries in their area, and especially that at Abergarw. The clerk was instructed to write to the Superintendent at the ROF to ask him to advertise the facility to the workers. In the August 1942 edition of the Factory newsletter an anonymous writer had expressed amazement that the five wartime day nurseries visited in the Rhondda were almost empty. The writer believed patronisingly that the reason was a failure on the part of women workers 'to understand all that their children will gain by attending these excellently run centres.' In fact there were other factors that made attendance at the nurseries low. Mothers had to pay a charge – about 1s. for a full working day or 9d. for school hours. In addition, the nurseries were actually not very convenient for those for whom they were designed. The hours that the nurseries were open did not fit real work patterns: the nurseries usually operated from 8.00 to 5.00, which did not match any of the three shifts at the Arsenal. In any case travel extended the working day beyond the hours that the nurseries were open. For many mothers it would be difficult to get their children to the location of their nearest nursery before the start of their shift. As a result many women ignored the nurseries and instead relied on their own private systems of childcare while they were at work – usually involving grandparents, neighbours or teenage sisters – which was cheaper and more convenient.

The management, assisted by government policies, had made huge efforts to maximise the number of employees at Bridgend, and these efforts had been very successful. According to Hornby, of all the filling factories, Bridgend got the nearest to its optimum establishment: others like Chorley constantly struggled to secure a full complement. The highest recorded figure for labour at the Arsenal was 32,577, in March 1942.

In the Forward to the June 1942 edition of *ROF 53 News* the Senior Labour Manager, Mrs Edna Shields, congratulated her colleagues on their combined achievement so far.

> After only two and a half years, this factory appears to have got into working order. Output is good, teething troubles are far less conspicuous. At the end of the war you will have every reason to be proud of the part you played in this, YOUR factory.

Badge issued to ROF workers – August 1941

Notes

1 After the war Harry Fletcher moved from Woolwich to work at the Royal Mint, and so in 1969 he ended up in Wales after all, when the Mint transferred to Llantrisant.

2 Designed by Austin and Edge. Produced at Longbridge. 747 cc side valve engine. 290,000 produced between 1922 and 1939.

3 Only one Division was fully equipped, and that was a Canadian Division.

4 Pembrey was ready for the manufacture of TNT in November 1939; it was producing 220 tons of TNT by June 1940, as well as Ammonium Nitrate. The production of Tetryl started in April 1941: Tetryl probably came to Bridgend from Waltham Abbey in Essex until then. Marchwiel was not active till March 1941.

5 The numbers employed at Chorley actually dropped by a thousand the following month.

6 At one point in the summer of 1941, officials of the Ministry of Labour complained that they 'were trying to fill a leaky tub'.

7 According to MacNalty 'a complication in the early stages of the war was the prevalence of louse infestation and scabies'.

8 In June 1941 the *Western Mail* reported that only 5% of women in one unidentified south Wales ROF had any experience of working in a factory. This contrasts with the situation at Chorley; Lancashire girls had been working in textile factories for generations.

9 Is there perhaps just a hint here in Hughes' choice of words that not all recruits were equally willing to cooperate?

10 See Chapter Nine.

11 Jack Jones, who was later to write the novel *Off to Philadelphia in the Morning* wrote several such scripts for radio, including one patriotically entitled:'Wales Marches On'.

12 A prominent clothing shop in Dunraven Place, Bridgend.

13 Shop wages were as low as 3s. a week for young girls; 'live-in' domestics received between 4s. and 10s.

14 In 1939 well over 80% of females in southern Wales were classified by the Government as 'unoccupied' – an insult to all those women who managed children, husbands and the home, and often carried out casual and poorly paid work (such as dressmaking, knitting and washing) from the house.

15 William Beveridge: 1879-1963. Lawyer, economist and social reformer. In 1942 published the Beveridge Report, which was the basis of the post-war Labour Government's Welfare State.

16 It seems that mothers had no need for the nurseries on Saturdays – in October *The Advertiser* reported that for four consecutive Saturdays there had been no children present at the Cowbridge Road centre.

5: Contraction and Consolidation

Decrease in the Workforce – March 1942 – March 1943

Over the twelve months to March 1943 a number of important changes took place, both in the total numbers employed at Bridgend, and in the sort of people who worked at the Factory.

First of all, as soon as the number of workers at Bridgend had reached the peak recorded in the spring of 1942, the total employed began to fall rapidly. There were a number of reasons for this: one was simply a statistical adjustment designed to reflect more accurately the actual number of workers in the Factory. In March the method of calculating the total workforce was changed to produce a more exact figure of those in work by excluding the number of absentees. So the 'net' figure for March is nearly 4,000 fewer than the 'gross' figure, at 28,707. It is worth noting that in the same month Chorley's workforce was nearly 2,000 less than Bridgend, at 26,922.

Over the next twelve months the number of workers at Bridgend declined steadily: by December 1943 it had already reduced by around 5,000 to 23,853, and it continued to decline into the next year. Chorley's workforce was also reduced, continuing to be smaller than Bridgend's, at around 20,000.

Numbers Employed at the Bridgend Arsenal March 1942 - June 1943

Date		Total
1942	March (Gross)	32577
	March (Net)	28707
	June	27180
	Sept	25238
	Dec	23853
1943	March	20620
	June	19537

There were two main reasons for this considerable reduction in the number of workers at the Bridgend Factory during the twelve months from March 1942. The first is that the armed forces had hugely overestimated the amount of ammunition that they would require. The second was that the ROF management in Woolwich had considerably underestimated the potential efficiency of the workforce and the factories.

During the planning of the armaments factories, the government had asked the Army, the Navy and the Air Force how many weapons, and so how much ammunition they would need in order to conduct the war. Unsurprisingly the three forces had made estimates which, in the understated words of Postan, were 'far from modest.' But it was on the basis of these inaccurate demands that the size of the filling factories, and the number of their employees had been based. The Minister of Supply, Herbert Morrison, began to argue that the production of the quantities of ammunition originally required was impracticable. He was supported by Churchill who had pointed out that the Army's proposals were for far more ammunition than had been used in the whole of the First World War, and that gun ammunition was liable to be consumed at a far lower rate than the planners had assumed. By May 1941 the forces produced more realistic and considerably reduced requirements, as this table shows[1]:

Some War Office Ammunition Requirements

Type of Ammunition	Original Demand	Reduced Demand
25-pdr HE	48,684,000	14,100,000
18-pdr HE and smoke	2,724,000	150,000
4.5inch gun HE	3,456,000	580,000
25pdr Smoke and Gas	11,400,000	4,300,000

The Battle of Britain, the Blitz, and the Desert campaign in north Africa meant that the only type of equipment where the demand was actually increased was for anti-aircraft and anti-tank ammunition such as 3.7-inch HE and 40-mm HE.

This huge overall reduction in the forces' demands for ammunition in turn meant a reduction in the planned outputs from the filling factories, and so a reduction in the number of workers needed in each factory. Indeed in the spring of 1942 Lewis Silkin[2], the chair of the Select Committee on National Expenditure (eager to save money[3] even as the Japanese were triumphant in the far east, and the British Eighth Army was struggling in north Africa), made the criticism that there was substantial excess capacity – around 37% – at the factories, and therefore surplus labour equivalent to several thousands of workers in the larger manufactories like Bridgend. The Minister of Supply, Andrew Duncan, was forced to admit in the House that there was 'some surplus of filling capacity,' though he did go on to claim that the 'surplus constitutes a necessary, valuable and wise insurance.' In addition the planners in Whitehall had decided that workers should now be diverted from army supplies, and into a higher priority – naval stores and the building of aircraft. It was, of course, from the March of 1942 that the reduction in the workforce at Bridgend began.

The second factor to cause the fall in the number of workers at Bridgend was the early date at which an unexpectedly high level of efficiency was reached at the Factory. According to Postan, 'Greater excess [of capacity] was bound to result from the conservative planning of the ROFs.' The management at Woolwich had originally identified a number of factors, which they had expected would hinder production in all the new factories, including the one at Bridgend:

> Huge numbers of people would have to be recruited over a considerable period, and this would cause disruption for some time.
>
> The new workers coming in would be unaccustomed to factory processes, and totally unskilled in the manufacture of ammunition.
>
> There were insufficient experienced staff at Woolwich to be deployed to train the new workers.
>
> Manufacture would be largely by hand or by small tools, in small, widely dispersed workshops.
>
> There would be constant changes in the requirements of the armed forces and so in the specifications for munitions, so it was rarely possible to mechanise the processes[3].
>
> The incoming supply of components would be intermittent for some time.
>
> Factories were not working for 24 hours a day as there were to be only two shifts.
>
> For obvious reasons bonus schemes could not be used in the Danger Areas and would be difficult to introduce elsewhere.
>
> Bombing and explosions were expected to hinder production.

Overall, then, the planners in London assumed that production per head would start at a very low level, and that it would take over eighteen months to reach the rate normally achieved at the original ROFs. Indeed, except for the last of the concerns listed, it is true that these factors did have an effect on production at Bridgend. But the Woolwich management entirely underestimated the ability of senior staff to organise the new factories, and of the new workers to acquire skills, learn the tasks, and so rapidly increase the production of munitions.

There are several factors that explain this rapid increase in productivity. The management at Bridgend very quickly gained experience, and soon succeeded in introducing more effective ways of working.

In the spring of 1941 (probably on 23rd March) the two-shift system – or long shifts – was scrapped[5], and a three-shift system[6] introduced in ROF 53. Thus the hours worked by each operative fell from 60 hours a week to 48, with no loss of pay. The change was popular: the reduction of hours in each shift from ten to eight reduced absenteeism, and initially output increased by over 33% – though this improvement could not be maintained. According to Myra Jenkins

> The afternoon shift was the most hated, because you would be finishing work when everyone else was going home after enjoying a night out.

Myra didn't mind having to work the night shift – 'I was one of those fortunate people who could sleep during the day.'

Also during 1941, efficiency engineers were appointed in the Arsenal, and efficiency schemes were subsequently introduced in areas outside the most dangerous processes: there were time and motion studies, and piece rate and output bonuses were introduced. The method used was an incentive payment on a group fellowship basis[7]; i.e. the bonus for achieving more that the basic was calculated on, and paid to the group, not the individual. The scheme was popular with workers: Les Williams commented that 'If you were on bonuses you were smiling.' The unions agreed to the scheme 'to provide for increased output in provincial ROFs (filling) to meet the present emergencies,' though it was supposed to 'be introduced as a temporary measure.' Over the next few years extra payments were made to many different types of workers. According to Inman

> Generally speaking the Ministry of Supply was successful in introducing piecework pay gradually and with negotiation, and had thus largely avoided conflict. There had not been excessively high earnings, and the whole scheme had resulted in greater productivity.

As other factories came on stream, the supply of components into Bridgend became increasingly reliable. There were few explosions, and not a single bomb dropped on the territory of the Arsenal, so there was in fact little disruption to production because of these factors – and air raid alerts ceased to cause any loss of production after the summer of 1941.

The workers of south Wales proved far more adept at learning the ways of factories, and the skills of manufacturing ammunition than Woolwich had imagined. Between mid 1942 and mid 1943 the output per head of the filling ROFs as a whole increased by 60%. All this meant that it was now possible to obtain the required output with a much smaller labour force. According to Postan, efficiency in the filling factories continued to grow, and total output did not fall even as the numbers employed at Bridgend dropped throughout 1942.

Improvements in the welfare and in working conditions provided for the workers also helped to increase productivity. The Ministry of Labour had complained that the arrangements at ROFs were not up to the standard of private firms because no staff had been appointed to deal with welfare problems. To remedy this welfare officers were installed at all ROFs, including Bridgend, during 1941[8]. Administrative staff of management status, and paid £775 pa were appointed to assist the Superintendents in dealing with welfare, and in September labour managers were selected, and paid £750 pa. These officers dealt with appointments; reception of new employees; allocation to suitable task; the welfare of individuals; control of absenteeism; discipline: transfer within the Arsenal to other groups; the release of workers from the Factory. The aim was to make every worker feel important. Thus attention was given to details such as seating, changing and washing facilities, canteens and social activities. According to Inman, writing after the end of the War, 'In general the standard of personnel management in the ROFs was high.'

The Senior Labour Manager at Bridgend was Edna V. Shields[9]. She had a huge impact on the life of the staff at the Factory: she was involved in recruitment, welfare, absenteeism and discipline, she appeared in court when workers were prosecuted, she presented cups for competitions and a standard to the Home Guard, she wrote in the Factory newsletter, she met the King and Queen, and she visited and comforted the families of those killed in accidents. When Sally Loveday started at the Factory she was interviewed by Mrs Shields:

> She was a Tartar! Oh, a terrible name she had, but I didn't mind her. She was very strict with the girls. Well, you can imagine the thousands that were under her.

Edna Shields

One worker recalled the uncomfortable interview in the aftermath of a dance in Porthcawl. She and a friend missed the last bus back to Bridgend, and so lost a shift at the Arsenal. The two girls were brought to Mrs Shields' office:

> We were both on the carpet. She laid down the law to me. My boyfriend was in the forces, and she said, "If it wasn't for you making bombs, he won't come back from the war." She really frightened you. That's what her job was.

Redwood admired Mrs Shields' effectiveness at inspiring the workforce:

> She had great ability. There is no doubt about it, a great organiser, a great campaigner. She could whip into people like an old-time Welsh evangelist would; the fervour of patriotism: "you're all working for the boys," and all that sort of thing. Mind she was a terrible disciplinarian – she had to be, handling all these women – and she could get you on 10 days suspension quite easily.

But he also understood she treated workers with consideration:

> You had a complete welfare system where a woman could go and say "I've got a certain amount of trouble at home this week, so I

> can't come in." The whole place was a community run in different sections by different welfare people. Mrs Shields was definitely in charge of all the women's side of the factory.

Trade Unions

A major factor in the efficient development of the Arsenal was the cooperation and hard work of trade union officials. Unions played an important part in the success of munitions factories across Britain during the war. Inman believed that: 'In general industrial relations in the ROFs were good.' As evidence she pointed to the infrequency of strikes at government establishments. Her interpretation was that this high standard of worker/manager co-operation was due to the intentions and efficiency of the managerial staff at the factories – though others might give some credit to union officials. Redwood recalled that

> Any grievances were aired on the joint councils. Very rarely were there any disputes. It was ironed out and settled. There were no strikes.

Several unions operated at ROF 53. They came together on the Factory's Whitley[10] committee, where representatives of the different unions and of the management met to discuss wages, conditions, welfare, training and production at the Arsenal. One agreement, for example, was to the introduction of bonus schemes to encourage increased production. Writing in the June 1942 edition of *ROF 53 News*, Edna Shields, enthused about the extent of cooperation between all groups in the Factory:

> There would seem to be a general atmosphere of solidarity. No one section of the community can claim all the credit – workers and management have indeed combined to make our ROF a formidable contribution to the War Effort.

Mrs Shields had no hesitation in paying a generous tribute to the part played by the unions:

> Only a very democratic body could meet to so good effect on Whitley and Production Advisory committees.

In July 1942 the authorities recognized the importance of the unions to Bridgend ROF by awarding Morgan Evans of the Transport and General Workers Union the BEM[11].

Morgan Evans' daughter, Sally, also worked at the Factory. According to her, 'He had an office in Admin which he shared with two others.' Apparently, Morgan was a good negotiator:

> A lot of his work was settling disputes. I've seen him on a platform at Time Fuze when there was an uproar – something had gone wrong, I don't know what, and he was speaking to the workers there.

Of course a great deal of union work involved welfare:

> He used to support the workers in the Factory, and he went to court for some people who had been involved in explosions to get compensation.

The only strikes at the Arsenal seem to have been small scale, and about relatively trivial issues. One ex-employee recalled an occasion when she arrived at the canteen for her break to find that they were out of buns, so she and her friends refused to return to their workshop till a fresh batch had been baked.

Roy Davies described another 'sit in' at the canteen:

> One of the boys, from Maesteg, I think he was, his sister was blinded on the initiators, and he didn't want to go into work, so all us boys, we stopped work, and we went to the Textile Canteen, drinking tea all night, and the police were looking for us, and they caught up with us about five o'clock in the morning, and they sent us home. The next night we had to go in front of the manager. He came in special. And he could have summoned us but he didn't.

In another incident Sally Evans was working as a waitress in the managers canteens; the staff there were given food from the workers' canteen. Sally objected because she wanted the better food served in the managerial canteen. She was

> leading the others, and refused to go in and serve the people at table. There was a dining room full of people, and nobody going in to serve them.

Presumably the protest was short lived, because the management sensibly sent for Sally's father – none other than Morgan Evans!

Above and opposite: Women workers with trays of detonators

NO STAMP
20
ONE HOLE
20
DEFECTS
20
EXAM

Top: In Textiles, sewing cartridge cases
Bottom: Workers tie bundles of cordite

Top: Weighing sticks of cordite
Bottom: Packing cartridges of cordite

Although the unions were important to the smooth running of ROF 53, they seem to have had great difficulty in organizing at the Arsenal. This was probably because of the huge size of the Factory, the distances people travelled to work, and the predominance of women in the workforce. The minutes of the National Union of General and Municipal Workers give some indication of the problems and successes of recruitment. In March 1941 the union's district officer, RG Cook, reported that 'extreme difficulty has been experienced in organizing [the Arsenal], due to the fact that the holding of meetings upon factory enclosures is strictly prohibited.' This prohibition was later lifted and in May Cook was able to report that 'by the end of this quarter there will be a 100% increase over the March quarter.' Things were even better by August when Cook reported that 'organization has been steadily improved here, and our membership has increased by some 400%.' So much optimism: a year later a minute recorded that 'Much dissatisfaction must be reported with the numerical strength of our membership at this factory.' Pontypridd Labour Party minutes suggest that by May 1942 the total membership of unions at ROF 53 had reached 10,000 – a little over a third of the workforce.

Of course around 70% of employees at the Arsenal were female. The workforce in May 1942 totalled about 27,000. Around 8,000 were male workers. If we assume that the vast majority of men would be unionised, then the number of women who had joined a union would be in the region of just 2,000 out of 19,000 female workers. Recruiting women presented union officials with special problems. Writing after the war, Inman commented that

> Filling factories employed large numbers of women unused to factory life, who had no long term desire to stay in, and who were difficult to organize.

A speaker at a joint union meeting at Cardiff in 1941[12] agreed with this diagnosis – he accepted that many women 'were working for the duration of the war only, and were not very concerned.' There was recognition at the conference that the distances women had to travel had an impact on recruitment and participation. Few would stay behind in Bridgend after a shift for union business when there were long journeys home to be endured. One representative commented that there was 'The difficulty in contacting the women at the various factories because many of them lived in scattered and distant areas.' There was some attempt to recruit women workers on buses and trains: in November 1941 the *Aberdare Leader* reported that members of the local Trades Council 'had been busy distributing leaflets among women workers travelling to the war factories.' There was criticism, too, of the women that did join. An officer of the NUGMW complained[13] that the union

> had to contend with the problem of women taking the place of our male members which ... reduces the financial returns because the women were mostly paying only half the contributions which the men were paying... With the wages they are receiving, they should pay full contributions.

Pay at the Arsenal

One of the most important tasks of the unions was to negotiate wage increases. Calculating how much workers at the Arsenal were paid is complicated. There was a variety of different grades of basic pay depending on age, experience, skill and task. Few received just the basic wage – there were extra payments: for shift working; as compensation for lack of overtime (when the three-shift pattern was introduced); for special ability work; for group productivity. And, of course, the actual amount taken home would be reduced by tax and other deductions. This helps to explain the variety of rates of pay per week remembered by former workers. Roy Davies was 17 when he started at the Factory: his judgement was that 'The pay wasn't good, not my money, I was only a boy – I got £1 10s.' Kitty Bishop remembered that 'the first pay I brought home was £2 19s.' Rowena Harris remarked that 'pay was poor. The canteen was the lowest paid in the whole of the Arsenal. When I started there I was on about £3.' Marjorie Heaver worked in an experimental workshop, and received £4. Myra Jenkins got even more: 'The pay was good – when we started it was about £5, and that in those days was good money.' One of the girls interviewed by BBC Wales started at £2

15s, but by the end of the war she was earning between £6 and £7. Margaret Plummer recalled that she started at the Factory on £4 10s, rising eventually to £7 19s. 6d.

The following chart gives some official figures of rates of pay. The second column shows women's basic rates with the addition of the compensation for lack of overtime. This is based on figures for all ROFs quoted by Inman in her history of labour in the munitions industry. The third column is from a document at Kew listing men's basic wages at Bridgend ROF.

Date	Women	Men
Dec 1939	£1 12s.	£2 10s.
Aug 1940	£1 18s.	£3 3s.
Feb 1941	£2 1s.	£3 8s.
Nov 1941	£2 6s.	
Mar 1942		£3 12s.
Dec 1942	£2 13s.	
Apr 1943		£3 16s.
Aug 1944	£2 19s.	£4 2s.

Both men and women earned more than these basic figures. For example, Inman listed extra ability payments of up to 4s. for machine work, and as much as 8s. for special ability work. Mari Williams quotes figures for average total women's pay calculated by the Miners' Federation of Great Britain in 1942[14]: £3 10s. for unskilled, £4 10s. for semi-skilled, and £5 for skilled female workers.

What is immediately apparent from these figures is the difference in wages between men and women. Inman reported that the principle was established in ROFs that

> women taken on to replace men did not automatically receive the full men's pay, even after a probationary period, and even if they could do the men's work unaided.

She went on to confirm that 'The Ministry of Supply had no women eligible for full rates paid to men in the same job.' Today this would be seen to be an unacceptable injustice, but in the social context of the time the difference caused little concern. As we have seen, women did not flood into the unions in large numbers, and equal pay was certainly not on the agenda of any union. Most people accepted that women were temporary workers in industry, and that it was only natural they should not receive the same pay as men. The wages paid to women in ROF 53 were very much higher than anything they could earn in any other job, and the vast majority of women were more than satisfied with their remuneration. One of the participants in the BBC Radio programme confirms this:

> It was well-paid work for girls of our age. It was about the best-paid job, and that was so why so many girls went there. It was good money, money that you would not have got anywhere else.

The usual concern about women's wages in the valleys of Glamorgan was not that they were too low in relation to men's wages in the Factory, but that they were too high: too high, that is, in relation to the wages of male workers in other industries, and especially in mining. The wages available to women before the war were always lower – much lower – than the wages available to men. Hence the shock when young women working at the Arsenal returned home with higher wages than their brothers and fathers. William Gibson's fiancée was

> having almost treble what I was earning...when I started I was only having fourteen and sixpence a week.

Marjorie Heaver testified that she used to bring home more money than her father, who was a guard on the railways. Kitty Bishop's father was a miner: she recalled that her first pay

> was more money than my father was earning in the colliery. I'll never forget his face when I brought my pay home – terrible it was.

In May 1942 Superintendent May recorded that there was a strike at the Ballarat Colliery,[15] Blaengarw, of 'boys who were alleging that girls of a younger age are earning more money than them at the Royal Ordnance Factory.' Miners' leader Will Paynter[16], in a speech at Aberdare in 1942 spoke of the 'fedupness' among miners who were told how vital coal was to the war effort, and who then

> came home after six days of hard grind at the coal face with less money in their pay packets than a girl of 18 working in a munitions factory.

The frustration of miners was compounded by the fact that they were prevented from getting jobs at the Arsenal (and hence accessing higher wages) by an Essential Work Order[17] which tied them to the pits. There may have been widespread resentment amongst male workers in other industries at the wages that could be earned by women at ROF 53, but the situation had to be accepted for the duration of the war – the expectation was that at the end of hostilities the women would lose their well-paid jobs, and proper pay differentials would be restored.

Transfer to England

As well as the reduction in the total number of workers at the Bridgend Arsenal, there was a change in the nature of part of the workforce. This was because hundreds of 'mobile' women were transferred from Bridgend, and partly replaced by 'immobile' women and male ex-miners.

One important aspect of female conscription was the distinction between 'mobile' and 'immobile' women. In essence mobile women were those with no domestic responsibility – so they were usually unmarried and young. Wales was classified as an area with a surplus of potential female workers available; these women could be directed to areas of England with labour shortages. Of course very many females who had started to work at Bridgend in 1940 and 1941 were young and single, and in order to free up these to be sent away in 1942, the Ministry of Labour made efforts to attract immobile women into the Factory, thus releasing the mobile females.

Joan Hunt was working in Cordite, but as she was single, and had no domestic duties, she was classified as 'mobile'. The process appears to have been simple, as she remembers.

> Then they wanted 40 volunteers to go to the Daimler works in Coventry, where they were making aeroplanes, and the supervisor turned round to me and said, 'you're going.' So I did.

Joan was lucky in that she knew many of the other women who went to Coventry, including her sister. After the war Joan married and settled in England; today she lives in Hook Norton.

Not all transfers to England were as satisfactory. In October 1943 the *Aberdare Leader* reported the case of a 20-year-old munitions worker from Robertstown who was transferred to Coventry. She had been very nervous about going so far from home, so her father had travelled to the city with her, and had even gone to the factory with her on her first morning. Nevertheless, she worked just one shift and then insisted in returning home. The magistrate decided that being homesick was not a sufficient defence, and she was fined £4 and costs. A girl from Cwmbach ordered from Bridgend never went to her allocated factory in England. In court she said that she was looking after her totally incapacitated father, and that her mother was constantly ill in bed – so effectively she was not 'mobile.' The law took no account of people looking after their parents, so the magistrates fined the worker £5. There is no record of whether these girls were subsequently directed back to the English Midlands.

One source of mobile females that could be targeted was the Irish recruits. According to Inman, the recruitment of Irish workers for the Ministry of Supply had begun in 1942, organized by a member of the Labour Management Department at the Bridgend Factory. Agents were placed in the main Irish towns and over 11,000 women in total were encouraged to come into the British ROFs, which reported satisfaction with their quality. The Irish girls who came at first to Bridgend were by definition mobile, and so in 1943 and 1944 many of them were moved from ROF 53 to English factories.

'Sub-standard' Men

Another way to release mobile women for transfer was to replace them with men previously regarded as unemployable. As we have seen, by June1942 the Factory was already employing some 3,000 ex-miners, most of them fit for light work only. Les Williams' asthma had forced him to leave the pit at Gilfach Goch: he came to work in the Arsenal in 1942. The Ministry of Labour continued to get many letters from other former colliers complaining that they could not get positions at the Factory, even though their daughters were working there, and these complaints were reinforced by local MPs.

A government order of May 1941 had forced all miners to work in the pits for the duration of the war, but in 1943 the government released those certified with pneumoconiosis from this obligation. The Ministry of Labour then began to recruit these colliers 'unfit for the mines,' plus men who had been discharged from the armed forces for various reasons. These people were denigrated in official papers as 'sub-standard'. One document[18] describes the position thus:

> ROF Bridgend had to recruit and train several thousands of men who were, quite naturally at this stage of the war, not the pick of the labour market.

In the August 1943 a memo[19] to the Senior Medical Officer at the Arsenal, Dr JP Elias, mentions that the Factory was 'taking on a good deal of labour recently, much of which is of a poor physical standard.' In that year the shortage of workers nationally was such that a large proportion of those available were over 50, and according to MacNalty 'their physical condition could only be described as pathological.'

Many ex-miners had respiratory problems, and so could not be risked in contact with the various chemicals used in the Arsenal. Those 'light' jobs that were available were often already filled by disabled workers. The Factory management was particularly concerned that any lowering of the entry standard would simply result in an increase in the overall sickness rate, and so of absenteeism. In the end the administrators of the Arsenal had no choice. The hope was that improvements in the environment, and in methods of filling and handling toxic materials introduced since 1940 had reduced the risk of sickness. Medical Officers were urged that 'discretion should be exercised' in the enforcement of the fixed standards; but some 40% of applicants were still rejected. Those that were appointed were carefully screened so that they could be specifically allocated to tasks within their particular abilities. The problems for ex-miners are illustrated through a description by

Eunice Jones of the difficulties of one former collier with calloused hands faced with inserting very small screws into a component. 'Oh, Mrs Jones,' he said, 'tis a shovel I want in my hands, not this tiny screwdriver – I can't feel it.'

To cope with these problems Dr Elias developed a system of sorting the male entrants. They were classified according to their general health, their eyesight, their fitness for contact with powders and their previous work. Then they had to undertake a series of tasks to test their aptitude. These tests included:

> Handling of tweezers to pick up dummy detonators and to place them in holes.
>
> Extraction of small discs of uniform size from a pile of assorted discs.
>
> Insertion of a pointer into holes of different sizes.
>
> Inserting as many matchsticks as possible into a cribbage board in 60 seconds.
>
> Weighing accurately inert powder.

Patronisingly, the official government paper goes on to claim that

> It proved possible with careful selection and training to beat the output of some of the best of the mobile women, despite the fact that these men had an indifferent or poor industrial record.

Between 4,000 and 5,000 men were recruited to the Arsenal using this process. An inevitable result was that the proportion of men and women working at the Factory began to change – women were still in the majority but the percentage of men increased throughout 1943 and 1944.

By the spring of 1943, the total number of employees at the Bridgend ROF had stabilised at around 20,000, and it remained consistently at that level for the next two years until victory had been won in Europe. Thus after an extraordinary rise in numbers during 1940 and 1941, and a rapid fall back from the highest statistic during 1942, the Factory enjoyed just over two years of stability in employee numbers during 1943 and 1944, and into the spring of 1945.

Numbers employed at the Bridgend Arsenal March 1943 – October 1945

Date		Total
1943	March	20620
	June	19537
	Sept	20281
	Dec	19928
1944	March	19982
	June	19856
	Sept	19928
	Dec	19798
1945	March	19921
	June	17133
	Sept	8520
	Oct	5000

It is today impossible to find out how many worked at the Bridgend Arsenal altogether. There was a constant flow of people into and out of the Factory, so the highest figure of 32,577 recorded in March 1942 does not actually represent the total number of those who at some time worked on the manufacture of munitions at the plant: tens of thousands more of the people of south Wales must at some time between 1939 and 1945 have contributed to the war effort at ROF 53.

Notes

1 Adapted from Table on p135 of Postan, *British War Production.*

2 Lewis Silkin: Labour MP for Peckham. Chair of the SCoNE sub-committee investigation into ROFs.

3 The Civil Service was also made to feel the pain of economies – in March pencil sharpeners were withdrawn from offices 'to conserve pencils.'

4 In November 1942 a Ministry of Production report concluded that if all processes were fully mechanised, changes in design of the weapons would have made filling workshops 70% ineffective, and fuze workshops 50% ineffective.

5 The hours of the two shifts were:- Day shift 7.30 – 18.30 : Night shift 19.30 – 6.30. There was one hour meal break midway through each shift. Employees worked six shifts per week.

6 The shifts were labelled Red, White and Blue.

7 The Bedaux principle.

8 See Inman, *Labour in the Munitions Industry.*

9 Several interviewees claimed that she had worked in the Prison service before arriving at Bridgend.

10 Named after John Whitley, MP for Halifax, who chaired the Parliamentary committee of 1916 which recommended the setting up of joint industrial councils where management and workers could discuss contentious issues.

11 British Empire Medal (Civil Division) 'In recognition of services with the Royal Ordnance Factory, Bridgend.' Morgan Evans was invested by the King at Buckingham Palace on July 21st, 1942.

12 *Aberdare Leader* 11.10.41.

13 Minutes of NUGMW: 6.8.41 (NLW3FN20/2/5)

14 The Miners' Federation was trying to achieve higher wages for their own members, so these figures should be treated with caution.

15 Also known as Glenafon or Glengarw Colliery.

16 Will Paynter 1903-1984. Communist. Leader of Hunger Marches in 1930s. Political Commissar with the International Brigade in Spain 1937. General Secretary, National Union of Miners, 1959–1968.

17 The Essential Work (Coalmining Industry) Order, May 1941.

18 Kew (AVIA 22/2513)

19 *Gazette* 13.1.39

6: Trains, Buses, and Hostels

In an article on ROFs in south Wales, a correspondent to the *Aberdare Leader* gave a rather idealised description of workers on their way to the Arsenal.

> Women and girls of all ages, married and unmarried, wearing turbans and slacks, smoking, laughing, haversacks slung on their shoulders, or little attaché cases in their hands – contrasting rather incongruously with permed hair and lipstick – hurrying in large numbers to the bus and railway station, or, at the end of the day, pouring out of them in a swarm, tired, work-stained, but still laughing and cracking a joke. An unfamiliar sight surely in Wales, where women's place was always regarded as being in the home.

It was recognised very early in the planning of the Arsenal that very many of the workers would have to be transported from some distance. The nearest town to the Factory, Bridgend, had a population of just 9,000, and could not supply the bulk of the enormous workforce needed. In fact people travelled every day by train and by bus from considerable distances. The problems that workers had in travelling to the Arsenal was recognised in Hornby's official history of the war factories when he wrote that the Bridgend Factory was able to recruit sufficient labour for its needs 'even though transport in that area was very difficult.'

Workers came to Bridgend from all over the county of Glamorgan and beyond: from the Rhondda and Cynon valleys, from Pontypridd, from Port Talbot and from Swansea. Some journeyed from Ammanford in the west, and from Merthyr Tydfil in the north. According to Inman, about 1,500 of the Bridgend workforce 'travelled more than three hours daily, excluding their walk to and from the bus stop or station.' It is perhaps not surprising that in February 1941 a government report suggested that some 1,000 women had stopped working at the Arsenal because of the length of time taken to get to and from Bridgend. In November 1941 the Factory management reported to a conference at the Arsenal the identification of a 'new disease which might be termed "travel tiredness" suffered by those who daily' travelled many miles to work. It was some compensation that these employees had their fares subsidised; the Assisted Travel Scheme meant that travelling expenses of more than 3s. a week were paid by the Factory. This cost, plus the consumption of scarce commodities such as tyres and petrol, and the anticipated problems of travelling in wartime led the authorities to plan two huge hostels for the workers near Bridgend.

Rail

One of the reasons why the Bridgend site had been chosen in the first place was its proximity to the GWR's main line through south Wales. But a proper railway station with direct access to the Factory was not included in the original plan, and to start with provision was rudimentary. As far back as July 1938, complaints had been made at an Ogmore and Garw Council meeting about the lack of good transport to the site of the Arsenal. The fear was expressed by one concerned councillor that the terrible consequence might be that the people of those valleys could be forced to live in Bridgend.

In the summer of 1940 the authorities tried to save fuel by rationalising services to the Arsenal: bus traffic was banned from places served by railway stations. This decision brought a flood of

Workers arriving at Tremains Platform

complaints. At a meeting of the Maesteg Council on 20th June it was reported that 'people employed at the Arsenal at Bridgend were now greatly inconvenienced and delayed,' because 'they had to travel by train instead of by bus as hitherto.' Modern passengers might sympathise with the complaints that ensued. Apparently conditions in the carriages were appalling: 'The train was always overfull, and the people travelled in great discomfort.' Punctuality was also a problem – it seems that 'the train did not arrive in sufficient time to allow the employees to clock in at the proper time,' with the result that 'their wages were cropped accordingly.' The Council complained to the government, and received the assurance from Herbert Morrison[1] (then Minister of Supply) that everything was being done to provide adequate travelling facilities for the operatives at the Factory.

A minute[2] of a meeting in London on 12th October 1940 gives some indication of how important the management at Woolwich considered the provision of improved railway facilities to be:

and boarding trains at the end of their shift

> It has become a matter of extreme urgency that the extension to and covering over of the passenger platforms at Tremains Halt should be completed at the earliest possible moment.

There were obviously murmurings of discontent from the seven thousand strong workforce, because the minute goes on to record a severe warning of trouble ahead:

> With the large increase in the number of operatives, and the approaching winter, the position is becoming rapidly worse, and may lead to labour troubles.

The GWR provided an estimate of the costs at £23,070 for the platforms, with another £3,000 for an additional footbridge to the Factory. Optional Platform Shelters would add £2,000 to the total.

The workers at Bridgend were forced to endure a winter of inconvenience, because the new station was probably not available until around 16th March 1941, the date upon which the two new platform loops were brought into use. The station did have the platform shelters, and two island platforms, providing four platforms for passengers. Special screening walls were built to shield workers in the unlikely event of low-level aircraft attacks. The total paid by the Government for the station was £25,458.

It was just as well that these facilities were eventually provided at Tremains Halt. When the station opened 16,000 people were already working at the Arsenal, and this was to increase to nearly 33,000 within a year. By 1942 58 trains a day stopped at Tremains; at the main shift change time ten passenger trains left the station in the space of 20 minutes. 30,000 passenger journeys a day – around nine million in a year – started or finished at Tremains, making it one of the busiest stations in Wales.

Of course all this passenger travel to ROF 53 was in addition to the extensive freight traffic to the Factory sidings, and the normal wartime traffic on the main line through Tremains Halt. Yet despite this, the author of *It Can Now Be Revealed* was able to claim that 'a remarkably high degree of punctuality' was maintained. He went on to declare that 'of the trains serving ...ordnance depots, less than 1% ever arrived more than 10 minutes late' – a performance that today's railway companies can only dream of!

One reason for this success may have been that very long journey times were timetabled. Mair Davies describes her travel to work experience.

> We would catch the 5.10 bus up to Nantymoel station to catch the 5.30 train, Although it was only ten miles from there [to Tremains] we would not get there till seven. We had to wait about on a siding to let the main line trains from Swansea through.

An hour and a half to travel from the top of the Ogmore valley to Bridgend does seem a bit excessive. Mair did not arrive back in her house till 4.30pm, so she was away from home for nearly 12 hours. The afternoon shift was marginally more convenient. She would leave the house at 1pm, and get home about 11pm. For the night shift she caught a train to Tremains at 8.15, and returned home at 9.30 the next morning.

Nantymoel was relatively near to Bridgend. Other workers travelled from further afield. Rosina Davies lived in Cwmafan. She had to leave her house at 4.30 in the morning to catch a bus to Port Talbot station. There she caught the 6.00 train to Tremains where she arrived around 7.00am. Since she did not get back home till 7.00pm, she was away for over 14 hours.

Travel to work by train was not always a pleasant experience for other reasons, judging by the comments of members of the Ogmore and Garw Council in February 1944. They complained that the carriages were unlit at night, and demanded that the GWR do something to rectify the situation. The Company replied with asperity that the problem was theft and cited the example of a fully lit train on the line that had had the light bulbs in 21 compartments stolen within a week. One peevish councillor complained, perhaps unreasonably, that 'the railway company should supervise their own property as they used to do. The talk about lack of manpower was being very much over done.' Not much awareness that there was a war on, then.

But there were compensations. Betty Cartlidge enjoyed her journey with friends from Caerau: 'We all teamed up, and travelled in the same compartment every day.' Joan Hunt caught the train at Trefforest. Her friends who got on further up the line always kept a place for her in their compartment 'by standing up at stations so that it seemed it was full!' Mair Davies and her friends from Nantymoel often entertained themselves on the journey to work with a sing-song. Redwood reveals that

> We heard all manner of tales of what went on in the carriages. You can imagine the devilment now with some of those women after the shifts – although they were tired they were full of spirit going home.

Mair Davies gives a slightly different story about the homeward trek after the night shift:

> We wouldn't be able to keep our eyes open as the movement of the train rocked us to sleep.

Not all workers travelled to work in pleasant companionship. The *Aberdare Leader* reported a court case that followed an altercation between two women on a Factory train. Both accused the other of starting a fight. There was an argument about a pay packet, and then one was alleged to have pulled the other's hair and kicked her in the stomach. The second was alleged to have struck the first several times in the jaw with her fist so that she fainted. It must

Articulated bus

have been a vicious fight, because both women were off work for three days.

In addition to the passenger trains there was heavy freight traffic to and from the Arsenal. Explosive materials and components could conveniently be brought in to the Factory, and the finished products could easily be sent out to their destinations. As we have seen, some of the very first work to be started on the Arsenal site was the laying down of the sidings and signal boxes adjacent to the main line, and the construction of a line and sidings to the location of the magazines under Brackla Hill. Much of the materials used in the construction of the Arsenal had been brought in on these new lines.

When the Factory was fully functioning, 64 wagons of explosive materials and other components arrived every day. Logistically it was a hugely complicated operation to ensure that the correct items arrived in the right quantities at the appropriate time. TNT, Tetryl and Ammonium Nitrate came from the ROF explosives factory at Pembrey, a few miles west of Llanelli. Cordite arrived from a Royal Naval propellant factory at Caerwent just to the east of Newport, and a factory at Marchwiel near Wrexham in the north of Wales. Fuzes were brought from Theale, near Reading. Every day 51 wagons left the Arsenal, loaded with the completed products[3]. Many of the artefacts leaving Bridgend were filled components for Glascoed (near

Pontypool) or Hereford ROFs, where they were fitted into the complete weapon or piece of ammunition. Some items, especially primers and initiators, were booked out to the Royal Naval armaments storage depot at Trecwn in Pembrokeshire, or to the testing station and firing range at Aberporth in Cardiganshire. In addition to this munitions traffic, each day 14 wagons of coal arrived from nearby collieries to feed the Factory's power station.

Buses

Buses were as important as the railway in the transport of workers to and from the Factory. Many people in south Wales lived in communities without a convenient railway station, and buses could tackle the steep roads leading to many villages. When the Factory was in full production, more than 32,000 passenger journeys to and from the Arsenal were made every day on 864 timetabled trips, aboard 144 buses.

But in the early days there were many problems. Just like the railway station so the road transport arrangements were unsatisfactory at first. According to Mari Williams, organising workers' buses was an extremely complicated business. This was partly because there was a large number of small coach companies in the area, and they usually did not have the capacity to provide back up vehicles or drivers in an emergency. To begin with insufficient buses were available, so the Ministry of Supply came up with an extraordinary solution. Their engineers took a Fordson articulated tractor unit[4], designed to haul lorry-type trailers: to this they attached a passenger trailer unit apparently made in the engineering section of the Arsenal. Photos exist of this most unusual hybrid apparently on its way to Abergwynfi and Ferndale in the Rhondda with a cargo of female employees. It could not have been very comfortable.

Many workers travelled from the Cynon Valley, and towards the end of 1940 there were frequent complaints about delays and the time taken to complete the journey to and from Bridgend. The Aberdare MP, George Hall, became involved, and in December the local Ministry of Transport Commissioner, CP Clayton, wrote a letter to him outlining the problem.

Bus park at the end of a shift

> The number of employees at Bridgend who have to be conveyed from the Rhondda, Aberdare and other areas has risen very rapidly, and this has caused the bus companies considerable difficulty. The lines of approach in the vicinity of the works tend to be congested, and in the complete blackout it takes a considerable time to marshal the vehicles and see that they get away without completely blocking some of the roads.

Hall also received a letter from the manager of the Red and White bus company, Norman Taylor. He agreed that there were logistical problems at Bridgend, especially the absence of a purpose-built bus park. 'There are no facilities for loading and unloading passengers at the works,' he wrote. But Taylor went on to blame some of the delay on the workers. 'To a considerable extent the delay in getting away is caused by the girls themselves,' he explained. Firstly he had had to forbid the departure of individual buses for safety reasons:

> if a bus pulls out immediately it is full, there would be a tremendous rush for the first bus, and in consequence serious injury to some of the workers.

Secondly:

> whilst probably 90% come straight to the buses, the remainder go to the canteen and do not present themselves until often as late as 7.50am and pm.

There were two shifts at the Arsenal at that time, and they finished at 7 am, and 7 pm. So if this assertion is accurate some people were spending nearly an hour in the canteens before arriving at the buses. Taylor assured the MP that the company had tried several methods to deal with this problem, but that

> these have failed: this again mainly through the behaviour of the women themselves.

Clayton indicated that there had been discussions with the Arsenal management about the difficulties, and that a bus park would be constructed. Presumably this did in due course reduce the problems. At the time of these letters the workforce at ROF Bridgend was just 10,000, and would increase greatly, so it was imperative that better facilities should be provided. The introduction in March 1941 of three shifts instead of two must have reduced the pressure at each change of shift by 33%. Whether the problem of people staying on in the canteens at the end of the shift was solved is not known.

Once these initial complications had been dealt with, bus journeys do not seem to have been as time consuming as those by train. Les Wills, an ex-miner, worked at the Arsenal from 1942. He took a bus every day from Williamstown, and got to the Factory in about 45 minutes.

One reason why bus journeys were quicker is suggested in an entry in Superintendent May's Diary. In February 1942 May met with Barber, the traffic officer at the Arsenal, and Walter Howells of the Transport and General Workers Union who were concerned

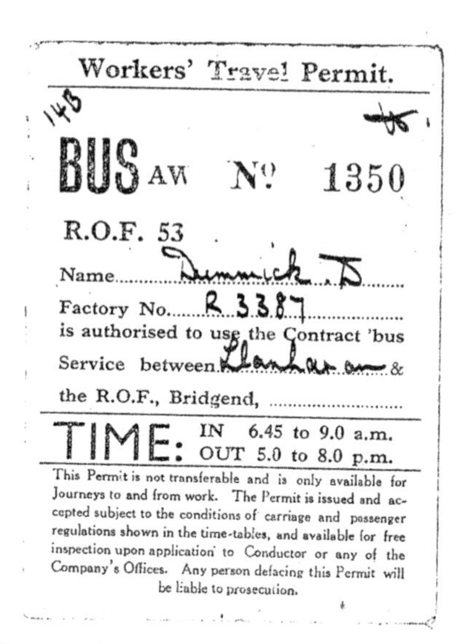
Workers' Travel Permit.

BUS AW No. 1350

R.O.F. 53

Name.........Dummick D.........

Factory No.......R 3387..................

is authorised to use the Contract 'bus

Service between Llanharan &

the R.O.F., Bridgend, ...

TIME: IN 6.45 to 9.0 a.m.
OUT 5.0 to 8.0 p.m.

This Permit is not transferable and is only available for Journeys to and from work. The Permit is issued and accepted subject to the conditions of carriage and passenger regulations shown in the time-tables, and available for free inspection upon application to Conductor or any of the Company's Offices. Any person defacing this Permit will be liable to prosecution.

about 'the police action of dealing with speeding by factory buses.' Presumably the Police were acting vigorously against buses that broke the speed limits. May was in no mood to be conciliatory, and

> urged on them in the interests of the successful prosecution of the war that the buses, petrol, oil and tyres should be conserved from the ravages of unnecessary high speed.

Despite May's best efforts, matters do not seem to have improved. In January 1943 *The Advertiser* reported a case in which it was alleged that two buses travelling from the Arsenal to the Rhondda were racing. Evidence suggested that the buses had driven abreast of each other round a bend between Coychurch and Pencoed. Superintendent May told the court that the dangerous driving of buses was common and that passengers put bets on which bus would reach the destination first. Indeed on some other occasions his officers had been threatened

> not only by the driver and the conductor, but by some of the passengers, who were very hostile.

The 14-year-old Gwyn Davies also experienced the ire of homeward bound workers. He used to drive a herd of 24 milking cows from fields on one side of the Coychurch-Pencoed road to Torcoed Farm on the opposite side at around 3.15 every day - and every day the buses from the Arsenal would be forced to slow and stop. Gwyn remembers the female passengers shaking their fists at him and mouthing obscenities through the windows of the vehicles.

Local bus companies made considerable amounts of money out of running bus services to the Factory. An example of these Welsh entrepreneurs was Wally Carpenter of Blaengarw, who owned a company called Garw Luxury Buses. According to Grafton Radcliffe, in his book *Back to Blaengarw*, Carpenter's coaches were not luxurious, and not even reliable. The local children sang a version of a song that went

> You'll never get to heaven in Wally's bus – it'll get half way, then the thing will bust.

Nevertheless, claimed Grafton, Wally 'became really affluent after winning a contract to transport local workers to and from the Arsenal in Bridgend.' In fact he became so well off that for a time he was able to become a racehorse owner whose colours were registered with the Jockey Club. Perhaps inevitably in such an unpredictable environment the money was lost, and Wally died a relatively poor man.

The number of workers commuting to Bridgend by bus from surrounding areas inevitably caused an increase in the amount of traffic on the roads. One manifestation of these new difficulties occurred over a year before production had started, on the morning of January 12th 1939. Just outside Coychurch a bus taking construction workers home from the Arsenal to the Rhondda collided head on with a bus bringing children from Llanharan to school in Bridgend. Both Western Welsh buses were badly damaged; children were showered with flying glass and thrown from their seats – no thought of seat belts on buses in those days. Thankfully no one was seriously injured; 19 people were taken to hospital, including 13 children, but only the driver of the workmen's bus, from Tonypandy, and 12-year old Roy Piggott of Llanharan were kept in overnight. The *Gazette* described this accident as 'the most serious bus accident that up to this time has occurred in the Bridgend district.'

Top: Island Farm Hostel
Bottom: Pencoed Hostel

A yet more serious accident occurred on 28th April 1942, when a bus carrying Arsenal workers – mainly from Maerdy in the Rhondda – crashed into a Llanharan Co-op lorry, at Cog Hill. The force of the impact tore the side out of the bus, and women workers were pinned in their seats. Fourteen were injured, and one passenger, Phyllis Davies was killed. She was a twenty-year-old from Maerdy, who had been married for just five weeks.

One easy way to reduce travelling was the exchange of workers between factories. It was sometimes the case that people had started to work in an establishment opened a long way away, but that another factory closer to home had started production subsequently. In that case it was relatively easy to arrange a transfer. Thus many people travelled originally from the north of Glamorgan to the Arsenal at Bridgend – but a small-arms ROF was opened at Hirwaun at the head of the Cynon Valley, involving a much shorter journey to work for those transferred to this new factory.

The Hostels

The planners of the new Ordnance Factory had always intended to provide living facilities in the vicinity of the Arsenal to deal with anticipated transport problems. During 1941 the workforce at the Factory increased dramatically; between March and November that year the number of employees at the Arsenal doubled to over 30,000. It was known that the bulk of these employees would live considerable distances from Bridgend. According to Inman, it was believed that there would be major disruptions to transport from air raids and the other inconveniences of wartime, and that therefore workers whose houses were more than 12 miles from ROF 53 would much prefer to move into places near their work rather than travel for hours every day. In addition it was thought that all possible lodgings in nearby towns and villages would have been taken up very quickly, and so the locality would not be able to cope with the expected huge demand for rented rooms. At the same time Factory managers were increasingly concerned about high rates of absenteeism, and the damage which that was causing to production. In July 1941 a report from the Select Committee on National Expenditure cited 'transport difficulties over the long distances which workers have to travel,' and 'absence of adequate accommodation near the factories,' as the most significant factors contributing to absenteeism.

That summer there was, therefore, a sense of crisis over the issue of accommodation. The Select Committee's report to Parliament insisted that 'a sufficient number of hostels near the factories should be provided as matter of urgency.' Even the planned provision at one factory of places for about 12% of the workforce was deemed to be inadequate. In the first year of the conflict building war factories had been the priority for men and materials: by the spring of 1941 much of that programme had been completed, and so resources could be diverted to the provision of this apparently desperately needed living accommodation.

On June 20th 1941 the *Glamorgan Advertiser* had announced that 'dormitory shelter accommodation' was to be provided in Bridgend for 1,000 people. Up to twenty-five shelters were being erected, each intended to house around 45 workers. The site for this hostel was off the new by-pass A48 road to the south of Bridgend, at the point where it cut across the road to the village of Merthyr Mawr. The forty or so acres for the hostel had been purchased from land farmed by John Davies of Island Farm. A month later an advert in the *Advertiser* designed to encourage women to work in the Arsenal promised that 'Good hostel accommodation is provided for those whose homes are beyond travelling distance.' In fact two hostels were built to serve workers at the Bridgend Factory – the one at Island Farm, and one at Pencoed, just to the south of that village.

The two Bridgend hostels did not look particularly prepossessing to an outside observer. The living accommodation consisted of a number of plain, single storey, long blocks made of pre-cast concrete sections, thrown up rapidly to the minimum standards demanded by the exigencies of wartime, and inevitably looking rather like an army encampment. Near the gate was a brick-built administration and welfare block, which included a concert hall/cinema, dance hall, kitchens and a cafeteria. Additional facilities included a shop, a library, medical centre, a laundry with ironing facilities, and recreation rooms. The female residents were initially charged £1.5s a week, which covered accommodation

Darts, table tennis and a sing-song in a Bridgend hostel

plus two meals a day. Rooms had central heating, and were fitted with bunk beds, wardrobes, and chests of drawers. Senior staff of the hostels had the privilege of living in individual bungalows.

The facilities were built by the Ministry of Supply, but they were managed by the YMCA/YWCA Joint Committee. The two youth organizations had considerable experience of managing hostels, but nothing on the scale of those planned at Bridgend and Pencoed. Inevitably there would be teething problems. By this stage of the war it was difficult to find workers with the administrative, social or catering skills to staff the new hostels. The Warden at Pencoed must have been delighted to acquire the services of the young Sue Roberts who had just completed a catering course in a Cardiff College – she earned 10s. a week. The managers did work hard to create pleasant institutions. According to Inman,

> everything was done... to encourage the growth of smaller communities within the larger unit – such as the use of the house system, and the creation of small groups for leisure time activity... WEA[5] classes, cookery and needlework classes.

One eventual change was the provision of small common rooms within each sleeping block.

Early in January 1942 a Ministry of Information photographer took a number of pictures of life at the hostel at Bridgend – presumably as propaganda to show how welcoming the hostels were, and so to encourage women to move into them. Included were scenes in the canteen, the laundry room and the sewing room. There are representations of activities in the recreation room where two girls play table tennis with two male guests, while others play darts. Another photo shows the lounge, equipped with comfortable chairs, a piano, a gramophone, a wireless – and male guests from the RAF.

Not even the romantic allure of the blue-grey uniform could ensure the success of the hostels. The first public acknowledgment that there was a problem appeared in November 1941, in a *Western Mail* report on a conference at the Arsenal. Eight local MPs, plus trade union officials and Factory managers had come together to discuss various issues in connection with ROF 53. The article led

Entertaining in the Hostel lounge and canteen

with the complaint about 'The reluctance of Welsh girl war workers to utilise hostels specifically constructed for their benefit.' Superintendent Corbett informed the delegates that there was a capacity of 2,000 in one hostel, but that there were only 300 people living there. As Corbett said, 'The girls prefer to travel 30 or 40 miles a day, with all the inconvenience of the blackout, rather than stay at the hostel.' It was almost as if these ungrateful and wilful girls were being accused of being deliberately spiteful.

The visit to the Factory of the King and Queen a few weeks later was utilised by the management to try to promote official accommodation. The *Western Mail* reported that the Queen asked about the hostel facilities, and that the Royal couple were then driven to the Pencoed hostel to see the facilities there. When a resident, Daisy Markham was asked by the Queen 'Do you like it here?' Daisy replied with the officially approved answer, 'Yes, it's splendid.' The *Western Mail* went on to report that 'Others assured her Majesty that they were very pleased with the hostel.' But not even the stamp of Royal approval could persuade people to live in the hostels.

Despite the low numbers taking advantage of the accommodation provided, the Warden of one of the hostels gave an optimistic report on its activities in the June 1942 edition of *ROF 53 News*:

> The hostel has now been open a year. It has been a year of experiments: foundations of policy had been laid, and a community spirit created...Thanks to the assistance and co-operation received from the Factory, the future happiness of the residents is assured.

The report goes on to list the activities organised for the inmates. These included music concerts, drama productions, dances, classes in handicraft and dressmaking, lectures and talks. Sue Roberts remembers a 'beautiful ankle' competition at one of the dances. Religious services were being held every Sunday. The July copy of *ROF 53 News* included the information that girls from the hostel had 'offered their services free of charge to the local farmers,' and that 'the girls rendered valuable assistance in hay-making.' In the same edition it was reported that the Factory Amateur Dramatic Society had performed *Outward Bound*[6] at the Pencoed Hostel, which had been received by 'enthusiastic audiences.'

Top: Modern electric irons in the Hostel laundry
Bottom: Hot and cold running water in every bedroom

Despite these positive articles, the hostels continued to be rejected. A more realistic appraisal of the situation was given in an article in the *Western Mail* in that July where it was reported that work had been suspended on a partly finished hostel – presumably Pencoed. The journalist went on to explain that this was because of the 'disinclination of the girls for whom it is intended to leave their homes and take up residence there.' In a clear reference to Island Farm the correspondent wrote that

> for more than a year now efforts have been made to fill another hostel associated with the same factory, but despite considerable publicity and many attempts to persuade the girls to reside there it is doubtful whether it has attracted anything like its full complement of residents.

In a vitriolic assault (reminiscent of Tory attacks on single mothers at the end of the twentieth century[7]), the article went on to blame most of the problems of the war on these recalcitrant girls. They were apparently affecting food production by wasting the agricultural land used for the hostels; they were costing the country valuable resources in the unused buildings; they were draining the country of petrol, rubber, coal and vehicles in insisting on travelling to work; they were diverting manpower to the driving of passenger trains and buses. The journalist compared the Arsenal girls unfavourably with those in the Forces who 'willingly and cheerfully leave their homes for a far more Spartan camp life.' The righteous indignation of the writer knew no bounds:

> It may seem incredible, yet girls, themselves without responsibilities or serious home ties, in private conversation scorn the idea of hostel life even to aid the war effort.

The failure of official accommodation was not confined to Bridgend: it was a national problem. In an extraordinary attack on Government policy in July 1942, the Select Committee on National Expenditure reported to Parliament that the excess provision of hostel places adjacent to war factories was a 'remarkable miscalculation.' Lewis Silkin, the chair of the Committee characterised the civil servant who had made the original estimates as 'some academic person sitting at a desk who may have been good at arithmetic but was not good at anything else.' He went on to accuse officials of a 'fundamental error,' in assuming that those living more than 12 miles from factories would want to move into hostels. All this invective was a bit rich coming from a group which twelve months before had been so insistent on places being provided as fully and as rapidly as possible. Why were the hostels so underused?

One reason was the drop in the demand for labour. Although the figures of those employed at the Arsenal rose up to the end of 1941, as we have seen, a number of factors resulted in a reduction of over 30% in the workforce by the summer of 1943. This in turn took the pressure off the demand for accommodation in the local area. When Gwen Lloyd was sent from Borth to Bridgend in 1942 she was at first housed in a hostel where she quickly made friends with another girl who had come from Blaina. The hostel obviously did not suit them, because the Gwent girl said 'we're not staying here,' and the two of them found digs in the village of Coity, just a few hundred yards from the Brackla site. Obviously getting rooms near the Factory was not difficult.

A second reason for the unpopularity of the hostels was the cost. In south Wales the national weekly rate of £1.5s. was probably seen as excessively high. Inman commented that the figure would seem 'more to a Welsh girl than to those in more prosperous districts,' and that 'many Welsh girls made a practice of sending money home.' Apparently some consideration was given to introducing differential charges, but it was decided to keep rates uniform across Britain. In November 1941 the national charge was cut by 2s. 6d., but this was not enough to make a significant difference. Those workers who did need accommodation in the Bridgend area could probably get lower charges from a landlady.

A third factor was the Assisted Travel Scheme. Workers who lived at a distance from the Arsenal did not have to pay transport costs above 3s a week. Technically the fares were paid only if there was no appropriate accommodation available near the Factory, but in practise this regulation was never enforced. Thus there was no financial incentive to move into the hostels: in effect the workers were actually being paid not to live in them. In November 1941 the *Western Mail* quoted Corbett as declaring that as much as 24s. a week was being paid to individuals to subsidise their fares to the Arsenal. Inman revealed that an attempt was made in

1942 by the Ministry of Supply to end fare subsidies 'beginning with small nibbles at journeys of three hours and more at Bridgend, Glascoed and Hereford,' but the restrictions proved unworkable, and in the end nothing was done to end the travel subsidy.

In any case the real problem was that people simply preferred all the disadvantages of travelling long distances each day to avoid living in the quarters provided. As Lewis Silkin declared in the Commons, the Government seemed to have taken no account 'of the fundamental question: would the workers be willing to live in the hostels.' These places might eventually provide good standards of food and care, but, as Inman wrote,

> Hostels were unpopular because they were not, and could not be made the same as, homes.

Essentially the hostels were huge, even intimidating institutions. Workers, especially young girls, did not want to sleep in soulless dormitories, to share common washing facilities, to eat in cafeterias. They wanted to go home to their own family, their own kitchens, their own hearths, their own privacy and their own beds, and were prepared to put up with great inconveniences to achieve that.

A report in the *Glamorgan Gazette* of a meeting of the Bridgend Town Council in February 1943 sheds a light on resentments in the town towards the underused hostels. Officials reported that exceptional hardship was being caused to people in a house in Nolton Street which was in an overcrowded and unhealthy condition. Councillor Oakes pointed out that 'there were hostels in the area which are not nearly full,' and he

> thought it unfair that Bridgend should be overcrowded while many such buildings were unoccupied.

Councillor Williams was even more incensed at the situation:

> I don't see why we should turn houses in this town into hovels when there are such hostels empty. It is disgusting that people should be pushed into rooms with a few sticks of furniture and charged enormous rents.

He proposed that the council contacted the 'authority in charge of the hostels in question.' Presumably the residents of the house were not workers at the Arsenal, and so not qualified to live in Island Farm, or at Pencoed.

By September 1943 the Factory management had given up on trying to persuade workers to live locally, and instead were celebrating those who travelled distances and yet did not miss shifts. That month the newsletter highlighted J.M. Davies, who had worked in Time Fuze section for nearly two years. She travelled over 90 miles each day to and from Bridgend, and she was able to write that she had 'only been absent from duty when transport failed on two occasions,' so she was proud to think that she was 'not a "missing cog" in the wheel.'

The hostels may have largely failed in their original purpose, but the costs of their construction were not to be wasted. In August 1942 the Minister of Supply, Andrew Duncan, was able to announce that nationally, 14 out of 16 completed surplus hostels had been allocated for alternative government use, and that seven hostels on which building work had been suspended were now to be completed for other departments. The Pencoed hostel did continue to house Factory workers, but it had ample room for other categories of residents such as Land Army girls. The hostel also operated rather like a hotel, and welcomed members of the armed forces, civil servants, groups of workers from other factories, and others visiting the Arsenal or government installations in the area. Pencoed was used as accommodation for refugee families from bombed out homes in the east and south of London after the V-1 and V-2 campaigns. According to Sue Roberts there were about 1,000 residents in all: 'It was a complete world on its own – one happy family. I never worked so hard in my life.'

Island Farm was to have uses perhaps more appropriate to its design, and to have a unique history: it would become infamous throughout Britain. In 1943 and up to the invasion of Europe in June 1944 it was used as an American army camp. In July 1943 Superintendent May wrote in his Diary that he had 'Received information that about 1200 troops of a field construction unit arrived at hostel under Col Hancock 5 p.m.' Presumably these were British troops who were to prepare Island Farm for its new male military residents. Next month the exotic visitors arrived: May wrote on 15th August that 'Inspector Fitzpatrick reported the conduct of the coloured troops at the by-pass hostel was excellent last night.' On the 22nd May received the news that 800 American troops of the 28th Infantry Division had arrived at Island Farm Hostel.

Once the Americans had departed for Normandy, Island Farm was converted into a prisoner-of-war camp able to hold over 1,600 captives. Its moment of nationwide fame came on 11th March 1945 when 67 German officers escaped – the biggest escape from a British POW camp, though all the prisoners were recaptured within a week. Island Farm was then converted into Special Camp 11, a prison for high-ranking German officers including luminaries such as Field Marshal Von Runstedt, commander-in-chief of the German armies in the defeat of France and the BEF. The history of Island Farm as a prisoner-of-war camp from 1944 to 1948 has been well documented in two books, *Come Out Wherever You Are*, by Herbert Williams, and *Island Farm, Special Camp 11,* by Sue Hawthorne and pupils of Brynteg School.

Today there is a modern housing estate in the shadow of an M4 embankment on the site of the former Pencoed Hostel. The Island Farm site has been cleared of almost all its buildings, but awaits its next incarnation as a Technology Park. Meanwhile it serves as wildlife sanctuary, and a source of sloes and blackberries. One original building remains, Hut 9, protected by a formidable fence. By looking at that it can perhaps be seen why the workers at the Arsenal chose to travel, rather than living in the hostels.

Notes

1 Herbert Morrison: 1888–1965. Labour party politician. MP for Hackney South. Deputy Prime Minister to Clement Atlee, 1945-1951.

2 Kew (AVIA 22/2513)

3 Safety regulations on carrying ammunition and explosives by rail were considerably relaxed once hostilities started. Pre-war the maximum number of wagons per train that could carry such items was 5: during the war this was raised to 60. In addition the amount that could be carried on each wagon was raised – for open wagons from 2,200lbs to 4,000, and for covered wagons from 10,000 lbs to 16,000.

4 With 3.6 litre sidevalve Ford V8 85hp engine, capable of hauling 8 tons.

5 Workers Educational Association.

6 1923 play by the English writer, Sutton Vane, about a group of passengers who find themselves on a ship without a crew voyaging to an unknown destination. Slowly they realize that they are all dead, and bound for heaven – or hell.

7 E.g. Peter Lilley in 1992.

7: Workers' Playtime

In 1949 Ian Hay's official story of the Royal Ordnance factories was published. On page 92 appears a hagiographical eulogy to the workers:

> There was nothing whatever to criticise in the spirit of the ROF operatives – men or women. Their effort was unceasing; they were inspired by but one aim and purpose – to do their part and back the fighting forces to the limit. Nothing deterred them – long hours, perpetual hours, air raids.

It suited the authorities to paint this picture of unstinting dedication on the part of the workforce. The reality was more complex.

There were many factors which tended to depress morale at ROF 53: the fatigue caused by travelling long distances; the shift pattern; the safety, health and cosmetic problems caused by explosive chemicals; the strict discipline; the pressures to increase production; the rejection of unsatisfactory components by inspectors; the monotony and boredom of repetitive unskilled work. Betty Nettle was working in Pellets: 'I had a piece of paper and a paintbrush and paste – it was like wrapping a sweet. I've never been so bored in my life.' Peggy Rowlands felt the same: 'It was a long day, and the work was monotonous. You couldn't chat a lot, you had to concentrate. We didn't like it.' The high rate of absenteeism,[1] especially among the female workforce, gives some

indication of the extent of low morale at the Factory.

To overcome such feelings, and so ensure maximum production, it was important for the management to maintain and raise morale: to create a belief that everyone at the Arsenal was working together towards the common goal – victory. This was relatively easy when news of triumphs was announced from the various fields of battle, but it was difficult to generate enthusiasm throughout the workforce at Bridgend – certainly before the victory at El Alamein late in 1942, and in between the good news that followed.

Those in charge at ROF 53 used a variety of methods to try to keep their workers satisfied. In particular they facilitated the organization of sports teams and other social activities, and attempted to inspire effort through music, propaganda and the example of hard working colleagues. Other factors could also lift morale – satisfaction with pay, perks such as food free of ration coupons, propaganda, patriotism, the visits of celebrities, and friendships made in the Factory.

Sporting and Social activities

One of the ways in which workers at the Arsenal were given a feeling that they were part of a community was through the creation of clubs and societies covering a wide variety of activities. Of course, as we have seen, Corbett, Superintendent from 1941 to 1945, brought with him the Quaker ethos of Fry's chocolate factory in Bristol where the welfare of workers was as important as the work that they did. Woolwich allowed the Superintendent to use Factory buildings and land for recreational schemes, and he was given a small grant for the purpose. The May 1943 edition of the Factory newsletter announced proudly that 'Our Sports Pavilion is now available to all.' This pavilion seems to have been built off Felindre Road in Pencoed, adjacent to the Hostel there.

There was a cricket square, and tennis courts. Apparently there were facilities, too, for darts, bridge, dominoes and refreshments. The pages of *ROF 53 News*, are full of information about the activities of sporting and other groups.

Field Sports

The first Annual Sports Day was on August 15th 1942. There must have been a major crisis on that day because the following year *ROF 53 News* wrote about 'last year's unfortunate experience.' Probably the problem was the usual curse of a Welsh summer – rain – as the writer goes on to comment that 'None of us can determine what sort of weather we shall have.' The second Annual Sports Day in 1943 was held in the grounds of the Bridgend Boys' Grammar School (now Brynteg School) at Ewenny Road.

There were teams representing ROF 53 in the sports of rugby, soccer, hockey and cricket. In fact hockey players were able to field three Factory teams – ladies', men's and mixed. There were hard-fought internal competitions in all these sports, as well as in tennis and golf. The many contests seem to have been very well supported and intense. In 1943, 18 sections and departments put teams in for the cricket competition[2]. The cup was won by East Group, who defeated Engineering in the final by 158 runs to 85. This is not surprising since a Glamorgan player, Cyril Smart[3], was a member of the East Group's team. According to *ROF 53 News* Smart 'knocked up a lively, albeit at times lucky 84, and did his usual damage with the ball.' In 1943 a Factory golf tournament was held at Southerndown Golf Club. The standard does not seem to have been very high: the *ROF 53 News* reporter commented wittily, if cruelly, that 'Colonel Bogey was too much for the bulk of the 17 competitors.' The final of the 1943 soccer cup was described in tragic verse:

> On Newbridge Fields one Friday night,
> Time-Fuze placed their soccer might
> To battle with a team from Smoke
> And win the cup; but here's the joke –
> Smoke beat 'em, yes! One nil!
> And it's made them feel quite ill.

Nora Roberts, Factory Beauty Queen

They walk around forlorn and broke,
Their future plans all gone up in Smoke.
When asked the cause of their defeat
By what they thought was easy meat,
The captain said, 'Oh don't provoke,
We couldn't see the goal for Smoke!!

Corbett was determined to actively encourage sporting activities. On Easter Monday 1943 he turned out to referee a charity rugby match at the Brewery Field between two teams of over 40s: £100 was raised from the large crowd that turned up to see the top man blowing his whistle.

Other Competitive Activities

Darts was even more popular than the field sports: thirty departmental teams entered for the Factory Darts League in 1942. The following year a cup competition was won by Textiles, and the Textiles team, representing the Arsenal, went on to win the District Wings For Victory competition. An Interdepartmental miniature rifle shooting competition was held at least once, in

1942. The Canine Society was busy in 1943, organizing two dog shows, in May and October. In May the winner of the LJ Corbett cup for best in show was the cocker spaniel 'Vyasma', owned by Messrs. Long and Hadfield. Mrs Shields gave a cup to the Society – for the best Terrier in show. There were also boxing and table tennis sections in the Factory Sports Club.

In August 1944 the front page of the *Rhondda Leader* was adorned with a misty photograph of the lovely Nora Roberts. She was a 21 year-old girl, of Church Street, Ynyshir, who had been chosen above 17 other girls as Beauty Queen of the Arsenal. The crowning ceremony was performed by no less important a character than the Superintendent, Len Corbett, on the steps of the Embassy Cinema in Bridgend. Strangely, neither the Bridgend *Gazette*, nor the *Glamorgan Advertiser* saw fit to report this triumph for the Rhondda Valley.

Music and Drama

There was a great deal of stage work based in the Arsenal. Thus the Factory Operatic Society presented *The Vagabond King* (by Post, Hooker and Friml) in 1942[4], and the patriotic operetta, *The*

Rebel Maid, (by Phillips and Dodson) in May 1943, both at the Porthcawl Pavilion and Maesteg Town Hall. Redwood, was a member of the cast of *The Vagabond King* :

> Bear in mind you had people who were great singers from West Wales. Val Jeffrey from Swansea was a wonderful Contralto…we had a cast of 250, all on a stage the size of the one at the Pavilion. The firemen…were the French archers. The costumes were hired from London. We had all the uniforms and big bows.

During April 1945 the Society produced *The Student Prince* (by Donnelly and Romberg), starring Val Jeffrey and W Cobbley, again at Maesteg and Porthcawl.

In October 1944 a newly formed Factory Choral and Orchestral Society gave a rather more sedate programme of music from the *Messiah* in the English Congregational Church in Bridgend (today a pub!). The Superintendent, Corbett, was chairman of the concert.

The Home Guard Band, under the baton of Mr P Durrant, played 'popular programmes at various canteens during morning meal breaks.' These programmes were broadcast around the site. According to the Factory newsletter, the performances were 'greatly appreciated,' as the Band was 'better than ever.'

The ROF Amateur Dramatic Society presented *Outward Bound* (by Sutton Vane) in July 1942 at the Pencoed Hostel. According to DAC, writing in *ROF 53 News*, it was 'very well received by enthusiastic audiences.' The critic considered that 'it would be invidious to select any player for special praise from a team which worked so well together.' The following year the Society performed *George and Margaret* (a comedy by Gerald Savory) at Pontycymer, Maesteg, Porthcawl, and in the Miners' Welfare Hall, at Cymmer in a drama festival, in which the company won second prize.

An Inter-Factories Eisteddfod was held in City Hall and the Cory Hall in Cardiff in 1943, 1944 and 1945. A writer in *ROF 53 News* claimed that in the 1943 Eisteddfod Bridgend's 'combined successes exceeded those of any other individual factory,' and went on to list four first places: Tenor Solo, T Joseph Thomas; Contralto Solo, Blodwen Morgan; Elocution, Olwen Wynn; Violin

Solo, Colin Timberlake. Megan Hall of Porthcawl was an enthusiastic participant. She

> started a Ladies choir [at the Arsenal] and we used to meet in the lunch hour; we would rush our lunches and then have a choir practice. We competed in the interfactories competition where we sang Brahms Lullaby. We came second, and we were quite thrilled with that.

In 1944 an eliminating concert was held to determine who should represent the Factory in each of sixteen competitions. Despite this, in a report of that year's event, the *Western Mail* was able to record only one Bridgend victory – that of Mrs A Gwilym and Mrs B Morgan in the Soprano/Contralto duet.

Soldier, airman and sailor at Hostel dance

Rather less serious than these activities were the numerous departmental troupes organised within individual sections to entertain their fellow-workers in canteens during meal breaks. In June 1942 the Factory newsletter records that HE Fuze Concert Party worked their shift, and then gave up their afternoon to give a show to 40mm. Workers in Pellets organized a troupe which they called the Pelleteers.

Talent, or 'Go-as-you-Please' competitions seem to have been very popular. *ROF 53 News* records a number held in the canteens of the various sections, including Textiles, T&P, and Brackla 'A'. One of the winners at the latter competition must have been well worth seeing – it was Mrs H Jones, an acrobatic contortionist.

Individual sections also organised dances – some in Bridgend's Palais-de-Dance, some at the Casino, Porthcawl[5], and some in the hostels. The profits usually went to a charity such as the Red Cross or the Merchant Navy Fund. The October 1940 minutes of the Maesteg Council recorded that the proceeds from an ROF dance at the Town Hall were to be 'for the sole use of the Maesteg Comforts Fund.'

Music While you Work

According to Redwood

> You would have music while you work, you see. You would have it in the canteens while you were on your break, you would also

> have it while you were on production. You'd have speakers in the workshop. You had different records and, well, Vera Lynn – she was the one. You'd have all these going – purely morale boosters.

Undoubtedly the workers at the Arsenal would have enjoyed the music broadcast to the workshops. They would have sung along with the programmes, shifts would have appeared to pass more quickly, and the rhythm of the music would have encouraged faster production. It was not only the melodies of the Factory Home Guard Band that were heard in the many buildings of ROF 53. To keep up morale, and speed production, the Factory system relayed BBC radio programmes. One such, broadcast every morning and afternoon from 23rd June 1940, was *Music While You Work*, a non-stop medley of popular and lively tunes[6] played by a different band every day.

Another radio programme heard throughout the Factory was *Workers' Playtime*. This was broadcast first in May 1941, and went out live three times a week from the canteen of a different factory 'somewhere in Britain.' The format was always that of a variety show of singers, musicians and comedians. Twice during the war the factory somewhere in Britain was ROF 53: these were the line-ups on those two occasions:

> June 6th 1942
> Bruce Merryl and George Myddleton – Pianos
> Alda Campbell and Vic Wise -Double Act Comedians
> Dickie Hassett – Comedian
> Laelia Finneberg – Classical Soprano
>
> June 8th 1944
> George Myddleton – Piano
> Trefor Jones – Tenor from Cymmer[7]
> Eddie Connor and Vernon Drake – Double Act Comedians
> Dorothy Carless – Singer[8]

There were four other broadcasts from Bridgend using local amateur, rather than professional, talent. These were: *Factory Canteen* on September 17th 1941, and *Works Wonders* on 5th September 1942, 5th February 1944 and 25th July 1945.

ENSA[9] put on shows at ROF 53. In *The Times* in October 1942 the reporter writes that he saw a party of ENSA entertainers

> in a vast Royal Ordnance Factory giving three shows a day – the first at noon, and the last at 1.30am – for a week in different canteens on this site.

According to Margaret Plummer,

> Every day there was something on. Every shift while we were having our food in the canteen there would be entertainment – no rubbish, top class entertainment.

Rowena Harris, who worked in Textiles Canteen, has a somewhat different memory.

> We had loudspeakers in the canteen. They played music and the radio most of the time. We had ENSA concerts with singing and dancing, comedy. The canteen would be packed. We didn't have one every week, it was months between them.

Sue Roberts remembers a production by CEMA[10] at the Pencoed Hostel.

> It was Puccini's Madam Butterfly, but the soprano was so enormous that the stage creaked when she walked: the girls called her Madam Moth!

Margaret Plummer recalls the visit of one very special entertainer:

> We had Clark Gable[11] come there one day. He was selling war bonds for a kiss. Of course you had to buy the bond first... I didn't kiss him, I didn't buy any bonds – we were a big family that we had to support.

Home Guard

On the surface the Factory Home Guard Battalion was a military organization, but it performed an important social function as well as providing morale-boosting privileges to its members. Some of the real motives for workers joining the Home Guard were expressed by Roy Davies:

> I was working in the initiators then, and I was there one Friday night, and all this bloody stuff was coming through, piling up, so

> I said, "Where's the rest of the boys then?" Well, they'd all gone to the Home Guard. So next Friday, I was in the Home Guard and the bosses had to do the job then. They used to moan like hell. We used to do drill and arms like, with the guns and Lewis guns. And then on a Saturday and Sunday (we used to get paid for all this mind, double time) up off the A 48 across the fields there, we crept along the hedges like; it was great.

Over a month this weekend camp was occupied by each of the four companies at the Arsenal in turn; facilities for recreation and entertainment were provided once the training was complete. *ROF 53 News* reported that a summer camp would be held near Trecco Bay at Porthcawl in the first week of August for the 250 officers and men of the Battalion, and that 'training will be combined with a reasonable amount of leisure.' An added incentive was that 'some additional uniforms are expected very shortly.'

The considerable privileges accorded to members of the ROF Home Guard caused resentment amongst employees in other work places. According to complaints from councillors in the minutes of the Penybont Council, men who joined the Arsenal Home Guard trained for only two hours a week, yet they were excused the nightly Fire Guard duties that others were compelled to do. And as Roy Davies explained, the ROF Home Guard units did their training in their normal paid working hours, while members of other units outside the Factory had to train in their own spare time. No wonder the Factory Home Guard was popular.

In fact Fire Watching was another source of resentment at the favoured position of Arsenal workers compared with those outside. The minutes of the Penybont Council for April 1942 reveal that 'increasing agitation had been caused amongst men enrolled for Fire Guard duty under Civil Defence regulations,' because ROF Factory watchers were being paid 27s.6d. per night duty, while other watchers were receiving just 3s.

Women workers were not excluded from Home Guard activities. In 1940 the *Gazette* reported that a standard for the Arsenal Home Guard 'had been subscribed for by the girls working at the Factory.' In a ceremony which the *Gazette* reporter claimed was unique, because it was the first in the country, Mrs Shields, the Female Labour superintendent had presented the new standard to

Captain Barbour, the commanding officer. It seems that later, women employees were allowed a more active role; the November 1942 newsletter reported that a large number of men and women were being trained to shoot in the Battalion indoor shooting range.

Propaganda

To keep up production the Ministry of Supply felt that it was vital to impress upon workers in filling factories the importance of their work. The size of the factories, the huge number of workers, the monotony of the relatively unskilled processes, the often very small part of any component worked on: all these factors tended to prevent the individual appreciating their own essential part in the grand scheme of things. In 1942 special Works Relations Officers were appointed to educate the workforce.

There were two main themes for the information given to the employees at Bridgend. One was briefings about the course of the war in general, so that workers might be inspired to work harder for specific objectives. This education process relied heavily on materials from the Ministry of Information. The second theme was to try to show something of the work of the Factory as a whole, and then how the parts worked on fitted into ammunition used by the armed forces. Peggy Inman wrote in her book *Labour in the Munitions Industry*, that the purpose of this programme of education was

> to overcome the monotony and feeling of uselessness in producing the same part hour after hour, day after day… Many of the workers had no real interest in the work that they were doing, which had no connection with their peacetime activities, and was in any case often boring... It was of particular value for women workers…who were unused to factory life, and to mechanical equipment.

The methods used to put across these messages included films, exhibitions, photographs, charts, posters, talks, guest speakers and visits to military establishments and to other factories.

One such visit is recorded in the August 1942 edition of *ROF 53 News*. A photograph shows thirty women, all dressed in their best, topped off with the inevitable fine hats. According to the caption, the girls were all from one section of ROF 53, and visited another ROF (possibly Glascoed) 'to see the fitting and make-up of the remaining part of the unit upon which they are engaged.' They stayed overnight at a hostel of the host factory. Opportunities were given to see completed ammunition in action. Eunice Jones had played an important part in the development of a new type of naval shell, and she was invited to visit a destroyer to see the round fired.

An example of a talk – and its dramatic effects – is given in the Factory newsletter. Captain and Mrs Hammer spoke about their experience in Malta from 1938 to 1942. This so inspired one of the foremen present that he

> drew from his pocket his pay envelope, extracted the contents, and handed them over to the War Savings Collector,' saying, 'Make this a munitions for Malta week.'

It is not recorded if other workers followed his selfless example in full, though the article claimed that

> 'the War Savings amount for that day rose far above the usual collection, and exceeded the average by £30.

Direct thanks from the various fronts was particularly appreciated by the workforce. Teresa Barnett recalls that a letter was sent from the 7th Armoured Division (The Desert Rats) in North Africa thanking the workers at Bridgend for never sending out a dud mortar bomb.[12] According to one of Mari Williams' informants, the Admiralty sent a letter of thanks to workers at the Factory for the fuzes produced at Bridgend which had helped to sink German warships: photos of the destroyed vessels were shown alongside the letter.

In September 1943 *ROF 53 News* advertised a major exhibition entitled *Path to Victory*, which was clearly designed to show how the work done at the Arsenal fitted into the war as a whole. Great importance was obviously attached to the show, because the newsletter records that no less a personage than the Director-General of Filling Factories, CS Robinson, had come from his headquarters in Woolwich to be 'one of the earliest visitors.' The exhibition was set up in a marquee at the Factory and the approach was guarded by 'a brave show of flags of the Allied

Nations' accompanied by examples of light guns. Inside the marquee were displayed 'fuzes of many types, primers, and a variety of other stores all filled in our Factory.' Next there were 'a number of interesting exhibits of complete rounds, ranging from a .22 cartridge to a 15-inch Naval Shell.' The Factory's Engineering department presented 'an imposing display of tools and machinery wholly produced on our Factory.' The writer in *ROF 53 News* felt moved to comment that, 'The fact that 60% of this exhibit was made by female labour tells its own story.' Other highlights included a 4,000lb 'block buster', a captured Nazi flag, unexploded German bombs, 'arresting posters depicting many aspects of Factory propaganda and publicity,' and two stands on the work of the Factory's Surgery. Another feature on offer was the story of the war starting with 'vivid pictures of the Blitz on British cities' followed by the journey 'from El Alamein to the liquidation of Sicily in actual photographs.' If this were not enough a Cinema Annexe presented special films. The newsletter enthused that the exhibition 'is bound to arouse intense interest,' and encouraged employees to 'Come along and see what our lads are doing for us.' In fact this was not left to chance: arrangements were made for parties of workers to visit the exhibition to ensure that all employees could be properly inspired by the extravaganza.

Inevitably the Factory radio system was used to motivate the workers. A news bulletin was broadcast on each shift and into every workshop giving uplifting information about the progress of the war. Each bulletin started with 'Radio Bridgend calling – Hello ROF workers.' A script for 4th August 1943 detailed the successes of the Red Army in driving the Germans west from Stalingrad, successful British bombing raids on Berlin, France and Italy, details of German planes shot down over Britain, and Japanese setbacks in the Pacific.

ROF 53 News was frequently used to exhort the workforce. Two examples will suffice to give an impression of the character of these motivational writings. In the November 1942 edition Billy Hughes of T&P section writes

> When this terrible war is over, the workers of this Factory will be able to say with pride "I did my bit." So, as a worker in this fine Factory I say "Keep it up, fellow workers."

Left **BLUE SHIFT** Right

Back Row—M. Bevan, E. Williams, N. Brangham, B. Summers, P. Pickford. M. Currie, M. Miyen, T. Thomas, C. Musto, W. Pugh, E. Burns, M. L. John, O. Wilkes, L. Mitchell.

Front Row—D. Amos, M. Rees, K. Davies, M. Howells, L. Conovan, L M. Jones, P. Parsons, P. Jones, H. Waters, B. Rees.

Cordite Section Blue Shift – 100% attendees – April 1943

Writing in the August edition of that year, S Reynolds, Manager of West concludes

> Now before us is the harder task. This is not an endurance test; and so we must maintain our speed, our output, our efficiency and our enthusiasm.

In July 1942 the newsletter published a poem by KL designed to enthuse the workforce:

> Malta is raided every hour;
> Our friends there look to us for power.
> To chase the blighters from the skies
> We've got to make production rise.
>
> The heroes on the Russian Front
> Must not be left to bear the brunt.
> When Russia calls can you be deaf?
> Where are your heroes, ROF?
>
> When China made her Burma Road
> Each man or woman bore her load.
> Are Britons now less strong than they!
> Come, Wales, and shew them all the way.

Efficiency Cup Winners' Dinner with the Superintendent

To encourage others each edition of the newsletter included an example of a worker with perfect attendance. For example in June 1943 Miss Elizabeth Enoch of Nantymoel is singled out for praise. She had not missed a shift in the two years from March 1941 that she had been working in the Factory, and it is pointed out in the article that she 'does all the shopping and helps with the housework.' In the same edition two others with full attendance over the previous twelve months are listed, along with the facts that in one case the worker has four children to look after, and in the other an invalid father; presumably the management is trying to show that considerable domestic commitments need not prevent employees from getting to work every day. On the back page of the newsletter is a photograph of the members of Cordite Section who did not miss a day's work in April. Since this is in fact just 50 women out of a total of 407, the message that comes across is that only a minority of workers (12%) were giving one hundred percent attendance to the cause. Pyro's commitment was even worse than this: only 31 out of 470 (7%) had unblemished attendance in the same month, and the photos of the dedicated women on the back of *ROF 53 News* look rather sparse.

Another method used to motivate the workforce appears in the June 1943 edition, where much is made of the Superintendent's Efficiency Cup. Blue Shift of Pellets Section were the winners of the first and second week of the competition, and twenty workers from that shift were rewarded with a luncheon in the rarefied atmosphere of the Superintendent's canteen. Efficiency seems to have become a watchword at the Factory; in the September edition (in what seems to be more of a threat than a promise) it is announced that an efficiency song 'has been written as our Factory song, and will soon be heard in canteens, on the platforms and on the air.' Apparently there was to be no escape!

An example of a motivational film with ROF 53 connections was *Danger Area*[13], made by the Ministry of Information. In 1944 the *Glamorgan Gazette* advertised a free Ministry of Information film show at the Cinema, Bridgend, on the afternoon of Sunday, 23rd April. *Danger Area* was one of the films that was to be shown. Readers of the *Gazette* were told that the film was 'of particular interest to Welsh audiences' because it 'was recently taken in a Welsh factory.' In fact the story seems to have been a true one, because the plot follows very closely a report printed in *The Times* newspaper in November 1941 headlined 'Arms Workers Race Against Time' about a 24-hour shift in a south Wales Royal Ordnance Factory – presumably Bridgend. In essence the Admiralty needed a special batch of ammunition for a warship on convoy protection. The Saturday morning shift should have finished its work around lunchtime that day, but when told how vital the ammunition was, the twenty-strong all male team worked through till 3am the following Sunday morning to complete the task. The film was in fact partly made in a studio, partly in genuine workshops. According to the credits it was recorded at Merton Park Studios in southwest London. The principals are cut-glass accented actors, but the workers have genuine local accents, and seem to have been actual employees of the Bridgend Factory. At one point they sing a funereal 'Sospan Fach'. No doubt the film was shown in the canteens of the Factory as well as in the local town.

How successful was the education programme ? Peggy Inman was well placed to make a careful judgement; she wrote:

> There can be little doubt that the workers in the majority of the ROFs comprised some of the best and most consistently informed groups of any in the country.

'Keep Smiling Through'

There were other factors which tended to lift morale. As we have seen, the wages of employees were relatively high, especially for the women at the Factory. Before the war Margaret Plummer was working for just 10s. a week: in a videoed interview she claimed to have started at the Arsenal on £4.10s, a huge increase. Betty Cartlidge had been earning 18s. in service, but at the Arsenal she had £3 a week. The high wages could mean an enormous difference to the standard of living of families, and this in turn would ensure high morale. As one of the women in a BBC radio programme commented, the girls

> did enjoy the money. It was well-paid work for girls of our age. It gave them a pick up. They could buy things they couldn't buy before... They had money in their pocket for the first time ever in their lives. They didn't feel guilty because they were having a little bite, a very little bite of the cherry.

And of course, for many of the men unemployed before 1940, having a job at all was a positive factor. Another contributor to the BBC programme observed that

> There was very little employment in this village. It was an awful thing that this war had to come to get a decent living. It was only when the Arsenal opened that a lot of people ever had any money at all.

Jill John reminisced that

> I noticed the difference with families who had people working in the Arsenal. Suddenly you'd see improvements in the house because of more money coming in.

Everyone who worked in the Factory had a main meal in their canteen. This food was off ration, so they would eat much better than those not involved in war work. There were treats, too, available to workers in the Factory only. Rowena describes one instance:

> When you came in through the first gate there was little kiosks on the right-hand side, and every now and again we'd have an amount of face cream delivered, Snow Cream and things like that. And then we'd open that little kiosk and sell it, and then they used to queue up before they went into the danger area, or they came when they came out of the danger area. It was just makeup, you couldn't get it. We had long queues for it, just ordinary face cream, whatever was available; face powder, different things we had.

Redwood describes another treat:

> One perk was, they had a special ration of Cadbury's chocolate. The canteens dished them out – you had to pay for them of course, but at a cheap rate. Well oft times if you knew someone, who knew somebody, who knew somebody, you were able to get a few bars over and above your allocation, say for the fire brigade.'

Unofficial treats were available, too. Mair Davies came to the Factory from the Rhondda. According to her,

> Things were scarce – if you could get something for someone else, we did. One girl from Swansea would get nice cream sponges without coupons, and she would bring them in for us. One girl from Port Talbot would bring in empty seed bags; they were made

Workers waiting to greet a Visitor to ROF 53

The King and Queen with Mrs Shields and Len Corbett

> of good strong cotton. We used to boil them.... then embroider them and make afternoon clothes out of them. Perhaps someone who didn't like coffee would exchange it for something else.

Rowena tells another story:

> There was a young man working there. He was going into the Navy and he was getting married, and he didn't have a wedding cake. So we made a cake, and iced it. But we couldn't actually just give it to him, so we held a raffle and made sure he won it!

Most workers were patriotic – they genuinely felt that they were helping the men in the services fight, and their country to win the war. Margaret Plummer was 'determined to do something for the

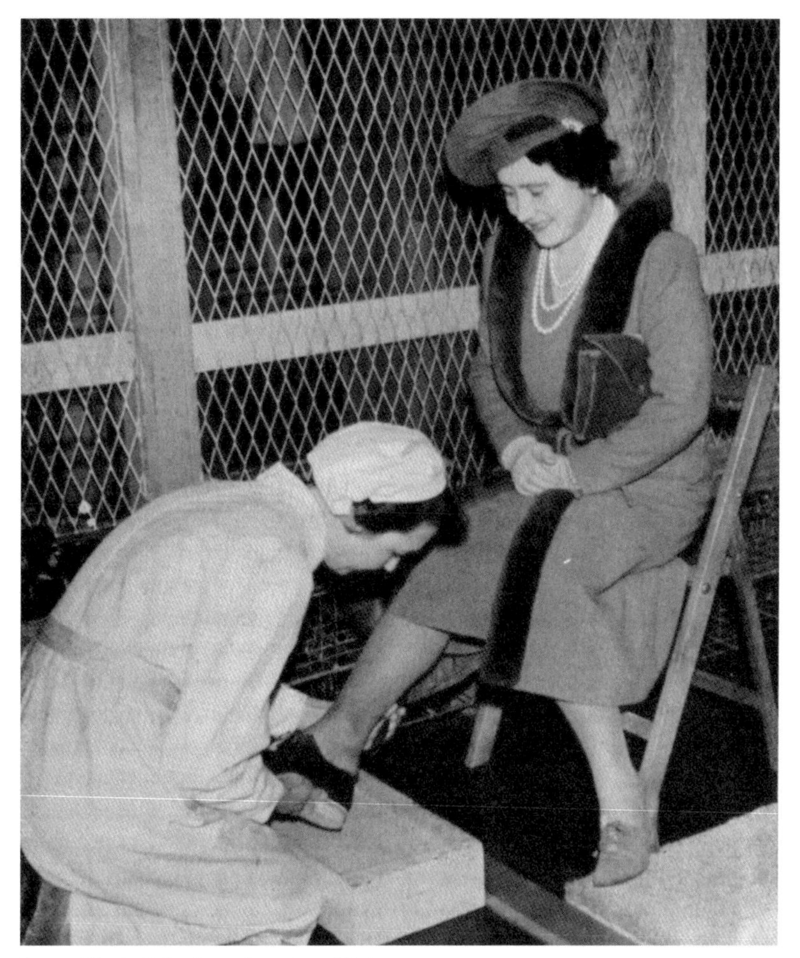

Queen Elizabeth having safety shoes fitted

war effort.' When her mother prevented her from applying to join the ATS, Margaret said 'Well, I'll go and make the ammunition for the men.' When Myra Jenkins worked there she 'felt we were doing our little bit for the war.' Writing in *ROF 53 News* in May 1943, Mrs R Jones declared that

> We feel that we're helping our boys as much as possible...Personally I think this is the best way that I can do my

> duty towards my country... We have helped in building up the vast supply of munitions which are now reaching our boys who are doing their best to clear the oppressed lands.

In August 1941 the Ministry of Supply tried to encourage this patriotism and to develop a sense of pride in workers through the distribution of special shoulder badges. These showed a crossed shell and a bomb on a navy background overwritten with the legend 'ROF Front Line Duty.' The badges were to be sewn onto normal outer coats. According to the management the insignia was supposed to indicate 'the supreme importance of the job' the employees were doing, which counted as 'front line duty.'

Some girls got unofficial encouraging feedback from servicemen. Peggy Rowlands (nee Hawkins) remembered that the workers used to 'slip notes into the ammunition boxes telling the soldiers that the girls were 'thinking about you' that they should 'keep smiling', and 'carry on with the good work.' According to Peggy, the girls would put their name and addresses on the notes, and would get replies, and sometimes photos from the soldiers.

Visits by VIPs were used to tap in to feelings of patriotism, and to inspire the work force. On 6th December 1941, the day before the Japanese attack on Pearl Harbour, Police Superintendent May received some important news from his Chief Constable: the King, George VI, and his wife, Queen Elizabeth, were coming to visit Bridgend in five days' time to visit the Arsenal, and then to travel on to the Pencoed hostel. Such short notice was necessary for security reasons, but it meant that May was busy for the next few days organising the policing of the visit. In the Arsenal there was frantic activity in the shops to be inspected. According to one worker 'they were painted from top to bottom, and all the girls there had new magazine clothes.'

The King and Queen made many such visits to different parts of Britain during the war. A journalist on the *South Wales Echo* expressed his understanding of the three purposes of this trip. First,

> The visit of their Majesties ... is a reminder that the British Empire is one family of nations of free people

presumably because the royal couple had come out of England to spend two days in Wales. Secondly, the visit showed common purpose between the different classes and the monarchy as

> The home country is held together by understanding and sympathy between the cottager and the throne.

Finally, warming to his theme, the journalist went on to explain that the journey would inspire the workers to greater effort since the trip would

> cheer on the workers in their great and laborious work of providing the means of defending the liberties and freedoms of the people from the aggressors.

The Royal train arrived at Bridgend station at 10.00 in the morning of 11th December, to be met with what May described as a 'large, orderly crowd.' He wrote in his diary that the couple 'looked exceedingly well.' The Queen was dressed in a beige suit with pink trim: the *Echo* reporter trilled that she wore clothes that were two years old. The King wore his Field Marshal's uniform. The Royal party[14] travelled by car to the Arsenal. At the entrance to the Factory, like any other entrant, the King was asked to surrender any cigarettes or matches: he handed over a silver lighter and a case containing the cigarettes that would eventually kill him. The Queen was then asked 'Have you anything to declare, your Majesty?' to which she replied, with what the *Western Mail* reporter described as 'her usual gracious charm,' 'No, I have no cigarettes.' A long life ahead for her, then. Gossip in the Factory was that Elizabeth was 'full of jewellery' which she did not declare or surrender.

At the main Administrative Building the Queen was presented with a bouquet by Miss Radford of Textiles – one of the first twelve girls to join the staff of the Factory. Then their Majesties were introduced to the Superintendent, Len Corbett, Mr F. Wakeham, his deputy, and Mrs Edna Shields, the senior Labour Manager. According to May, the King and Queen went on to visit a shifting shop: there is a photo which shows the Queen having the appropriate danger area footwear put on by a kneeling subject. They must then have visited workshops – Sally Evans was working in time fuze, and according to her

The Duke of Kent in RAF uniform

> they passed by me close enough to touch them. The Queen passed right by me and spoke as she passed. Oh, we were thrilled at the time.

The *Western Mail* reported that the Royals questioned women workers about how long it took to travel from their homes to work. When Mary Williams from Merthyr told them that she left home at 3.30 in the morning, the Queen asked about the hostel facilities. Corbett commented that

> we have one of the best equipped hostels in the country, but the girls do not use it as much as we would like.

The visitors were entertained by the works choir, who finished with 'Hen Wlad Fy Nhadau' – enabling Corbett, former captain of the England rugby team to say that 'that was how the Welsh used to intimidate the English on the football field.'

The King and Queen then went on to Pencoed, to one of the Arsenal's hostels, where they were greeted by the manager, Miss Coles. An 'impromptu' dance was in progress when the royals arrived. Then the visitors chatted with some of the residents. Daisy Markham responded positively with 'It's splendid,' when the Queen asked if she liked the hostel. In the kitchens the young

Sue Roberts was dishing up mashed potatoes with a scoop. The Queen showed her common touch by asking, 'How do you do that? I've always wondered.' According to Sue, Elizabeth was radiant, while George 'was a little man, and seemed heavily made up.' Another worker thought that his complexion made him look 'almost as if he had been embalmed – like peaches and cream.'

After they had left Pencoed the royals went on to visit other places in the area, including the carbide factory at Kenfig, Abercynffig Welfare Hall, Wyndham Colliery, a nursery at Nantymoel, and the Miners' Institute (where the King declined an invitation to a game of billiards).

George and Elizabeth were not the only important visitors for May to take care of. The Duke of Kent[15] was at the Arsenal in April 1942. Clement Attlee, leader of the Labour Party (and soon to be Deputy Prime Minister) addressed workers in the Textile Canteen in February 1941. May was very taken with another pilgrim to the Factory, Viscount Bennett, who had been Prime Minister of Canada (1930-1935). He was managing at the Ministry of Supply with his fellow-Canadian, Lord Beaverbrook. May described him as 'a very charming and typical Canadian.' Bennett addressed workers in the Textile Canteen, and then used the Factory broadcast system to speak to all the other workers in their workshops.

There were a number of military visitors to the Arsenal. Perhaps the most distinguished was Major General Dudley Johnson of the South Wales Borderers. He had four times been decorated for bravery, culminating in a VC for his courage in an attack on a bridge over the Sambre Canal in France shortly before the Armistice in November 1918. Just the sort of guest to 'cheer on the workers in their great and laborious work.'

Many former workers at the site expressed their enjoyment of their time there – some went as far as to say it was the best period of their lives – usually because of the friends that they made, and the fun that they had. Megan Jones of Pencoed summed her experience up with the exclamation: 'Oh! We had the time of our life.'

Many lasting friendships were made at the Factory. Betty Nettle (nee Reynolds) commented that

> I enjoyed working in the Arsenal. I made very good friends, and only death has taken those friendships away.

Lucy Hughes, who worked in Textiles, remarked that

> we had great fun; they were great girls – although it was wartime we made our own fun… the ROF taught me to stand on my own two feet. We had a foreman with a real baby face. When he walked down the room the girls would all start singing "You must have been a beautiful baby, you must have been a wonderful child.[16]" His face would go all red!

Betty Cartlidge (nee Edwards) also enjoyed herself. As she said

> We had fun down there. On the night shift, at break time we had parties in the Canteen – we all brought something to eat. Everyone scrounged something – tins of fruit and so on. They were a lovely crowd of girls – all the girls were marvellous. When I got married they all sent me telegrams. We used to go to dances together in Maesteg Town Hall.

Dances were a very popular recreation throughout the war, and even more so when the Americans came to the area. Their base at St Mary Hill was the largest staging post in the west of the British Isles. Peggy Rowlands was 'never short of dancing partners when the Americans came to Bridgend.' Workers who lived a distance from the Arsenal went to events in their own communities. Margaret Plummer lived in Swansea, so she went to dances at the Patti Pavilion, but she would go to Llanelli or Gorseinon if there was nothing on in Swansea. According to her,

> There were real bands in those days, not this disco business. We danced to Joe Loss, and Bert Ambrose, and even the band down the Patti was a damn good band.

Rowena Harris explained the social opportunities that working at ROF 53 gave:

> People worked hard, but some of them enjoyed it as well, because they made friends. If the war hadn't come, and the Arsenal hadn't been built I'd have stayed in Pontycymer. The Arsenal was a way of meeting people; most of the women working there were married and had children. They never went out to work, so therefore they didn't go and meet a lot of people. Once the war started, everybody met everybody – people from Swansea, people from the Rhondda – people you'd never meet otherwise.

Redwood describes the fun had after the last performance of the ROF's operatic society in Maesteg:

> There were a few drinks, you can imagine, cider and beer. And after a few pints, somebody brought in a Belisha beacon – the orange ball off the top and we are using this Belisha beacon as a rugby ball. The firemen scrummed down. Well it rolled through the curtain and crashed down into the orchestra pit. Fun, I never had so much fun in my life, oh boy, oh boy.

Roy Davies of Bridgend enjoyed his time at the Arsenal:

> The company was great. I preferred the Arsenal – There were a lot of young boys there. We had fun, a bit of a laugh. We enjoyed ourselves down there. I loved it. I was only a young boy. Wicked boys, we were.

These are just two of the stories that he told:

> One night two of us went up by the women's toilets and we got a sheet from stores, and I stood on his shoulder, we put it over me and over him. The lighting wasn't very good. It was a blue light, they were terrible lights, and we made a noise like a ghost. Wooo! The women wouldn't go to the toilet. Then we were caught and that was that... There were housewives there, and they were part-time, and they used to work in a certain shop, and we thought, we'll shake them now. And we stood outside, and the light switches were outside the building, and we switched them off and one of the boys made a noise like a bomb coming down from a plane. Well, the women had heart attacks! We had a hell of a row over that, so they moved us again.

It would be difficult to evaluate the success of the Management's efforts to maintain morale, or even to quantify the effects on production – so many factors were involved in output. Obviously many people would be unhappy with the work, or for personal reasons. Rowena Harris tells the sad story of a girl from Pencoed who committed suicide.

> She was a nice girl and she never had a boyfriend. She was a very quiet girl, and this fellow started making a right fuss of her. She went out with him for some months. She got very attached to him, and then she found out he was married. She went to the station after the night shift, and threw herself under a train.

But overall morale seems to have been good most of the time for most people. This is Rowena's judgement:

> It was a very good feeling in the war. Everybody felt as if they had to do something and we all did it and there was no question about are not doing this, or not doing that. In the canteen, if one girl hadn't finished her work the other girls would help so that you would all finish together.

Notes

1 See Chapter Eleven.

2 Initiators, Central Stores, Brackla 'A', Fire Brigade, Engineering, EDB, War Department Constabulary, HE Fuze, Chemical Inspectorate Toolroom, Central Admin., His Majesty's Office of Works, Time & Proximity Fuze, INO, Stores and packing, East Group, CIA, Transport.

3 There were at least two Glamorgan players working on the Arsenal: the other was Dick Duckfield, in Engineering, scorer of the County's then highest score of 280 (not out) against Surrey at the Oval in 1936.

4 According to *ROF 53 News* the company was short of tenors – some things never change!

5 Later the Stonleigh Club.

6 Slow and 'lethargic' melodies were banned lest they slowed production! The BBC instruction was 'There must be as little variation of tempo as possible, the ideal being to maintain the same beat throughout the programme.'

7 During his career he sang on the West End stage with Ivor Novello and Anna Neagle.

8 A singer with Geraldo's Band – the BBC's dance band during the war. One of her top hits was 'That Lovely Weekend'.

9 Officially – Entertainments National Service Association (set up by Basil Dean in 1939): unofficially – Every Night Something Awful.

10 Council for the Encouragement of Music and the Arts founded in 1940 to help promote culture in Britain. Originally chaired by Lord De La Warr. After the war CEMA became the Arts Council of Great Britain.

11 Star of many films including *Gone With the Wind*: in 1943 he was serving as a gunner with the USAF in a B-17 Flying Fortress.

12 Hardly surprising, given the rigorous inspection regime at Bridgend!

13 Produced by Henry Cass, and with music by Norman Del Mar: it ran for 20 minutes.

14 Accompanying the King and Queen were Col. The Hon. Piers Leigh (equerry), Major Sir Alan Lascalles (asst private sec) and Lady Nunburnholme (lady in waiting)

15 An Air Commodore in the RAF. Unusually for the royal family, he was familiar with factory life: in the 1930s he had worked for the Home Office Factory Inspectorate – indeed he was known as the 'Democratic Duke.' He was to die in a plane crash within four months of his visit to Bridgend.

16 Bing Crosby 1938 song written by Mercer and Warren.

Photographed in the 1980s: Top: Blast Wall
Bottom: Entrance through Traverse

8: Safety: Rules, Regulations, Risks and Reactions

Designed for Safety

One of the huge advantages the designers of Bridgend had was that the Factory would be built on a very large green field site. The mother Arsenal at Woolwich had developed on a restricted urban site over very many decades: at Bridgend the design could

Danger Area buildings with traverses: anti-blast earth embankments

incorporate the latest ideas on safety. During the First World War over 600 people had been killed in several disastrous explosions at armaments factories[1]. And since 1918 there had been considerable developments in munitions. According to William Hornby in his *Factories and Plant* many new types of ammunition had to be dealt with, and the increasingly sophisticated detonators and fuzes had to be filled with a variety of complex explosive substances. Most of these changes had the result of greatly increasing the possible hazards of filling factory work, and so more stringent government regulations had been enforced in the last few years. The principles involved had already been set out in the plans for Bridgend's sister plant at Chorley, and the Factory in southern Wales would be constructed to the same standard.

What were the safety precautions built into the design?

Over 1000 acres of land was purchased, so that the hundreds of individual buildings could be widely spaced.

Most of the buildings that made up the Factory were relatively small, so that any damage could be localised.

As much non-inflammable material as possible was used in construction: the workshops themselves were made of steel frames with brick walls.

The majority of the workshops had gabled or flat roofs constructed of light materials (wood and felt), both to lift in the event of an explosion to allow the blast to expand upwards, and to avoid heavy debris falling afterwards. As a fireman at the Arsenal said, 'the buildings would disintegrate to save life.'

Every building had its own lightning conductors, and earthed copper strapping down and around its exterior.

All doors opened outwards to allow for rapid evacuation, or the dispersal of blast. They were closed automatically by brass weights suspended in the doorframes.

To avoid accidental sparks, all nails, screws, locks and hinges were made of bronze.

Switch boxes for lighting or machinery were fixed to the outside of buildings. All movable electrical parts in machinery plus the switches, and certain sections of electrical cabling were made of brass.

Light bulbs were sealed in bulkhead units set in the walls, or suspended from the ceiling.

Workshops had sand buckets and fire extinguishers at Fire Points.

Most process workshops were equipped with an overhead drencher system connected to the high-pressure water main.

Telephones for use in emergencies were housed in cast iron pillars spaced along the clean ways, or within the porches of marked buildings.

Earthen embankments, called traverses or baffles, were built around buildings where dangerous processes were to take place. In the event of an explosion, this would prevent the blast travelling laterally, and force the discharge upwards – thus protecting adjacent structures.

The many storage facilities about the site (e.g. in the filled stores section) were made of reinforced concrete, and 'semi-buried', both to protect them from enemy action, and to limit the effects of any explosion.

'It's a Ticklish Sort of Job'

There were very many procedures theoretically stringently enforced to enhance safety. All employees were issued with a booklet which detailed the general Rules and Regulations that applied to all of the Royal Ordnance Factories. Those who worked in the Danger Areas in Bridgend were given a separate and specific 40-page booklet of Rules which they had to carry with them while they were at work. The Rules start with the sensible advice that 'experience has shown that danger may be found in the simplest things, and it is only by the most thorough control of everything that is done in the Danger Area that safety may be preserved.' The management acknowledged that the Rules were

NOTICE

This book is valuable. It must be preserved in good condition. It is not transferable, and must be shown on demand to any Constable or authorised Official of a Danger Area. When signed in ink in the space below by the employee, endorsed and dated with the special stamp of the Royal Ordnance Factory Bridgend, it constitutes a VALID PASS for the person named, enabling him to enter the Danger Area in the performance of his official duties. It will remain current for a period of three calendar months following the date of the last endorsement. It must be given up on demand to an authorised Official of the Royal Ordnance Factory Bridgend, and in all cases when the person ceases to be employed in the Danger Area of the Royal Ordnance Factory Bridgend.

Name of Employee..........

Ident. No. of Employee..........

Employee's Signature..........

Date of Issue..........

Dates of Examination :

RULES

OF THE

DANGER AREA

ROYAL ORDNANCE FACTORY
BRIDGEND

CARDIFF
Printed under the Authority of His Majesty's Stationery Office
by William Lewis (Printers) Ltd., Penarth Road, Cardiff.

4TH EDITION
1941

restrictive (they 'border on severity'), but insisted that this 'was essential for the safety of all.'

There was a list of things that could not be taken in to the Danger Areas. The prohibited items were fairly obvious:

Matches, spent or unspent
Tobacco including snuff
Food, sweetmeats, beverages
Private Bag or Parcel
Stick or Umbrella
Chemicals or Explosives
Lighters or any means of producing light
Pipe, Cigarette or any smoking materials
Medicine
Bicycle Equipment
Knife, Scissors or File
Inflammable oil or solvent

Women workers in Danger Area clothing

The worker was encouraged to

> turn out all his pockets and shake out his handkerchief before arriving at the entrance to ensure that he is free from prohibited articles

a process which could not have improved the general health of the workforce!

Every operative working in the explosive filling groups had to pass each day from the Dirty Side to the Clean Side. Before the shift change-over people arrived at a changing room called the Shift House[2], or the shifting room. There the normal outer clothes and outdoor shoes would be taken off, and personal effects removed 'including belts, waist straps and braces (except those worn for health)'. These would all be placed on numbered pegs or in lockers. This would leave the workers with 'undervests, shirts, collars[3], neckties, drawers and socks.' Employees were not allowed to use 'articles of steel or other metal on their private undercloth-ing', and metal buttons or fastenings had to be covered in fabric. Workmen were 'strongly advised not to wear clothing made of inflammable materials, e.g. artificial silk, flannelette.'

These instructions seem to be rather masculine: this is because when the Regulations were originally drawn up it was intended that the workforce in ROF 53 would be male. In an earlier list of definitions it is helpfully laid down that the 'rules worded gener-ally as applying to males apply also to females, except where manifestly inappropriate.' Female workers did provide specific challenges. Margaret Plummer of Swansea relates that

> when we first started there we had Celanese underwear. When you take that off you'd see little sparks – the static electricity in your body would cause sparks. Well they found that was causing a bit of problems, so most of the girls wore satin or silk.

Sally Evans of Bridgend comments, 'we weren't allowed to wear anything other than cotton under our overalls.'

Properly denuded of their everyday clothing, the workers would proceed towards the Clean Side of the Shift House. They would be checked by a shifting room attendant, before being allowed to step over a low barrier or 'toeboard' into the Clean Side. Random searches took place to make sure that no forbidden materials were taken into the Clean Side.

On the Clean Side clean long sleeved white overalls were put on. Myra Jenkins didn't like these at all:

> they were like prison clothes, they were horrible, rough old flannel things.

At first these were secured with ribbon tapes; later rubber buttons were introduced. There were no pockets in these overalls, but workers were allowed to take money for food and drink to the

Clean Side in a special bag, which was hung around the neck. Hair was covered with small woollen pillbox-style hats for the men, and turbans or mobcaps for the women – no hairpins or hair clips were allowed. Long hair had to be tied back with ribbon. Special anti-static nailess footwear (with no metal tags on the laces) was put on to reduce the risk of friction sparks.

Margaret Plummer detailed the process:

> We'd come over the bridge from the station and go through the security block, where the officers would make sure that you didn't take cigarettes and matches into the Factory…You went into your own section and block, in through the door into a cloakroom with a barrier halfway across, You would take off your shoes and clothes, and put them in a special locker…go over the barrier barefoot, and put on their overall which was thick, woolly…like a Welsh wool blanket. It had long sleeves and buttons down the front…rubber buttons, not bone or anything, because bone would cause friction. You weren't allowed clips in your hair, no hairpins, no rings…if your hair was very long you pulled it right back with a piece of ribbon not elastic. Your hair was covered with an old dust cap, and you wore special shoes… you were then on the clean side.

The paths leading to the various Danger Buildings were specially constructed of the smoothest asphalt, top-dressed with a shellac-like resin (a low conductivity insulator), which made it smoother still. In fact in the opinion of one worker, Mair Davies, the clear-ways were so smooth that they were dangerous: they

> were very slippery; we would be walking like on an ice rink, skidding all over the place. It was extremely dangerous for those carrying the dets. We had to scratch the bottom of our shoes to save us from falling.

In the initiator group, some of the compositions were so sensitive that there were special rules for their movement. They could not be transported on the dillies[4] used elsewhere, but had to be carried everywhere by hand. The carriers were not allowed to walk side by side, nor were other staff allowed to walk with them. Roy Davies of Bridgend remembered

> We used to carry the detonators on the clearways, and in the day you carried a little red box with a flag, and in the night, a little red lamp, and the boys used to shout, 'Watch out, the brothel boy's coming!'

When the delivery arrived at the workshop, the boxes could not be taken directly in through the doors, but had to be placed in special hatches in the walls. Once in the building caps were normally stored on wheeled trolleys. When filled the caps had to be passed through an internal serving hatch to a separate room with small armoured cubicles for packing, and from there through another hatch out to the carriers on the clearways; all to prevent any accidental bumping into a swinging door, or another worker. Failure to use the hatches would result in disciplinary action.

In some workshops where particularly sensitive materials were dealt with employees were protected by metal boxes with panels of safety glass. Operatives were supposed to work on the detonators with tongs. Rowena Harris recalled what the arrangement looked like to her:

> They were in small sections, like telephone kiosks. There was a barrier above, and on either side, and you worked with your powder in there individually, so that if there was a blow up other people would perhaps be protected.

Stringent cleanliness was enforced in the workshops to prevent the tiniest spark coming into contact with any particle of explosive material. The asphalt floors of the workshops were covered with speckless rubber matting, frequently swept or vacuumed, and the wooden workbenches were covered with thick brown linoleum. There was an official regulation that Danger Building clothing had to be washed at least once every six months. This last instruction does seem to be entirely inadequate, and there was a laundry on site to ensure working clothes were uncontaminated. Only special non-ferrous tools could be used in the Danger Areas.

Once the worker arrived in the Danger Building, every action was controlled in detail. Thus to prevent items falling on to components and into powders, pencils were not to be placed behind the ear and pince-nez were not to be worn; any 'skylarking' was expressly forbidden. Instead staff were enjoined to 'perform the work entrusted to them in as gentle and careful a manner as possible': there was to be no 'undue haste.' Perhaps unnecessarily, employees were instructed that explosives should 'never be thrown down, or allowed to fall or drop on a bench or floor.' In each building the Overlooker had a heavy responsibility for the maintenance of safety. In the Rules of the Danger Areas it is written that

> the lives of the men he supervises are largely in his keeping and depend on his firm determination to allow no infringement of regulations.

Overlookers were

> in the best position at once to notice irregularities of conduct, which though not expressly forbidden, may yet be objectionable.

And in the event of an accident the Overlookers were to

> prevent workmen from rushing aimlessly about, needlessly leaving the cleanways, or crowding to the scene of an occurrence.

All employees had to take part in regular Fire Drills organized by the Factory Fire Brigade. According to Redwood, each shop had

> their own little squad, using stirrup pumps, and having little practices, especially if production was up to quota, and they had a little bit of time to do it.

The Fire Brigade had to check that the equipment was in good condition.

> One duty on the shift was to go out on fire examination of the shops to see if protective implements were in order.

But not everyone treated the facilities with respect:

> People used to throw rubbish in the sand buckets, and instead of going to the toilets some men would do it in the buckets.

Breaking the Rules

Regulations are effective only if they are adhered to strictly. Fire buckets were not the only safety factors treated with disrespect. Almost every week local newspapers printed lists of those fined for introducing contraband into danger areas. Margaret Plummer claimed that 'there were those who did take cigarettes in, with one tucked in their hair this side, and a match on the other side, and then they would smoke them in the toilets.' Another trick was to hold items between toes. Betty Reynolds recalls how the clean side rules were circumvented on a regular basis. Women workers would slip their metal hairgrips to INOs (Inspectors of Naval Ordnance), who would put them in a little pocket in their uniform, and then return them when the operative had reached their workplace.

Richard Rees, a worker at the Arsenal described his experiences there in a series of articles in the Sunday *Empire News* in 1957. This is his account of the consequences of contraband:

> The urgent whisper 'Women searchers on the line' would send the lasses everywhere scurrying to find the nearest man. 'Searchers, Dick, Mind these for me…hurry please' it was no use arguing. Into my little canvas money bag hung round my neck went rings, lipstick, face powder, hair clips – all the female bric-a-brac imaginable. Ivor, my mate had the misfortune to spill over his clothes a box of face powder hurriedly passed to him. His wife didn't speak to him for a fortnight.

Greater risks were taken in the actual processes in order to increase production. Margaret Plummer maintained that

> if there was an accident I would say it was more the operator's fault that the actual Factory's fault because they were very keen on safety measures. But some of the girls would want to do things quicker, so they neglected the safety measures… Some of the girls were anxious to get as much stuff out as possible, and they took one or two little risks.

Joan Hunt from Pontypridd described how the regulations were ignored in her workshop. She worked sitting on a stool at a bench, and received 40mm fuzes from the girl on her left; she then levelled and pressed the powder into the component. Everyone was aware that there was a competitive atmosphere between workshops.

> The supervisor would come in, and she would say 'the next shop has done 2000 yesterday, and we've only done 1500, we must do more.'

Joan was sensibly careful:

> I always worked to the rules for safety. I thought, 'They won't blow my hands off. What will I do for the rest of my life? If I've got my hands I can work.'

But keeping to the rules meant that she was working at a slower pace than the rest of the line. In any case the girl to Joan's left had an easier job; scooping powder into each component. Joan persisted in keeping to the regulation way of handling the fuzes.

> You were supposed to pick them up by holding them between thumb and first finger, so any explosion would go up. Other girls just picked them up with their whole hand, which was quicker, but I wouldn't.

Fuzes would pile up beside Joan – far more than the regulation five. This got her into trouble:

> The supervisor would come to my position, she elbowed me in the side, she nearly pushed me off my stool, and she would grab handfuls.

There were regular checks by safety inspectors, but the supervisors conspired with the staff to hide breaches of regulations. As Joan said, 'When the supervisor heard that the Danger Man was coming round, she made us hide the extras under our overalls.' Eventually the supervisor got Joan transferred to Detonators, but she refused to go there.

> Dets were much worse than fuzes. I knew a girl from Pontypridd who was badly injured there. So then they sent me down the doctors.

Joan was eventually sent to work in the Cordite Group.

Roy Davies of Bridgend was one of those responsible for delivering supplies to the workshops. There was an official limit to how much explosives could be held in a workshop at any one time, but Roy used to stack up far more boxes of detonators than were allowed:

> I used to pile them up in the shop and then go off to have a kip among all these dets in the magazine.... I used to sleep in my clothes for a couple of hours. It was okay as long as the Danger Buildings Visitor didn't catch you. Otherwise I'd be up in court –

> some were, and they were sacked. But people would tip me off – 'The DBV's about, Roy.' If she was, I'd be running about taking the detonators out again. And sometimes as she was coming into the shop through one door, I'd be going out of the shop through the other door with the detonators, taking them back.

A fireman at the Arsenal confirms the breaking of regulations in another context:

> Dets were carried in a tray of oil to keep them stable, and they were to be handled with tweezers. But a lot of these girls used their long fingernails instead.

He also confirms the competitive element:

> It was all a matter of production; one shop would beat the other shop for production this week. And this was an honour, and it was seen as a good thing to do because it was war. But there are no shortcuts when it comes to explosives. If you took the risk you were risking your life and other people's lives.

The details of a different situation in which the rules were apparently ignored were recorded in the *Gazette*. A 43 year old worker from Penygraig in the Rhondda was prosecuted 'for failing to comply with the general safety regulations when operating a machine' at the Factory. According to the prosecutor, 'Every precaution had been taken [by the management] to minimise the danger from explosives.' He went on to denounce the operative for failing to follow the proper procedures.

> It was the old story of familiarity breeding contempt. The defendant did not do what he should have done, and there was an explosion, but fortunately no-one was injured.

The accident is not described in detail, but was said to have been caused in some way by a screw on the machine. The worker's defence suggests that cutting corners was happening in a similar way to that in Joan Hunt's workshop. He claimed that 'by doing what he did, he was able to do more work,' Unsurprisingly, the management denied that this was the case, and the operative was fined £10 with £5 5s costs.

Another processor at Bridgend, quoted in Mari Williams' *A Forgotten Army*, was known as a fast worker, but she could only achieve this by ignoring the regulations:

> I used to do it not the safety way. I used to have the detonators in my lap!

Some breaking of regulations had nothing to do with increasing production. Roy Davies describes one incident:

> We used to play about: boys are boys. I got back to the shifting house one day, and we used to throw our boots at each other, and I threw mine, and it exploded. I had a det in my boot! We had wire cages where you kept your shoes, and all them blew apart. I'd been walking about all night with a det in my boot! One of the boys had put it there: I could have lost my foot. We never thought a thing about it at the time but I've thought about it since. Of course there was an Inquiry on then. I had to go in front of the boss.

The Official Attitude

Despite the emphasis on safety, the attitude of management to pressure on the workforce seems to have been ambivalent at best. One fast worker, Marjorie Heaver from Abercynffig describes the job as it should have been done.

> The live detonators were in a box. I used to sit at a covered box with a glass panel, which was to protect me. How I should really do it was, take one det out of the det box, close the box, put the det into the casing. Then, turning a big wheel, fixing the little det into the casing, which then would go into the trench mortar. One at a time, it used to be and then you had to take one out from the box at the right-hand side of you. Then you open the box and put one in, and that was the routine. It could be boring, but I was doing it so fast that I didn't have time to be bored. My particular job was putting the detonator into the detonator case. And I used to go on to the line, but they were always crying out for detonators, so it was always 'Marge, get on the detonators', because I used to do it the quickest. We did work at quite a speed and safety rules were broken, but I think that really on the sly they knew that we were doing it. They didn't care as long as they were getting the output.

Whether or not the management was aware that Marjorie was

breaking the safety rules, they were so impressed with her achievements that she was rewarded for her speed. She was named the British War Worker for 1941 for manufacturing detonators at a rate of 500 an hour. She was presented with a certificate and a cheque for £25 from the Factory manager. Then she was collected from the Arsenal gate by a chauffeur-driven limousine and driven to the studio of Ernest Carver in Bridgend for an official photograph.

Inspection

There was a thorough system of inspection of finished parts. There were two types of inspectors: CIA[5] (Central Inspectors of Armaments), who checked produce destined for the Army and RAF, and INO (Inspectors of Naval Ordnance). When Myra Jenkins joined the Arsenal she was chosen to be in CIA, but she does not recall that the selection process or training were very rigorous:

> I was in CIA from the start; they must have been looking for inspectors. We didn't have to qualify in any way. I don't remember having any training. It was just as if they said 'this group will be CIA and that group will be INO, and the rest will be ROF.'

Sally Loveday, also a CIA examiner confirmed this impression, though she does recollect a little more preparation:

> We didn't have much training. They gave us a week or two of telling us what to do; they didn't give you longer than that.

Myra remembers the great pressure that was put on inspectors to pass faulty material:

> I was inspecting the pellets. We had tools to measure: the pellets had to be a certain depth – exactly right, just dead on because it was forming part of the fuze. The pellets were very small, about a centimetre in diameter. The girls were putting the powder in, and then putting them under a press to make the pellets. We in CIA would take a tray, and we would take our time, because we had to make sure they were dead right. Otherwise, we had to reject them, and we did our share of rejecting them, as I remember. And that would bring the number of boxes down that were

> finished in that workshop.
>
> You had to be very strict. They used to say to us 'Oh that'll do,' and I had to say no. Then the overlooker would come down and he would try to get you to change your mind. And then he would go and fetch his boss. I was only 21, and it was a big responsibility. You had to be quite determined. I must admit I didn't like it. You had to go such a speed. It was killing and the trays would be mounting up and mounting up and I'd think 'Oh, I never can get through this'. And you would try and keep up with them and they would bomb them out.

Sometimes the workers in a shop were so keen to beat the output of rival workshops that they would try to circumvent the regulations, and push through components that had been failed by inspectors. This was the experience of Sally Evans, another CIA inspector. Her account is so graphic, it is worth reproducing in full.

> I used to quarrel a lot because I refused to let stuff go through. The boss in time fuze, it was Mr Vincent; I used to fight like anything with him when I was in time fuzes because he was ROF and I was CIA. Well, we never agreed. … They had to put felts around the rings, and if they were loose at any part they were rejects, and if you failed too many the girl used to get really narked. I remember this particular time…I rejected them, and I had discovered that when we was out to break they were passing them, so I got wise to that; I marked the ones I'd failed where they couldn't see the mark. So this night when I got back from break these trays had gone. I went all down the corridor, and I found them all – there must have been about 15 trays of them, and there was about 25 on each tray. I went straight to the bosses then, and I told them exactly what had happened.

The reaction of the operatives to this is astonishing:

> Oh, the workers played hell with me; I had them all fired up. They played heck, and I thought they were going to mob me. One woman was going to hit me. They told me that I was holding up the war. My fiancé had been killed, I had 3 brothers fighting, so what did they think, it was ridiculous to suggest that I was holding up the war. I had an awful time after that with the girls in that shop! I didn't care though, I still wouldn't pass them.

Richard Rees confirms this attitude.

> Others got angry when batches of dets on which they had been working got rejected. No amount of arguing by the inspector would convince them that the detonators were faulty and therefore dangerous. Repeatedly I heard these awkward types telling an inspector of the loud reports coming from the Burning Ground where the rejects were being destroyed. 'They're our dets going off all right; hear 'em? And you rejected them,' was the scornful cry.

Health Problems

Explosions were the most evident danger while working in an armaments factory. But there were other hazards faced by those working with the many varied chemicals used in the manufacture of weapons. Contact with TNT, Tetryl, Fulminate of Mercury or any other of hundreds of compounds could cause health problems. Sally Evans was a CIA inspector in the time fuze section, where black powder was used, but she worked there just for a year, because she 'was allergic to the stuff that they were using there,' and she suffered from asthma attacks. Eventually she ended up as a waitress in one of the dining rooms. Margaret Plummer claimed that some of the girls had an allergic reaction which caused their faces to 'swell right up,' and 'their eyes would go yellow inside.'

One worker, from Penrhiwceiber in the Cynon Valley, had obviously had enough of working with explosive materials. When she was prosecuted for absenteeism in 1942, she declared to the court

> Do they really expect me to work when I am not fit to go? I have been working there for two years in powder, and it is nearly killing me.

The magistrates were unmoved by her appeal, and fined her £15, plus three guineas costs.

Yellow Skin

To an outsider the most obvious manifestation of health problems was the yellow appearance of workers handling powders, and especially that pressed into pellets. Betty Nettle from Stormy

Down hated working in the Pellets section.

> It was such a hell house to work in. My hands turned yellow straight away. The powder was finer than talcum, and got everywhere. It came out of your skin at night, and you could see the shape of your body on the bed sheet.

Rowena Harris of Pantygog described what happened:

> The people who worked with powder, their skin was yellow, their hair was yellow, their eyebrows were yellow, even their nails were yellow. When I worked in Pyro canteen only handling the money my hands were stained yellow.

Not surprisingly, working in pellets was unpopular. As Mair Davies said, 'the Pellets section wasn't dangerous, but nobody wanted to go there because the powder turned the skin and hair yellow.' In fact some workers were so desperate to get out of Pellets that they were not above rubbing their own skin with abrasive material or irritants to create a rash!

Some workers turned different shades, depending on their original colouring and on the chemicals they came into contact with. Jim Westrop worked at Bridgend station during the war. In 1975 he recalled,

> often girls would come out after a day's work, their skin coloured bright orange. I had never seen anything like it. The entire face, hands, hair and even the eyes and teeth were discoloured a kind of nicotine shade, but much brighter.

According to Margaret Plummer from Swansea 'if you were blonde you went green, if you were light brown you went orange, if you were deeper brown you went yellow.' Betty remembers that 'I worked in Pellets, and I was yellow, but my sister in Pyro was pink!' Her mother couldn't get the sheets the girls slept in white.

> My mother always hung our sheets behind the house, she wouldn't hang any of those sheets for the neighbours to see, or anybody walking by on the road; it was just the perspiration at night that brought it out of your body.

Nothing seemed to get rid of the colour. Betty 'tried everything to get rid of it – including rubbing ourselves with bread dipped in milk, but nothing worked.' Margaret remembered 'we'd put a solution of bleach in our washing water, it was a surprise how it paled down.' Girls were prepared to believe anything. In a BBC programme, one recalled,

> We were all like idiots there; somebody would come in and say, 'Guess what, cold tea, marvellous. Gets a load of it off.' So you'd go home, then you'd get some cold tea, and you're wiping it all over your face. And you ask your mam, 'Am I any better, Mam?' You knew very well you weren't, but it was a psychological thing, so it did a bit of good.

There was perhaps only one advantage to all this: as Betty Nettle said, 'mind, if you went to a dance, you looked suntanned!' When Roy Davies went into the army after working in the Arsenal, he

> was as yellow as a guinea pig because of the powder. And when the doctor saw me, he said, 'you shouldn't be going into the British Army, you should be going into the Chinese army!' Never did me any harm as far as I know.

In the last year of the war, Emily Cumming (originally from Llanhari) worked in the textile section of the Factory. Later, she published a book entitled *Llanharry with a Y* which includes a poem that describes both the physical appearance of those in Pellets, and their attitude to the work: -

On Munitions

Yellow hands, Yellow hair,
Yellow faces everywhere...
Blissfully dozing on train or bus,
Travelling to 'Danger' without any fuss.

Sitting jaundiced in J.1[6]
Sipping tea with a tasteless bun,
Night shift pouring into day,
Tired and glad to be away.

Past the searches:
What no smokes?
Only 'Pasha'[7]
Spare the jokes!

Yellow hands, Yellow hair,
Yellow faces everywhere...
It made the daffodil look grey,
When the Arsenal got underway

Dermatitis

But workers were affected by far more than appearance. Peggy Rowlands from Pontycymer started in the Arsenal Laundry at the age of 16. When she became 18 she was moved to Pellets.

> I had chest problems, I was wheezy. And skin problems, irritations that were itchy. My hands were terrible – all white little blisters.

In fact the incidence of Dermatitis was far higher in filling ROFs than any other industrial disease. Contact with any compound could cause skin complaints. In the six months between June and November 1942, the medical staff at Bridgend reported 914 cases of Dermatitis – and presumably these were the more serious cases[8]. The problem for the administration was that the only way to cure the condition seemed to be to remove the worker from contact with the offending material and to apply camomile lotion. Those less seriously affected could be put to other work, though Peggy says that she was sent home till the problem had cleared. The difficulty was that other workers had to be transferred in to fill the vacancy and keep up production, so that there was a constant and complicated flow of staff from one section to another – a process which adversely affected efficiency, and hence production.

The management made strenuous efforts to prevent the loss of production threatened by Dermatitis. Much had been learnt from the First World War, and the new factories, like Bridgend, had every modern facility. Barrier creams were provided, as well as special clothing. Women had make-up rooms in which they could put on protective face powder and the barrier creams in front of mirrors. On completing their work, the staff could clean up at rather magnificent large circular sinks with multi spray systems which allowed staff to stand around them to wash. To encourage them to be thorough paid time was allowed at the start and end of each shift to apply and remove the ointments. Teresa Barnet remembers washing 'at a special round sink with taps, using pink soft soap.' David Lazell used the sinks after the war. He commented that

> the washrooms and toilets were almost palatial. Liquid soap dispensers were abundant, and always well topped up, and the user of these facilities washed his or her hands via a circular sink a few feet in diameter, with sprinklers that had a rare precision.

Propaganda was used to encourage the workers to follow the rules. An article entitled Keep Young and Beautiful[9] appeared in the Bridgend Factory magazine of November 1942. The article began by referring to the skin problems experienced by workers at Woolwich in the previous war which had led to them being nicknamed 'Canaries', and suggested that 'this discoloration was a high price for any woman to pay.' Since then there had been 'intensive research' and so, enthused the writer,

> well fitted ablution rooms were built and washing accommodation was provided together with a plentiful supply of clean towels.

But this was not all: providentially, 'research provided a suitable cream that we now know as Rosalex, and afterwards special solutions were introduced.' So now the ladies at Bridgend were encouraged to 'make all use of the facilities that are freely provided by the Factory Management.' The presumably grateful employees were then given 'some Factory Beauty Hints:

> Use the special soaps that are provided for contact workers.
>
> Apply Rosalex to the hands and face before going to the shops and again when returning from meal break. It is really important that you should follow this procedure regularly.
>
> Keep hands and faces clean. There is an abundant supply of clean towels available.

Next the anonymous writer appealed to the workers' sense of a bargain. 'It may interest you to know,' trilled the author,

> that Rosalex is an expensive skin preparation, and had the chemist who formulated this cream sold his secret to a commercial firm, it would have been an expensive cosmetic to buy.

Finally, this was followed up with an appeal to the vanity of the workers:

> Welsh women have always been known for their beautiful skins...are we going to end the war less lovely than when we started at the Factory? Now girls, it is up to you.

During the war there was some research to try to find alternative chemicals that did not have the same damaging effect on skin, plus the development of machinery which would mean that workers would not have to come into contact with the filling compounds. There were also regular inspections by medical staff, and workers could be moved from contact with chemicals before the problem became excessive.

Poisoning

Much less common than Dermatitis, but far more dangerous was poisoning caused by exposure to TNT, Composition Explosive (CE), or the wide variety of other chemical compounds used in the Arsenal. This could cause a variety of conditions from nausea and coughs to toxic anaemia [too few blood cells], gastritis [inflammation of the stomach], toxic jaundice [damage to the liver] and Aniline poisoning [damaging the stomach and heart]. There was a death rate of some 20% among those affected.

Already in March 1941 one of the trades unions active at ROF 53 was expressing concern. A minute of an area meeting of the National Union of General and Municipal Workers[10], in a reference to ROF 53, recorded that 'A number of our members ...have become incapacitated through inhaling TNT fumes.' Between June and November 1942, 43 cases of TNT poisoning were reported at Bridgend, along with 60 cases of white spirit poisoning[11]. We do not know how many people died as a result of such illnesses at Bridgend, though in MacNalty's *The Civilian Health and Medical Services* it is claimed that there were only 21 fatal cases in British ROFs as a whole during the entire war. There was constant effort to reduce the risk as the war progressed. The TNT in the atmosphere was regularly monitored. New methods of manufacture were developed, as well as improved ventilation systems. There were regular medical checks for workers at risk. A simple but effective change was to replace the cleaning brooms (which had simply spread the TNT particles into the atmosphere) with vacuum cleaners. The figures for all the ROFs does seem to show a reduction in cases as the war went on – though of course this can be partly explained by the huge reduction in the number of workers in filling factories in the last years of the conflict.

We know the details of only one person who worked at the Bridgend ROF, and who eventually died of TNT poisoning. This was Isaac Benjamin Rees, of Caerau, Maesteg[12]. He was not saved by any improvements to procedures. He worked with TNT powder on the Brackla site from 1941 to 1945. In 1943 he was diagnosed as having contracted TNT poisoning, and he was hospitalised for 4 months in Whitchurch Hospital and Cardiff Royal Infirmary. He recovered and actually went back to work at Brackla, though he continued to receive treatment: he was awarded compensation by the War Department. In 1949 he became seriously ill, and he died in November, aged 61. The coroner's verdict was that 'death was due to carcinoma of the

Surgery Staff July 1942

lung, accelerated by TNT poisoning contracted whilst employed at the munitions factory.'

Etta Lewis, a nurse at Whitchurch Hospital Cardiff during the war, described the illness of another Bridgend employee, this time a woman. Apparently the doctors had a special interest in her case because 'she had worked in the explosives factory at Bridgend, where in one part they used phosphorous.' According to Etta the woman 'was extremely yellow in colour, and her internal organs were deteriorating. She developed a very bad suppurating abscess in her side.' Unfortunately we have no information of the fate of this Bridgend worker.

'Normal' Accidents and Sickness

The tens of thousands of people working in a huge Factory like Bridgend would, of course, be susceptible to the normal range of injuries associated with industrial processes: injuries caused for example by incidents involving machinery, tools, equipment, vehicles and falls. We have one statistic that gives some indication of the frequency at Bridgend of non-explosive accidents causing loss of work. This is a figure of 315 incidents for the six months June to November 1942; an average of about 50 recorded accidents per month[13].

And naturally people would fall ill of normal sickness, such as 'flu, infections, gastric and dental problems. Thus at Bridgend in December 1944, 4.4% of male production, and 5.7% of female production was lost through illness.

It was obviously in the interests of the management at Bridgend to try to reduce the impact on production of accidents and illness. One way to do this was to provide proper health facilities on site for all Factory employees. To start with medical provision was insufficient; problems included unquantified personnel needs, inadequate salaries, undefined duties, the scarcity in wartime of properly trained staff, cramped facilities and the absence of satellite surgeries in the different sections. Initially the medical staff consisted of ex-servicemen, first aiders and St. John's Ambulance volunteers[14]. Soon better-qualified staff were brought in – though at first the authorities considered that just 6 SRNs were sufficient to care for the huge numbers working at Bridgend. Finally it was realised that Doctors had to be appointed to the Factory – though even then, according to MacNalty, when qualified Medical Officers were employed 'the need for them was so urgent that often they could not complete the specialist initial training on industrial health, and it was eventually dropped.'

Gradually things were improved. Proper surgeries were equipped, and hospital trained SRNs brought in. By September 1944 Bridgend had 6 full-time Medical Officers with a staff of around 60 nurses, dispensers and orderlies. The senior Medical Officer leading this team was Dr. Baird Milne. Facilities had improved: injured patients did not have to be transported to the Bridgend Hospital in Quarella Road since limbs could be X-rayed, and plastered in the Factory surgeries instead. By March 1944 there were 12 ambulances[15] based at the Factory – and 326 stretchers.

Over time other services were provided. The general level of health in southern Wales at that time was very poor – especially as most health care had to be paid for at the point of delivery. A survey of three large filling factories (which may have included Bridgend) found that in one establishment 87% of workers needed urgent dental treatment. Facilities on site would prevent both consequent sickness and absence, and time lost to attend dentists in the community. Some dental treatment was provided (at a fixed charge of 2s. 6d. per visit) though it proved difficult to recruit dentists for the work. Many workers had to stand at their benches for many hours, so a chiropody service was provided in the last two years of the war. Perhaps even more significant was the provision from 1941 of opticians especially to test and prescribe for those working with small components, such as detonators, which required great accuracy to minimise errors. In MacNalty's judgement 'this was undoubtedly one of the most valuable aids to production afforded by the Medical Services.'

The Factory health staff also dealt with other matters. In an article in the *ROF 53 News* of September 1943, headed 'Factory's Wonderful Response', the medical staff thanked

> all those who so readily came forward to offer blood to help our gallant Boys and Girls of the fighting services.

In the last months of the war, to improve safe working, automatic detonator filling machines were experimented with. Here a worker withdraws a detonator tray for inspection

Another major part of their work was monitoring and research into the particular health problems of a filling factory. An August edition of the Arsenal paper welcomed two scientists from the Ministry of Supply Medical Research Council, Warner and Chrenko, who were there to 'specially investigate and study the sections where C E is handled by the workers.' And of course it was the medical staff that carried out the huge task of examining all new applicants for work at the Factory.

Thus overall the medical care eventually supplied at the Arsenal was a vital element in the efficiency of the workforce and so in the productivity of the Factory. By providing services on site, problems were dealt with quickly, time was saved and absenteeism reduced. The medical staff contributed to the improvement of working conditions, and the prevention of work-related sickness. The comprehensive care on offer improved the general level of the health of those who worked at ROF 53. And because there was huge number from a very wide geographical area, no doubt the experience at Bridgend resulted in an expectation across south Wales that was to lead in a very few years to the creation of the National Health Service.

Notes

1 For example, at Chilwell in Nottinghamshire in July 1918, when 134 people were killed and 250 injured.

2 So-called either because this is where workers had to go at the start and end of each shift, or after the cotton shift which workers had to put on in munitions factories in previous times.

3 But celluloid collars were prohibited.

4 Dilly - an electric trolley used to transport components between workshops and stores.

5 Known sardonically as 'Churchill's Idle Army' by the rest of the staff. One worker commented that they 'always went to break 5 minutes early.'

6 J.1 – The building identification number of the canteen.

7 Pashas – Unpopular cigarettes made by Wills – variously described as made of camel dung, and smelling like ten cats locked in a small room for a week.

8 Kew (AVIA 22/1292)

9 'Keep Young and Beautiful': a popular song written by Dubin and Warren and sung by Eddie Cantor in the 1933 film 'Roman Scandals.' A particularly apposite line was 'Don't fail to do your stuff with a little powder and puff.'

10 NLW (3FN20/2/5)

11 Kew (AVIA 22/1292)

12 *Gazette* 2.12.49

13 Kew (AVIA 22/1292)

14 One of the few positive results of the Depression in Wales was that the unemployed had swelled the ranks of the St. John's Ambulance Brigade!

15 7 'standard', and 5 'canvas flap'.

9: Explosions, Death and Injury

How safe was Bridgend?

According to Percy Masters[1] , writing after the War (in *Safety in Royal Filling Factories*), during 1943 Bridgend was by some margin the safest of all the filling factories. Opposite are the figures for frequency of accidents per 100,000 man-hours at various filling factories in that year[2].

But ROF 53 was the largest Factory in Britain, and as we have seen, regulations were broken to speed up the processes: inevitably there were accidents, some fatal. Overall, from 1941 to 1945 Bridgend had the second highest number of deaths in any filling factory – at 17, compared with 18 at Kirkby (Liverpool), and 17 at Aycliffe (Durham). In contrast Chorley had just 7 fatalities, and Glascoed 2 in that period. See Appendix F for the statistics.

Bridgend	1.85
Kirkby	2.46
Swynnerton	2.48
Thorp Arch	2.51
Chorley	2.80
Risley	2.87
Aycliffe	3.80
Hereford	4.18
Glascoed	4.18

Courts of Enquiry

There was a thorough investigation after every explosion, whether or not anyone had been injured. These Courts of Enquiry were conducted by a team of about six or seven senior managers plus a workers' representative (at Bridgend often Councillor Hitchings). The site of the incident would be inspected, and witnesses, including scientific officers, questioned. The Court would try, not always successfully, to identify the exact cause of the problem, and would then make recommendations about any changes to procedures that might be required. Copies of these reports would be sent to every other filling factory so that the staff there could be made aware of the recommendations.

The most serious incidents would result in a Court of Enquiry presided over by HM Chief Inspector of Explosives or his Deputy. Only five incidents at Bridgend were so severe that they required the attendance of these officers:

17/1/41	Stove drying ASA detonators
18/5/41	Assembling and stemming no. 119 fuzes
1/11/41	Filling 3¾oz naval smoke boxes with SR 568
15/11/43	Filling and pressing stars for 1½ in. ctge Signal Green
20/12/43	Pressing 33¼oz CE pellets

But there were more incidents than just these five which resulted in deaths at Bridgend. We have been able to find information about 19 deaths attributable to explosions at ROF 53.

Known Fatalities at the Bridgend Arsenal as a Result of Explosions:

Date of Death	Name	Age	Living in	Reported in
3/10/40	Evan Williams	34	Maesteg	Gazette
5/12/40	Elizabeth Ann Hill	43	Trefforest	
17/1/41	Stella Healey	21	Merthyr Tydfil	
17/1/41	Ethel Mary Martin	22	Cymmer Afan	
18/5/41	Olive Doreen Bugler	19	Pontyclun	Gazette
21/5/41	Georgina McEllacott	36	Pontrhyl, Garw	Gazette
21/5/41	Audrey Lilian Mathews	19	Cefn Cribwr	Gazette
29/6/41	Thomas Charles Bevan	49	St. Bride's Major	Gazette
1/11/41	David George Davies	37	Merthyr Vale	Times
3/11/41	Doreen May Ray	19	Llansamlet	Times
8/1/42	Cecil George Couch	36	Maesteg	Advertiser/Times
8/1/42	Francis Edward Taylor	51	Pontypridd	Times
28/1/42	William John Hayes	41	Pontycymer	Gazette
18/9/42	David John Richards	60	Porth	Times
19/1/43	William Thomas Owen	35	Garth, Maesteg	
15/11/43	Harry Tantrum	42	Trealaw, Rhondda	
20/12/43	William Walter Hughes	54	Blaengwynfi	Times
14/03/44	David James Hopkins	43	Maesteg	
7/1/45	David John Rees	60	Caerau, Maesteg	
6/5/45	Thomas John Millward	52	Treorchy	

As far as we know this inventory is complete. According to Masters there were 17 fatalities at Bridgend between January 1941 and July 1945; 11 men, and 6 women: seventeen of our tally were killed in that period. The list of places which the deceased came from reads like a litany of the communities that served the Arsenal – though Maesteg does seem to have suffered disproportionally.

Deaths from Explosions

We believe that the first death caused by an explosion (or 'blow up') at ROF 53 was in October 1940. Evan Williams of Treharne

Road, Maesteg was a married man with four children. He was a junior over-looker in charge of 25 workers in a detonator workshop: it was his job to see that the people in his department did their jobs properly. No one seems to have seen what happened. A fellow worker in the same shop called as a witness at the inquest could not contribute much. She 'heard a noise, and turning round saw the deceased lying on the ground.' He had severe injuries to his right hand, so presumably he was holding detonators at the time of the incident. The severity of the injuries to his face meant that identification had to be confirmed by his pocket watch.

Evan's daughter Catherine still lives in Maesteg. She was just eight years old when her father was killed. She remembers him as a man who always had to be doing something: at the time of his death he was building a television in his spare time. And he did everything in a hurry: he was known to everyone as 'Ianto Full Pelt'. Catherine used to go down to the station every day to meet her father home from work. She remembers that on the day of Evan's accident a lady on the same shift got off the train, and seeing Catherine said 'O, poor dab'. Of course at the time she did not understand the comment, since the family did not yet know about the incident. Catherine can remember her father's coffin leaving the house draped in the Union flag. She did not go to the funeral, so she went into the cwtch under the stairs and cried herself to sleep on a sack of potatoes.

Catherine remembers the kindness of officials from the Arsenal to her and her siblings. Mrs Shields herself drove up from Bridgend each Christmas with clothes and toys and books for the children. Her brothers' school clothes were paid for, and Catherine had a lovely gymslip to go to Plasnewydd Primary School: 'I was the smartest girl in the class.'

The next fatality occurred just before Christmas 1940. Elizabeth Hill was 43 years old and lived in Long Row, Trefforest. She had a ten-year-old daughter, Audrey, from a previous marriage: Elizabeth's first husband, James Gardiner, had died in 1936. On 9th November 1940, less than a month before she was killed, she had married Henry Hill, who had been a postman before the war, but had joined the Navy. At the Arsenal Elizabeth was an Examiner for CIA. All we know of her death is that she received multiple injuries as the result of an explosion. The Superintendent of the ROF, Reg Edmonds, attended the funeral, as did Mrs Shields, and others of the staff at Bridgend. Elizabeth Hill is buried with her first husband in an unmarked grave at Glyntaff Cemetery above Trefforest.

In January 1941 two young women died in a major incident[3]. Stella Healey was unmarried, and came from George Street in Merthyr Tydfil. Ethel Martin was living in Heol y Glyn, Cymmer, in the Afan Valley. The overlooker spoke highly of their steadiness and reliability. Their job was to carry detonators between buildings. At the time of the explosion they were removing detonator trays from a drying-stove. The enquiry decided that a detonator must have fallen accidentally from the tray. The girls suffered terrible injuries; they were flung the full length of the workshop. The cause of death for both was given as 'fracture of the skull and multiple injuries caused by an explosion.' Betty Edwards of Caerau worked nearby, and she described the aftermath:

> We came in one morning, and the shop where they dried the Dets had gone – the whole building had gone. We heard that two girls from Cymmer had been killed, but they kept it quiet.

The incident was serious enough to be investigated by a court of enquiry conducted by HMCIE.

May 18th 1941 saw one of the worst accidents in terms of fatalities at Bridgend when three women died as a result of an explosion. Two were only 19: Audrey Matthews of Cefn Road, Cefn Cribwr and Olive Bugler of Graigllwyd Farm, Pontyclun. Olive was a farmer's daughter – one of six children. She had been working near London: concerned for her safety during the blitz, her parents had insisted that she return home. According to her brother, David Bugler, in her youth she had been a first class swimmer who spent as much time as possible in the pool, and loved diving in - her nickname amongst her friends was Lady Godiva! The third worker killed in this explosion, Georgina (Gina) McEllacott of Garw Fechan Road, Pontrhyl, in the Garw Valley, was 36, and married to Pierce McEllacott: she had two children. Three other people were seriously injured: Doris Gardner, Margaret Harries of Penygroes, Llanelli, and Thomas Rees – who lost an eye.

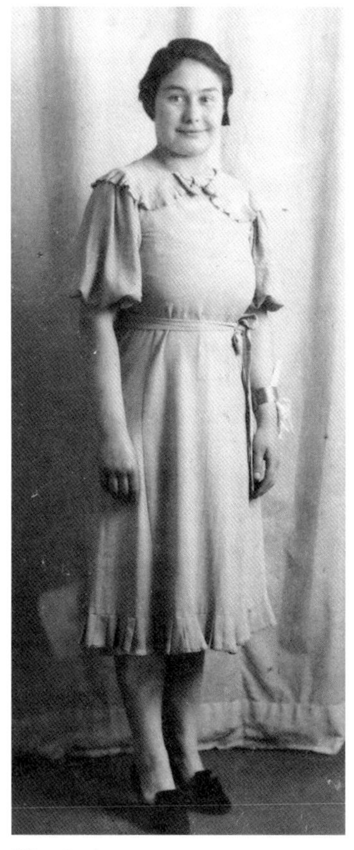

Olive Bugler

The accident happened soon after the beginning of the afternoon shift. There were 16 operatives in the workshop all engaged in making up initiators. The process involved putting detonators into the detonator plug, and then screwing the plug into the detonator holder. Boxes were brought into the workshop. Each box held papier-mache pots containing the detonators. It seems that the girls were getting ready to start work, and were passing the pots of detonators along the benches when the explosion occurred. According to the investigation it was probably while Audrey Matthews was withdrawing pots that something happened to trigger an explosion.

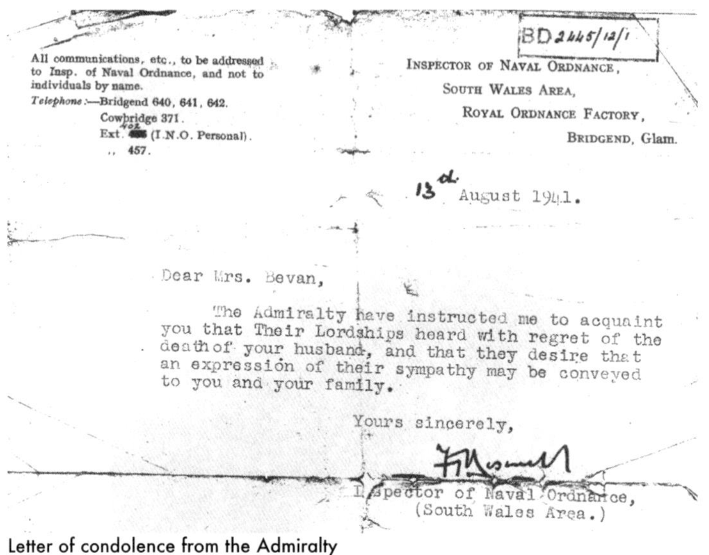

All communications, etc., to be addressed to Insp. of Naval Ordnance, and not to individuals by name.
Telephone:—Bridgend 640, 641, 642.
Cowbridge 371.
Ext. 402 (I.N.O. Personal).
,, 457.

BD 2445/12/1

INSPECTOR OF NAVAL ORDNANCE,
SOUTH WALES AREA,
ROYAL ORDNANCE FACTORY,
BRIDGEND, Glam.

13th August 1941.

Dear Mrs. Bevan,

The Admiralty have instructed me to acquaint you that Their Lordships heard with regret of the death of your husband, and that they desire that an expression of their sympathy may be conveyed to you and your family.

Yours sincerely,

[signature]

Inspector of Naval Ordnance,
(South Wales Area.)

Letter of condolence from the Admiralty

Although the subsequent report was critical of general procedures in the shop, the actual cause could not be identified. As the report pointed out, 5-grain ASA detonators were extremely sensitive – in fact there had been similar accidents at Chorley. A number of recommendations were made about handling procedures, but it is not known if these would have prevented the explosion. One would certainly have limited the effects – there were no screens between the workers in that workshop.

Presumably the recommendations were put into effect, because a witness at the inquest in July said that since the accident the procedure had altered considerably. The Coroner declared that 'it seems to me quite evident that if the rules and regulations had been complied with this accident would never have happened.' This seems a harsh judgement. Georgina and Audrey had both been working in the Arsenal for just a month and were thus inexperienced. Obviously the ROF management had not passed on the lessons learned from the accidents at Chorley. And since there were a number of safety recommendations in the Bridgend report, then it is clear that existing official procedures were unsatisfactory.

Thomas Charles Bevan, 49 years old, was well known locally,

especially in his home village of St. Bride's Major, where he lived in Mead Cottage. Tom had served in the Army throughout the First World War and he was a founder member of the Southerndown branch of the British Legion. He was accustomed to dealing with ammunition: he belonged to several rifle clubs, and had been a competitor at the 'Welsh Bisley'. Before he went to work in the Arsenal, he was the blacksmith in St. Bride's. He was married to Catherine, and they had four daughters – Irene, Esme, Annie and Edna.

According to his youngest daughter, Edna, her father was a Safety Officer on the Burning Grounds where faulty munitions were destroyed. Tom was connecting defective detonators before retiring behind the protective blast wall. Unfortunately something went wrong with procedures, and the explosion was initiated from behind the wall while Tom was still at work. The coroner exonerated the Arsenal management from blame, declaring that

> so far as the authorities were concerned they had provided everything necessary for the safety of their workmen, but however perfect a system might be it had to depend on the human machine, and there had been a flaw in the human machine in the case under consideration.

Tom was buried in the churchyard at St Bride's Major. As far as we know, Tom is the only person to be killed while working at the Arsenal that is remembered on a war memorial: his name can be seen inscribed on the memorial in the village

Redwood, was on duty at the main Administration Building on the next fatal occasion:

> it was a beautiful night, because it was like daylight – the moon was very bright. There was a huge explosion, you could feel the vibration in the ground.

Indeed, so powerful was the blast that it was heard by Superintendent of Police, William May, from his home in Merthyr Mawr Road over half a mile from the Factory. In his diary entry for November 1st he recorded that 'about 12.15 a.m., while listening to the news on radio, heard a loud explosion.' Redwood and his colleagues rushed to the site of the accident. He remembers:

Tom Bevan, with his daughter Edna in the foreground

> when we got there the whole of this building in Pyro was blown to pieces. There were only about two layers of brickwork left standing all the way round.

May listed the terrible results in his Diary: 'About 20 injured, 13 to hospital, one killed.' The dead man was David George Davies, a process worker, of Taff Street, Merthyr Vale, who died from multiple injuries caused by an explosion during the filling of 3¾oz naval smoke boxes with SR 568. It seems likely that two of the injured taken to hospital died later. The 19-year-old Doreen May Ray of Neath Road, Llansamlet received 'extensive burns of trunk and limbs' in the same accident, and she died two days later, on 3rd November. Another worker who was probably fatally wounded in this same explosion was 41-year-old William John Hayes, an assistant foreman, who lived in Oxford Street, Pontycymer. He died in hospital in Bridgend on 28th January 1942, and according to the

Gazette he had been injured three months before – which would put the incident in which he was wounded at around 1st November the previous year. The cause of his death was given as 'toxaemia [blood poisoning] due to multiple injuries due to an explosion at the Royal Ordnance Factory, Bridgend whilst following his employment.' Jack Hayes was survived by his wife Ceinwen, and his two daughters, Glenys and Linda.

Two men were killed in an accident that took place on 8th January 1942. Thirty-six year old Cecil Couch lived at Lansbury Crescent Park, Maesteg, and left a widow, two sons and three daughters. He had been a member of Bridgend Home Guard, and at the Arsenal he was an overlooker. Cecil was buried in Maesteg Cemetery. Francis Taylor, fifty-one, lived at Phillip Street, Graig, Pontypridd: his remains lie in an unmarked grave at Glyntaff Cemetery near Trefforest. Both men died of 'Multiple injuries due to an explosion.' *The Times* report did not name the dead but mentioned that three others were injured in the same incident. Readers of the newspaper would have been reassured to learn that 'Production at the factory will not be affected.'

David John Richards, a sixty-year-old of Gethin Terrace, Llwyncelyn, Porth in the Rhondda died on 18th September 1942 as a result of 'Profound traumatic shock due to multiple injuries received due to an explosion in a workshop (3.E.12) at the Royal Ordnance Factory, Bridgend.' He was examining, and apparently attempting to rectify a faulty naval fuze type 501 by applying pressure on the ignition screw: it seems that this fired the ignition pellet, causing the explosion. In the register of deaths his occupation is listed as an Iron Ore Inspector, though this was clearly a mishearing by the registering clerk of the letters 'INO'; so David Richards was actually an Inspector of Naval Ordnance. There must have been a huge explosion: *The Times* reported that, as well as the death of David Richards, seventeen workers were injured (seven seriously enough to be treated in hospital) 'at an ordnance factory in the west.'

The next fatal accident of which we have information caused the death on 19th January 1943 of 35-year-old William Thomas Owen of Mill Street, Garth, Maesteg. His death was caused by 'Multiple injuries due to an explosion.'

One of the worst blow-ups of the war occurred on 15th November 1943: Ian Hay in his book *The Story of the ROFs* describes the incident. In building 6.F.2 a worker was filling a Pyrotechnic Store with the usual highly sensitive composition – he was filling and pressing stars for 1½ inch cartridge (Signal Green). There was an explosion, which caused two other devices to detonate. The explosions were so severe that the roof came down, and parts of the walls collapsed, blocking two of the entrances. There were 17 people in the workshop at the time: the dense, chemical-filled smoke meant that the disorientated workers could not see how to get out from the burning building.

But help was at hand. About 50 yards from the workshop was Bryn Jenkins, a Maintenance Fitter from Llanelli. He threw down his bag of tools and ran to the workshop. The building was burning furiously, so he was unable to get in. Luckily an Auxiliary Fire Unit had been exercising nearby and was able to lay down a curtain of water to protect him. Hay describes Jenkins' heroism:

> Groping his way through the suffocating smoke, Jenkins contrived to find, lift up, and carry to the door not less than four injured men. He did not leave the building; he merely handed each of the victims over to the stretcher-bearers, and then returned doggedly in search of another.

Harry Tantrum (of Charles Street, Trealaw, Rhondda) was trapped under a large piece of concrete, part of a door arch. Fourteen others were injured or seriously burned. Ex-collier Dai 'Carnera'[4] Davies of Trebanog used his mining experience to try to free him. Eventually, with the help of others, the worker was released; but he was dead. Unsurprisingly, a year later, Bryn Jenkins received the highest honour that can be awarded to a civilian, the George Medal. This is from the official citation.

A hero of the Arsenal; Bryn Jenkins

> By his promptness in running to the rescue at the first sound of an explosion, by his cool courage in groping his way into the building not once but again and again, and by the speed with which he worked, Mr Jenkins undoubtedly saved the lives of at least four men.

Bryn Jenkins was living in digs in Bridgend with the Wood family of Cheltenham Terrace. George Wood remembers Bryn as

> a cheerful, strongish chap who liked his pint. He was modest, too. We didn't know a thing about his medal till we saw him dressed in his blazer to go up to Buckingham Palace to get it!

On December 20th, 1943 54-year-old William Walter Hughes of Tunnel Terrace, Blaengwynfi in the Afan Valley was killed while pressing 33¼ oz CE pellets in a Porter automatic press. He died as a result of 'multiple injuries due to an explosion.' According to the *Advertiser* William had come originally from north Wales, but had lived in Blaengwynfi for many years. He had worked at the Arsenal for 2 years and 8 months. *The Times* reported his death 'at an explosives factory in Wales,' and named four other men, Alfred Thomas, James Lee, Lewis James and William Wakelin, who were injured in the same accident.

David James Hopkins of Castle Street, Maesteg was an INO inspector in Group 1, the Initiator Group. On 14th March 1944 he was working in the annex of building 1.C.13, at the transit cupboard where components were transferred into the workshop from outside. There were a number of pots of composition explosive in the cupboard, and 6 of them exploded. The accident inquiry report was unable to determine exactly what had happened, but suggested that some action by the operative had caused one pot to be knocked in some way: this had set off the sensitive composition. David Hopkins was killed instantly – according to his death certificate he was killed by 'rupture of the lungs due to the blast of an accidental explosion.' One other worker in the shop, Margaret Jones, was injured in this incident.

The last fatality of which we have information is that of sixty-year-old David John Rees (of Gelli Street, Caerau, Maesteg) who died just a few months before the end of the war, on 7th January 1945. According to the death registration, the fatality was caused by

'Heart failure due to haemopneumothorax [Accumulation of air and blood in the pleural cavity] following injuries received due to an explosion.' the *Advertiser* gave no details of his death, except to say that it had occurred 'with tragic suddenness.' According to the paper 'He was a man of quiet disposition, but well known locally.'

Fatalities at Tondu House

Strictly speaking, Tondu House was not part of the Arsenal – but it was very closely connected to it. It was the location of the Pyrotechnic Research Department laboratories relocated from Woolwich after September 1940, and had close links with the Pyrotechnic group in Bridgend – even the midday meals at Tondu House were supplied from one of the Canteens at the Arsenal.[5] As far as we know there were two deaths through explosions at Tondu House:

Date of Death	Name	Age	Living in
6/10/41	Earnest Albert Roberts	45	Bridgend
22/12/43	Trevor John Stratton	42	Tondu

The first victim here was Earnest Albert Roberts, a 45 year old, living in Nolton Street, Bridgend. He was one of those who had transferred from Woolwich to Bridgend in 1940. The accident occurred while Earnest was destroying a large quantity of waste explosives. In his book about the history of Tondu House, Gwilym Rees reports that

> the general feeling at that time was that in all probability, the recognized safety procedures had not been followed. On going up to the burning grounds.... members of staff discovered the badly mutilated body of Roberts lying near a small crater.

The second Tondu death took place two years later. Trevor Stratton was a 42-year-old Laboratory worker living very close to Tondu House, in 'Ty Gronfa', Derllwyn Hill. He died of 'septicaemia and cellulitis [blood poisoning and infection causing acute inflammation of body tissue] as a result of burns received by following his employment at the Tondu House.'

With the exception of Tom Bevan, none of those who died

while working in the Arsenal is remembered on any memorial. Yet they are victims of war just as much as the service people whose sacrifice we rightly remember in stone and metal. It seems to us that a fitting tribute to all who worked in ROF 53 would be a memorial to those who made the ultimate sacrifice.

Injuries

It proved difficult to identify all the individuals who died as a result of accidents: there seems to be no complete count available of the number of those injured. Bridgend may have had a good safety record, but it was a very large undertaking, and very many people must have suffered injury. Because of the nature of much of the work – manipulating by hand at workbenches small but volatile quantities of explosives – injuries tended to include loss of finger joints or whole fingers, hands and eyes. Taken at random, these are the cold facts of injuries taken from two Courts of Enquiries into explosions:

10th June 1942 – Miss G Davies – amputation of parts of two fingers, and the whole of one finger, all from the right hand.

15th June 1942 – Miss M Phillips – injuries to both hands, and amputation of part of thumb and index finger of left hand.

Redwood describes the injuries to one worker that he had to accompany to the onsite clinic: 'Well, the face couldn't be recognised, and it was pitted with powder.' Mair Davies declared that

> the Dets Section was the most dangerous. Some were killed and others had hands or fingers blown off.

Rowena Harris of Pantygog, Pontycymer describes what happened to one of her friends:

> I knew one woman called Jane, who worked in dets, and there was a blow up, and she was in hospital, she had like shrapnel bits of detonators in her arms and back, and they had to take them out; it also affected her eyes.

We get occasional glimpses of the devastating effects of these terrible personal tragedies.

In 1998 the *South Wales Echo* featured the story of Gwen Obern, then 80 years old. In 1940, Gwen was 22, and had been

Gwen Obern, photographed in 1998

married to her husband Ernie for less than one year. She had been working at Aberdare General Hospital, but she decided to join the Arsenal workforce. She was to travel just three times from her home to work at Bridgend. On her third day, according to the *Echo*, Gwen was injured in an accident in which 5 people were killed, and 14 injured when a box of detonators exploded. We have not found a record of such a devastating accident, though we know that Marion Elias, also of Aberdare, lost her sight in the same accident. Certainly Gwen was severely injured: she was blinded, and she lost one hand, while the other was rendered useless. This is the moving account of her terrible experience and gradual realisation of the extent of her injuries, recorded in a BBC radio programme in 1989.

I was taken then, to the surgery attached to the factory and the first thing that I remember after the accident was, of course, speaking to my family, and the next thing I remember was my husband speaking to me. Now, I think it must have been very heartbreaking for him and my family when they came in, because they didn't know the extent of my injuries. There was quite a bit of argument about whether they were going to amputate my left foot. My dad had worked in the mines and he was very well up with first aid, and he wanted to see my foot before he would give consent for the operation. Of course, my family weren't there when I had my hands done. So, my father said he wouldn't give consent for that foot to be amputated. And then my husband wouldn't give consent either. Anyway, I can walk miles and ran miles ever since, so it's a good thing they didn't.

But the thing was, I didn't know that I'd lost my hand or that there was anything wrong with my left hand. It was so badly maimed and burnt; I didn't know that at all. Nor I didn't know about my eyesight, until one day my mother came in, and she said, 'Of course', she said, 'you know Da'cu', (that's what we used to call my granddad), 'that his left hand was very bad, wasn't it. You remember how his left hand was', because my grandfather had his left arm amputated when he was in the colliery, and I knew they were trying to tell me something. But there was no way that I would accept it.

Well, during the war, there was no chocolate or anything, but I must say that people from Trecynon and Aberdare were very good. They used to send me their rations of chocolate and things. And one nurse came in, and she said, 'well, what chocolate, have you got today, Gwen.' I said, 'you're not having any chocolate', and she said, 'why?' And I said, 'well, why didn't you tell me I'd lost my thumb on my right hand,' and she said, 'who told you?' and I said, 'it doesn't matter who told me, but you didn't tell me.' 'O Gwen', she said, 'it's surprising what you can do without a thumb.' So I was counting, and I thought, well, that's one gone. And throughout the night different nurses had to come back and forth for my dressings and so on. So I went down to my little finger, and one nurse said to me. 'You're very quiet tonight, Gwen, aren't you speaking to me?' And I said, 'no, I'm not. Why didn't you tell me that I'd lost my little finger?' 'Who told, you?' she said. So, I found out like that.

> So I thought, there's all my fingers and my thumb gone, but still I wouldn't give in to it. The thing was all this time I had no clothes on, just gauze over my burns. I was a bit of a mess, actually. And the thing I thought to myself was, it is a jolly good job I got married when I did because I wouldn't have a hope now. At least I've got a husband.

In the following years Gwen had to endure 76 operations. In 1943 she started to learn Braille and typing at St Dunstan's wartime training centre in Church Stretton. She had a talent as a singer, and St. Dunstan's arranged for her to have singing lessons once a week with the choirmaster at Hereford Cathedral. Gwen became the 'St. Dunstan's Nightingale,' travelling around Britain, giving concerts at venues like the Brangwyn Hall in Swansea, making gramophone records and appearing on the radio and television – all to raise funds for St Dunstan's. In the article she is

Mary Boundford and family

quoted as saying 'St Dunstan's gave me the will to live again.' Certainly, despite her horrific injuries, Gwen has had the courage to create a rich and fulfilling life.

Mary Jones of Tonypandy was another who was seriously injured but who was determined to be self-sufficient and capable. Her story was told in the *Empire News* in 1957:

> Mary was 18. She didn't mind seeing in the New Year (1944) at her workbench because she had been invited to a party at the house of a friend in Bridgend on New Year's Night. But she didn't make the party. Half way through the shift a tray of detonators blew up, and Mary woke up in hospital. All she had left on her left hand was part of a thumb. When she came home from the rehabilitation centre her family wanted to do everything for her. But she was firm. 'Look,' she said, 'I know you're only trying to help, but I've got to do it myself.' In the winter of 1945 Mary married Sam Boundford, a collier at the Naval colliery at Penygraig: the wedding ring was placed on her right hand. Together they raised a family of five children, as well as spaniels, budgerigars, a canary and a cat!

Mary is quoted as saying

> I do my best to take it all in my stride. I do all the household work myself, and the only thing that beats me is paper hanging – but I'll find a way round that one day.

Winifred Thomas of Cymmer, Porth sustained terrible injuries at the Arsenal. Winifred was an overlooker in the X-varnishing Shop. One day in May 1943, detonators that she was handling exploded. The circumstances were described in an article in the *Empire News* in 1957:

> The tray of detonators blew up in a blinding flash that rocked the building and hurled Winnie backwards. There was a moment of petrified silence. A solitary unshaded electric bulb miraculously untouched by the blast lit up the stark, smoky scene. Winnie lay groaning softly on the floor, blinded, with both hands smashed and bleeding. All around her women were screaming and fainting. Lily Long was the first to react. Quietly, methodically, she put a makeshift pillow under the Winnie's head, bandaged the mangled hands with towels, and comforted her until she was carried off to an ambulance.

Winifred Thomas

Winnie knew she was seriously injured, but she did not lose consciousness until anaesthetic was given to her. Both her hands had to be amputated, and she lost the use of her left eye. Her face and body were riddled with particles of the detonators. She became a patient at the Queen Mary Hospital, Roehampton, which specialised in working with patients who had lost limbs, and in the fitting of prostheses. In 1946 Winifred's story was told in the *Rhondda Leader*. The journalist wrote that he 'noticed that there were metal appliances where her wrists and hands should have been.' He asked Winifred how she managed to feed herself.

> Calmly she proceeded to fix curiously shaped cutlery into sockets in her artificial arms, and then demonstrated how easy it was to accomplish the seemingly impossible.

The article is upbeat: Winifred's right eye 'twinkled with good humour.' Soon she would 'have the latest type of artificial arms and hands. Then she will go to a rehabilitation centre where she will learn to write, and be trained to do handiwork.' She had been awarded the BEM for her work in the Arsenal. In a 1957 interview Winifred is quoted as saying

> 'I'm quite happy. I've always had faith. My life is centred about Carmel Chapel on the corner, and I never miss the Sisterhood.

But the overwhelming impression is of the price that she had paid, and would continue to pay for the production of armaments. The worker who went to Winifred's assistance, Lily Long, was a St John's Ambulance trained member, from Porth in the Rhondda. In 1945 she also was awarded the BEM for her first aid service in the Arsenal during the war.

Margaret Plummer, an inspector, described the psychological effects of the explosion that killed David Richards and injured 17 others.

> This fuze came down, and I said – 'this one's no good, this one's a danger, don't anybody touch this tray.' So I put it on one side. The chap in charge said 'that's O.K., that can be sorted out, that cap can come off.' So I said 'I wouldn't touch it if I were you. I'll go and get my boss now.' So I went through the blast door, and the outer door, when the thing went up. Who touched it I couldn't tell you... the one went off and set the others off. There were those who got away with it, that did live, but they were badly hurt. Three of us were lucky – two other girls were outside the blast door. They had shock. Well, I wasn't too clever myself, I admit it. I cried for days. You cried because you knew who was working there. They were your workmates.

Some explosions could be enormously powerful. Rowena worked in the Textiles Canteen, a good way from the Burning Grounds.

> But one day I was serving behind the counter, and then the next thing I knew I was hit against the wall. There had been an explosion on the burning grounds.

Sid Chilcott of the Arsenal's housing estate at Bryntirion was injured on the Burning Grounds in April 1945. He was destroying faulty detonators and had put a number of them in a wooden bucket of diesel oil. He was stirring the mixture gently when there was a flash, and Sid was thrown to the ground by the force of the explosion. He lost a hand and half a foot. After the war he got a job in the Remploy factory on the Industrial Estate at Bridgend.

Chance played a part in many injuries. Betty Edwards of Caerau was working in Dets with her friend Marion Walsh from

Blaengarw. They wanted a change, so they agreed to swap tasks for a while. Betty describes what happened:

> We'd only swapped a few minutes, and it blew up – it blew off the tops of the fingers on her right hand.

Of course there were very many minor accidents. One worker described what happened to her younger sister.

> She had the powder on her shoe, which was just one of those things, and we were walking along the clean way, and she tripped, and she burst her big toe open, and she had two stitches in it, because the powder that was on her shoe exploded. It wasn't a serious accident, but that's how dangerous it could be.

Roy Davies described the aftermath of another incident:

> Round the corner, there was a mixing shop for gunpowder, and I'll never forget, one day, this bloke was cleaning his machine for the break, cleaning this powder off, using a camel hair brush, and up she went, burnt all his eyebrows off; he came out as black as the ace of spades. Oh funny, it was. He was all right, though.

Apparently the Factory did look after people who were injured there. According to Rowena:

> We used to see a lot of them that had been in an explosion because they used to come to a day centre there, and then they used to come into the canteen and have a cigarette and a cup of tea, and then they'd go back to the day centre.

This centre that Rowena mentions may have been the Factory Rehabilitation Centre which is referred to in *ROF 53 News* for October 1943. In that edition is a list of the sums each section had raised towards the purchase of a piano for the Centre. The most generous department on this occasion was Fuze High Explosive with £11 15s. 7d.

The Press and Accidents

The management would not want press reports about accidents and fatalities at the Factory to discourage recruitment. Yet the start of the war, and the imposition of censorship did not mean information about such events could not appear in the *Gazette*. As in pre-war days, inquests were held on those killed, and journalists were allowed to report names, ages, addresses of the deceased, and the injuries that had caused their deaths. The Arsenal was not named but phrases such as 'a local works', and 'a Bridgend Factory' were easy to decode. The *Gazette* carried details of the funerals of prominent individuals.

Not all inquests were covered. If the deceased had lived outside the *Gazette*'s distribution area they were unlikely to appear. There is no mention of the deaths of Stella Healey from Merthyr, or Doreen Ray from Llansamlet. Earnest Roberts lived in Bridgend, but came originally from Woolwich, so perhaps that is why there is no mention of his inquest. Local people's details do appear, starting with Evan Williams of Maesteg in 1940. The last report of a death at the Factory in the *Gazette* is William Hayes of Pontycymer in 1942. Other local people do die after that date, such as David Rees of Caerau in 1945, but their inquests are not reported; so perhaps by this time the management had persuaded the *Gazette* not to print details of these later incidents.

Surprisingly, perhaps, *The Times* newspaper reported by name two of the deaths which do not appear in the *Gazette* – that of David Richards in 1942, and William Hughes in December 1943. These are statements of regret issued by the Ministry of Supply, and published the day after the accident. It would be difficult to identify the Bridgend Factory from the notices in *The Times* – one refers to a factory in the West of England (sic), and the other to a factory in Wales – not many people would have been able to specify the exact location from that. Even more surprisingly, *The Times* report even gives the names of three co-workers of William Hughes who were injured in the same incident.

Notes

1 Director of Filling Factories based at Woolwich during the war.

2 Cocroft says 134 people were killed in filling factories during the war, and perhaps 20 in explosive factories. The worst accidental explosion in Britain was at Fauld in Staffordshire on 27th November 1944, when 15,000 tons of bombs went up, killing 81 people.

3 Kew (HO 144/22490)

4 Primo Carnera: Italian boxer: World Heavyweight Champion, 1933-1934: 6ft 7ins, and 276lbs - Dai Davies must have been a big man.

5 A two-course meal and a cup of tea cost one shilling.

10: ROF 53 and the Luftwaffe

'So Prime a Prey'

Most people in southern Wales were convinced that the Arsenal at Bridgend was an obvious prime target, and so that it would inevitably be attacked by the Luftwaffe. Elliot Crawshay-Williams, in his poem denouncing the building of the Factory, predicted that it would be an irresistible objective for the enemy:

> And fellow-man, scenting so prime a prey,
> Some star-lit night may scatter down from heaven
> Death and damnation in a stinking leaven.

Certainly people in the Ogmore and Garw valleys believed that they were in great danger after the fall of France. The minutes of the local council for the 3rd July 1940 reveal that at that time there was considerable 'public agitation' for more protection (such as public shelters) for the population of the valleys 'owing to their close proximity to the ROF at Bridgend.'

In her book, *Sirens over the Valley*, Rachel Webb remembers that

Bridgend

Staatliche Munitionsfabrik

Länge (westl. Greenw.): 3° 33′ 25″ Breite: 51° 30′ 08″

Mißweisung: – 12° 04′ (Mitte 1940) Zielhöhe über NN 30 m

Maßstab etwa 1 : 37 500

1000 500 0 1000 2000m

Luftwaffe reconaissance photo 24 August 1940

every night in her house in the neighbouring valley she would pray with her children, 'Please God, protect our Arsenal in Bridgend, and our collieries in the valleys from the German bombers.' Doubtless the Webb family was not alone in seeking the protection of the Deity. Rachel goes on to claim that William Joyce[1] threatened destruction for south Wales in his broadcasts from Berlin:

> You people of Maesteg think that you are safe, but we're coming to blow up your collieries soon, and your Arsenal in Bridgend.

Eunice Jones claimed that the Factory was frequently mentioned in broadcasts by Joyce, who would say, 'Hello, you pretty girls up in Bridgend! We know where you are, and we're coming to get you.' Joan Stoker testified that Haw-Haw warned 'Next time you're walking down Adare Street, don't feel too safe – we know where you are!'

In fact despite these claims there seems to be no actual evidence that Maesteg, Bridgend or the Arsenal were specifically mentioned in broadcasts from Germany. Jeff Walden of the BBC is sceptical of these reported references. He has

> checked numerous local legends attached to Haw-Haw, and none of them really stands up. If the story goes that he threatened the Bridgend Factory with an air raid before the event, then I would discount it straight away.

Presumably the Luftwaffe high command would not have been foolish enough to declare their targets in advance of an attack. In his book *England 1914–1945* (p534) the historian AJP Taylor dismissed myths about the detail of Joyce's broadcasts as 'the manufacture of war nerves.'

It will be remembered that originally in 1935 the Air Ministry itself considered that Bridgend would be an easy target for aerial raiders. Indeed the town was initially rejected as the location for an armaments factory specifically on the grounds that it was relatively close to the Continent, and that the Bristol Channel, just four miles away, could be used as a convenient pathway to guide in enemy bombers to the Factory. The architects of the Arsenal had built in precautions to minimise the impact of an accidental explosion within the Factory – such as the use of widely dispersed

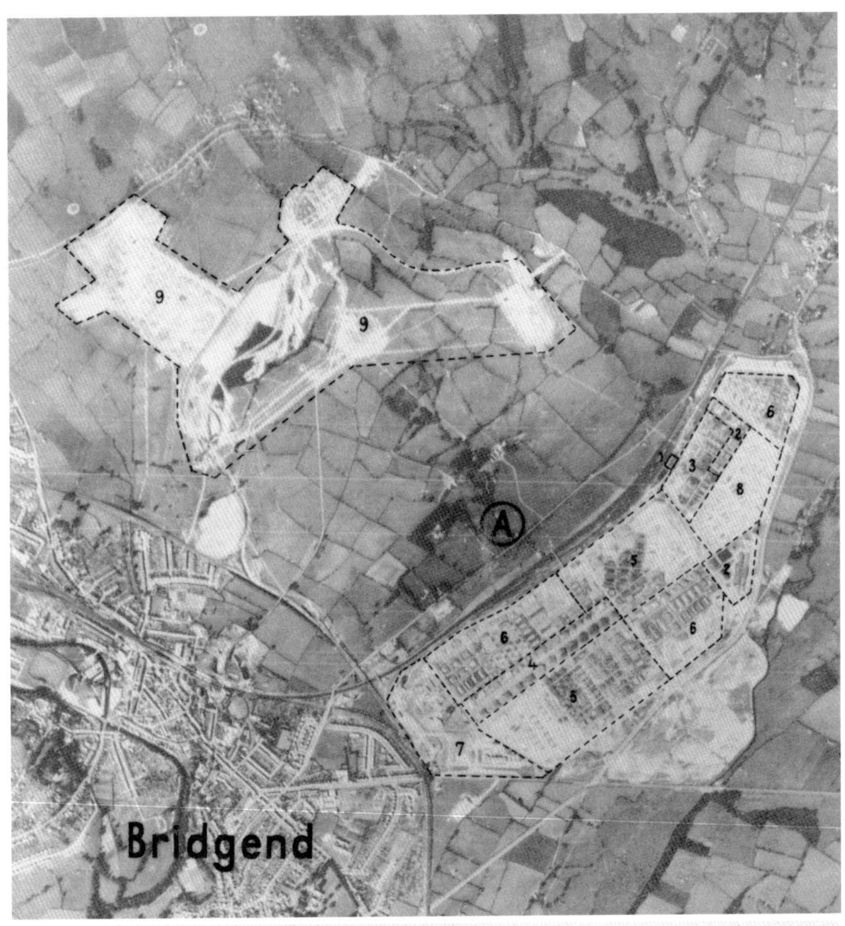

Munitionsanstalt B r i d g e n d. Metallverarbeitender Teil: 1) Kraftanlage; 2) Lager-u.Arbeitshallen; 3) Lagerschuppen Anlage für Pulver und Sprengstoffherstellung,Verarbeitung. 4) Füllhäuser; 5) Arbeitschuppen; 6) Sprengstoff-und Munitionslagerung; 7) Verwaltungs-u. Nebengebäude; 8) Baustelle; 9) Erweiterungsanlage im Bau (Lager), Gleisanschluß vorhanden.

Annotated Luftwaffe reconnaissance photo, 22 July 1940

small buildings, the raising of blast barriers, the covering of stores of finished weapons with earth, and the construction of explosive stores under Brackla Hill. These same features also ensured protection against any attempt by the Luftwaffe to damage the Arsenal. To provide safe refuge for workers in the event of an attack the designers of the Arsenal endowed it with plenty of air raid shelters. One worker, Mair Davies, did not have a very high opinion of this provision: 'I don't know what good they were as they were above ground in concrete buildings situated among the workshops.' On the outbreak of hostilities additional protection against aerial attack was authorised: in September 1939 over £100,000 was allocated for Passive Air Defence such as painting camouflage on to the Factory buildings[2]. A searchlight depot was established on Heol West Plas, near Litchard Cross – though Redwood did not

> remember it ever being used, because to use it so near the Factory would have drawn attention to the Arsenal.

Superintendent of Police May was certainly concerned about the threat from the Luftwaffe. This was what was exercising his mind in October when he conferred with the Chief Constable and Mr Frankton of the Ministry of Home Security on the danger that illumination at the Factory might show German pilots the position of the Arsenal. The lighting was inspected, and according to May, found to be

> satisfactory, with the exception of loading sheds and clearways. Former – too much volume. Latter – distance between standards is not sufficient.

Presumably the matter was rectified as May notes succinctly, 'To be remedied.' There were still problems the following year: in June 1940 May was concerned about the lights used by contractors working at night on the accelerated completion of the Factory. In November May was again discussing the lighting at the Arsenal, this time with the local MP, Ted Williams.

In the June of 1940 there was a terrible warning that armaments installations could be successfully attacked by the Luftwaffe. ROF Pembrey, 40 miles away to the west, produced TNT and other explosives that were used in the manufacturing processes at the Bridgend Arsenal. On 6th June 1940 the Llanelli factory was bombed; 11 workers were killed, and 15 wounded[3]. Forty miles to the East, ROF Glascoed was also attacked by day on three occasions, in June and October 1940: the damage, casualties and disruption were minimal. A couple of months later came the far more serious event that confirmed the wisdom of all those plans for moving the production of armaments out of London. On the very first day of the Blitz on London, September 7th 1940, the original factory at Woolwich was bombed – there were 300 casualties, the fuze section was destroyed, and the filling section incapacitated. These attacks at Pembrey, Glascoed and Woolwich must have caused very great concern amongst those responsible for the safety of the Factory at Bridgend.

In February 1941 the base commander at Llandow, Squadron Leader McQuire, complained to May about the glow of light over the Burning Ground at the Arsenal. Presumably his pilots could identify the Arsenal as they flew above, and so he was concerned lest the Luftwaffe might be able to do the same. On 29th and 30th April 1941 incendiaries fell near Coity, at Coedymwstwr, and on Pencoed, and flares lit up the sky over the Factory. May noted in his diary his opinion that the pilots were 'Looking for the Arsenal.'

The location of Royal Ordnance Factories in Britain was hardly a secret. Herbert Williams[4], admitted in the House of Commons in August 1942 that 'Herr Hitler knows about these factories,' and that he was 'certain that there were full reports in Berlin about their magnitude before the war began.' In fact we know that the Germans knew exactly where ROF 53 was. German agents could read the newspapers in which the building of the Factory was announced, and before September 1939 they could travel relatively freely about the UK. In any case, in the months before hostilities began German spotter planes flew unhindered high above Britain, and photographed the progress of the building of the Arsenal. Even after the war began the Luftwaffe continued to send its spy planes above southern Wales on a regular basis. An aerial photograph taken on the 22nd of July 1940 shows that the Germans were well aware of what was at Bridgend. The photo is entitled Staatliche Munitionsfabrik ('State' or 'National Munitions Factory'). The town and the

Arsenal are clearly visible: they were certainly not obscured by mist. The German intelligence officer who examined the photograph has, with varying degrees of accuracy, marked the different sections of the Arsenal, including the magazines at Brackla, on to the photograph. This table shows the actual sections of the Waterton Factory, the German identification of the sectors, and the English translation of that German label.

SECTION OF FACTORY	GERMAN LABEL	TRANSLATION[5]
Administration	Verwaltungs und Nebengebaude	Administration & Annexes
Power Station and Boiler	Kraftanlage	Power Station
Machine shops transport/textiles	Larger und Arbeit	Store and Works
Filled Stores	Full Hauses	Filling Houses
Initiator Group	Arbeit Schuppen	Transit Sheds
Cordite Group	Lager Schuppen	Store Sheds
Pellet Group Fuze Group Smoke & Pyrotechnic	Sprengstoff und Munitions Lagerung	Explosives and Munitions Storage
Fuze Factory 41	Baustelle	Construction Site

Reich intelligence was accurate about the location of the administrative buildings, the power station, and the machine shops. There seems to have been less certainty about what exactly went on in the various sections of the factory; but after all, most groups were producing Sprengstoff und Munitions. German agents were absolutely right about Fuze Factory 41 – in July 1940 it was still a building site. The reality is that it was impossible to hide from aerial detection the large rectilinear site of the Arsenal with its freshly dug earthworks and its many railway lines. The covering of the buildings with camouflage paint could not make the Factory disappear, and probably offered more psychological protection to the workers than any real concealment. So the Germans knew more or less what was at the Bridgend Factory, and they knew exactly where it was. Why, then, was the Arsenal not attacked?

The Myth of the Mist

All this concern and fear and preparation. And yet not one single bomb actually dropped on Factory land or on the nearby town of Bridgend during the whole of the war. This is remarkable, because from July 1940 to July 1941 bombs dropped all around. Many other communities within a radius of 5 miles of the Arsenal were hit – some of them several times. The table in Appendix B[6] shows the approximate location of the bombs that dropped in the area, and the distance that each was from the Factory. Bombs fell near RAF Llandow, Llysworney, Wick, Monknash, Southerndown, Ogmore-by-Sea, St Bride's, Ogmore Castle, Broadlands, New Inn Bridge, Ewenny, Stormy Down, Newton, Kenfig Hill, Penyfai, Abercynffig, Tondu, Betws, Blackmill, Heol y Cyw, Litchard, Coity, Coedymwstwr, Pencoed, Brynna, Llangan and Treoes. An unexploded bomb was discovered at Waterton Cross, within a few hundred yards of the Factory Administration building. Other places just outside the 5 mile radius were bombed: Llantwit Major and St Athan village experienced a number of incidents, presumably from planes seeking RAF St Athan; Port Talbot, Margam, Pontycymer, Caerau and Nantymoel received attention. But throughout all this Bridgend and its Factory survived unscathed. Indeed, if the 45 or so bombing incidents reported from within a 5 mile radius of the Factory in that twelve months are plotted on a map, the result looks like the record of a particularly persistent but inaccurate marksman, who could manage to hit the target area, but not the bulls-eye of the Arsenal and Bridgend.

Nearly every contemporary interviewed for this study repeated the belief that the reason why the Factory was not bombed was because it was protected by a miasma of mist which rose up from the river Ewenny and Waterton Moor, and rendered the Arsenal, like some twentieth-century Welsh Brigadoon, invisible to the German pilots: some even claimed that this was the reason why the Factory was located at Bridgend in the first place. This is a typical comment, from Mair Davies: 'People used to say the Factory had been built in an area where there was a great deal of mist so it could not be located by fliers.' Certainly there was marshy ground on the flood plain of the Ewenny River, and there are mists in the area on some still mornings in autumn and winter; but these are not frequent. Redwood reported that

> We had quite bad mist there round November, and February. You could hardly see your hand in front of your face – it was pretty bad.

Nevertheless, there would have been plenty of opportunities for the Germans to launch attacks on the site, unhindered by mists. There are plenty of other rather more serious reasons why the Arsenal seems to have had a charmed life.

In the first place, while the pilots of the Luftwaffe certainly knew the precise position of the Arsenal, actually getting to that point across hostile territory, at night and in the dark was very difficult. Their task was not made easier by their reliance on radio beams to navigate above the UK, rays which were routinely interfered with by British transmissions. The RAF experienced similar difficulties in reaching their target towns on the Continent – around one third of British bombers never reached the correct location.

If the planes did arrive successfully over a specific destination, it was almost impossible to hit an area as small as the Arsenal. We may think of the territory of the Brackla and Waterton sites as large, but to the bomb aimer high above Glamorgan they would have seemed insignificant. It is very difficult to strike such a target from a great height, and especially at night. The bomber's approach must be straight and level and the bomb has to be released when the plane is still some distance from the target. Once released the flight of a bomb depends on a number of factors, including its weight, its aerodynamics, the height and speed of the aircraft at release and the wind speed locally – which of course varies at different heights as the bomb falls. All these make accurate targeting almost impossible. To give some idea of the difficulties involved in hitting a specific factory, by early 1942 at least 66% of all bombs released by the RAF hit the ground more than five miles from the target town[7].

In any case an attack on the Arsenal did not fit in with either of the Luftwaffe's strategic objectives. Reichsmarschall Goering's first plan, attempted during the summer of 1940, was to prepare for invasion by gaining control of the air above Britain, and destroying communication and defence installations such as radar stations, ports and railway junctions. This involved destroying the RAF on the ground and in the air through daylight attacks on the airfields of the South and the East, and engaging British fighters in aerial fights. There was one such incident no more than four miles from the Arsenal when the aerodrome at Stormy Down was attacked by day, and at low altitude[8]. At midday on 21st August 1940, three Junkers 88s flew low above the runway, and released 12 bombs, 8 of which actually landed on the aerodrome. Two servicemen were killed, and eight wounded. The damage to the installation was minimal, and normal work had resumed by the next day. The incident showed that a specific objective could be successfully attacked even if the results were not always catastrophic. But daylight low-level attacks made bombers extremely vulnerable to enemy fighters, and could result in heavy losses. This was one reason why the Luftwaffe, after sustaining heavy casualties, turned from these daylight raids on specific RAF and defence objectives to a different plan.

The second strategic objective was carried on from September 1940. German planes attacked in large numbers and at night bombing indiscriminately large, more vulnerable targets such as major cities and towns like London, Swansea and Cardiff – the Blitz. These raids had the aims of destroying civilian morale as well as continuing to disrupt railways and docks, and interfering with war production. Neither of these strategic aims involved the specific targeting of individual factories like ROF 53 outside major urban areas. The sister filling factory at Chorley was not attacked, either – and no one there has suggested that it, too, was protected by mists. There certainly does not seem to have been any concerted large-scale attempt to attack the plant at Bridgend. The pattern and quantity of bombs that fell within five miles of the Factory seem to have been the product of accident rather than deliberate effort – perhaps the result of lost pilots, or the jettisoning of weapons not used in attacks on other targets.

There are other reasons why these important producers of weapons were not targeted. The German planners were well aware that armaments factories had been carefully designed to restrict damage from internal explosions, and that these measures would also minimise the consequences of any bombs landing on the Factory. Perhaps the commanders of the Luftwaffe decided that the potential damage was simply not worth the effort that would be required. Another possibility is that the German High Command did not want major armaments factories damaged, because after the expected surrender of Britain, they wanted to be able to use the munitions produced for their own armed forces. After all, the real goal of the Nazi government was the acquisition of Lebensraum, and the destruction of Communism. This meant the invasion and conquest of the Soviet Union, and German forces would require huge quantities of munitions for that project. Additional credence is given to these arguments by the fact that, apart from the Woolwich Arsenal[9], not one of the many other armaments factories in Britain was systematically attacked. Such damage as individual factories did suffer was the result of an occasional small-scale daylight raid, or perhaps a single aircraft either off course, or jettisoning unwanted missiles. As Cocroft points out in *Dangerous Energy*, 'surviving accounts indicate that in practice there was little systematic targeting of munitions factories by the Luftwaffe.'

Despite all these very good and logical reasons why the Arsenal was not targeted by Goering and his commanders of the Luftwaffe, it is still surprising that not one single bomb fell on the Factory – even by accident – when we consider how many missiles dropped nearby. Perhaps Rachel Webb had the right idea.

Panic in Pyro

The Arsenal, then was never bombed. Nevertheless, the Luftwaffe did have an indirect effect on production. This was as a result of the frequent air raid warnings that sounded during 1940 and 1941. The table opposite[10] shows the number of alerts heard each month at Bridgend in those two years.

Very many of these alerts must have been caused by planes passing on to attack other places, such as Port Talbot, Swansea, Cardiff, or English cities to the north. Each time the sirens sounded employees had to leave their workbenches and go to the shelters to wait for the all-clear. Obviously this interrupted

Month	1940	1941
January	0	22
February	0	19
March	0	41
April	0	32
May	0	40
June	5	12
July	36	9
August	65	5
September	75	3
October	61	11
November	62	4
December	41	0
Total for year	**345**	**198**

manufacture and reduced output. As Lucy Hughes commented, 'The bosses didn't like it when we went to the shelters as there was no progress or production being put out.' Sometimes there were as many as seven alerts a day. For example on the 27th September 1940 the sirens sounded at 05.19, 09.33, 11.45, 12.06, 14.44, 20.05, and 23.40, so that all three shifts were affected. Marjorie Heaver described how 'some nights we'd go straight from the train to the shelter because the sirens were going, and we'd be there all night.' Of course many workers may have seen the incidents as a break from the monotony of work. Sally Loveday remembered how they entertained themselves while they were sitting in the shelters: 'It was singing the whole time.' Lucy Hughes and her friends 'didn't mind going to the shelters because we had a workmate who told us our fortunes.' Huw Menai Williams, an INO Inspector, experienced time in shelters at ROF 53, and, according to one poem he wrote, seems to have succeeded in finding something to take his mind off the dangers:

During the Raid; Written in a Royal Ordnance Factory[11]

Martha makes for sweet forgetting
Of roaming devils and whistling death
Here, amid the stirred destruction,
With the fragrance of her breath
And the lightening of her beauty.
Welcome detonating dart -
Which through the fireproof suit I'm wearing
Finds its way to burn my heart.

Other workers were so fed up with conditions in the shelters that they wanted to go back to the workshops. Eunice Jones of Llangynwyd described what happened:

> Off we'd go to the shelters. They issued us with flannel waistcoats, but we'd sit there in the freezing cold nearly all night... You knew what a lovely warm shop you had there... then we thought about it – bugger it, why spend the night in the shelters – what about it girls? Well, the girls were all for it. It spread all round the Factory like wild-fire.

Apparently the management agreed that, as long as they were all volunteers, workers could stay in the workshops during an alert.

The nearest ROF 53 came to disaster as a result of action by the Luftwaffe came, not directly from the bombing of the Factory, but from a panic induced by the fear of an attack. This crisis occurred at the end of April 1941, and is described in detail by Redwood. By this time there had been about 30 bombing incidents within a 5-mile radius of Bridgend. All the workers at the Factory would have been aware of the attacks on Cardiff and Swansea, and the loss of life and injuries that had occurred in those places. Earlier in the month land mines had dropped near Treoes, and the huge blast had damaged the Priory Church at Ewenny, and smashed the plate glass windows of a clothes shop in Nolton Street, Bridgend. Redwood commented on the effect of this on morale:

> Mind it was really years of living on your nerves, there was no doubt about it. They say that people had moral fibre and all that sort of thing, but then Jerry started finding his direction and

> started dropping a few flares around a bit too close for comfort to the Factory... and when you've got women working there on night shift there were plenty of nerves there.

He describes the mode of operation of the air raid shelters in Pyrotechnics:

> Pyro was the biggest shelter on the whole Factory because there were several underground very deep shelters there; they were closed with steel doors and to open them you had to turn the wheel. When the alarm went the Fire Brigade automatically took charge of these wheels and opened them so that people could go in.

Access to these shelters was down concrete stairs, and it seems that the doors took several minutes to open, and that they opened outwards.

On 29th April many incendiaries landed in Coedymwstwr Woods, above Coychurch, just a mile from the Arsenal, and also in Pencoed only two miles away. The following night 12 incendiaries fell over Coity, hardly a quarter of a mile from the Brackla factories. Flares were dropped, and one in particular illuminated the night sky over Pyrotechnics. Redwood graphically describes the ensuing terrifying events:

> This one night, when they dropped this big flare and started bombing around there was panic, there is no doubt about it there was panic. What frightened the women, and a lot of men – frightened me anyhow – was the fact that flares came down over Pyro, and without exaggerating you could have read a newspaper, and we thought, well, if we can read a paper they must see the Factory – so, look out, they're coming. The flares were so brilliant, like chandeliers. We never had that before.
>
> As soon as the alarm went, as soon as Jerry was coming over, we had to make our way then to the respective shelters on the different sites. We're talking about something like thousands of people which had gathered from pyrotechnic and HE fuze, the nearest shops, would come to Pyro shelters. Anyway they all came down the stairs, a wide concrete stairs. There was myself and two other firemen with our backs to the steel doors and one was trying to open the doors, but the crush of people on us, well, they were going to kill us because we couldn't get our breath and we couldn't open the doors. We couldn't drive them back because there

was a tremendous rush of them, women and men.

Eventually – how, I don't know, don't ask me – we disengaged the two doors and the whole lot were pushed in so much that quite a lot of them fell on the floor. We were afraid of people losing their lives because that's the only time when I was working there that I saw panic, real panic because the bombs were so near and the lights were so bright and so it really frightened them, it really scared them.

And afterwards, once the all clear sounded, a lot of girls wanted to go home – that was unheard of, they were really frightened. Mind, they weren't on their own; we were frightened as well. But that's the only time that I saw panic which we very nearly failed to control.

The Factory Bomb Disposal Squad

Some of the UXBs that fell locally must have been dealt with by people from the Factory. The June 1942 edition of *ROF 53 News* has a photo of the Arsenal Bomb Disposal Squad in a wood with a 2,200 lbs unexploded bomb, which they have nicknamed 'Hermann'. According to the accompanying text, the squad, under the direction of Mr. DT Davies, 'has already done some tricky jobs with unexploded bombs in the district.' In the case of Hermann the squad 'dug it out and removed the fuze together with 1000lbs of HE.' By the summer of 1942 there were very few bombing raids over southern Wales, so it seems likely that Hermann had arrived in Wales the previous year.

Notes

1 William Joyce: born New York, 1906. Member of Oswald Mosley's British Union of Fascists. Anti-Semite. Went to Germany in August 1939, and broadcast propaganda in English throughout the war, earning nickname of Lord Haw-Haw because of his aristocratic nasal drawl. Executed for treason 1946.

2 Treasury Inter-service Committee approval of expenditure: Kew (AVIA 22/2153)

3 Even so, according to Ian Hay in *R.O.F.*, Pembrey was in full operation again within 48 hours.

4 Herbert Williams, 1884–1954: Conservative politician. MP for South Croydon 1932–1945, Croydon East 1950–1954.

5 Translation by Brian and Lyn Lewis

6 Information from Cottrell *Hostile Sky* and R Williams *Bridgend Report and Control Centre*.

7 See AJP Taylor Ch 14 for a discussion of the inaccuracy of bombing.

8 Cottrell *Hostile Sky*.

9 Woolwich endured a total of 25 major raids, in which 103 people were killed and 770 injured.

10 Based on figures in Cottrell *Hostile Sky*.

11 From *The Simple Vision*. Williams was an INO inspector in T&P section.

11: Policing the Arsenal

The arrival of such a large installation at Bridgend was bound to add to the workload of the local constabulary. Inevitably in such a complex site, and with so many people from so many different places working there, there were many temptations; some succumbed. The Arsenal was hardly Gomorrah, but the frailties of a few of the workers at the Factory are recorded in the pages of the regional press, and under entries in the war diary of Superintendent William May, the chief of the Bridgend police. In these documents we can read about theft, illicit gambling, fraudulent clocking on, absenteeism, the taking of contraband into Danger Areas, the consequences of drink, immoral behaviour, an indecent show, and the threat of fifth columnists, sabotage and sedition.

Theft

A number of cases of theft at the Arsenal are described in local newspapers. And judging by the comments of magistrates and police, it was obviously an extensive problem. During a trial in January 1939, while the Factory was still under construction, Inspector Beale of the Glamorgan Constabulary advised the magistrates 'that there was a great deal of pilfering being carried on at the Arsenal.' The actual offence of the defendant, a tractor driver from Waterton Lane, Bridgend, was receiving just 12s.

worth of tools (spanners, pliers and wrenches) belonging to Sunley's, one of the contractors building the Factory; but clearly this was but the tip of a criminal iceberg. A week later six men appeared before the magistrates' court, and all were found guilty of theft either from contractors, or from fellow employees. One enterprising worker from Pontycymer had managed to acquire illicitly an eclectic collection which included an oilcan, sheet copper, bolts, washers, a carpenter's square, a blowlamp, hammer, brace and bit together valued at £5. Unsurprisingly the Bench commented on the systematic thieving, and wondered out loud and threateningly 'whether they ought not to send some to prison' – though none were.

The notebook of Tom Bevan, the Senior Warden, describes an incident which suggests that the unfinished Arsenal was virtually under siege. On 15th February 1940 a stoker from the Boiler House had seen intruders inside the Danger Building fence, and had thrown a stone at them – which had caused them to run away. When the area was searched a ladder was found leaning up against the fence. Presumably on this occasion the thieves fled empty handed.

The problem was seen as so significant that a question was asked in the House of Commons by WH Mainwaring, the MP for the Rhondda East. He asked the Commissioner for Works 'to see that the War Office is in no way affected by the misuse of materials.'

The concerns of the authorities seem to have had little effect. In November 1940 during another case of theft – involving a youth from Aberkenfig and an oilskin coat – the Chairman of the Bench was still threatening 'if this sort of thing goes on, we will have to deal with offenders more drastically.' The prosecutor pointed out that 'larceny of clothing at the Factory is increasing very much', and requested the Bench to 'make it known to the Press about the prevalence of stealing at the Factory' – presumably to encourage others into the straight and narrow path.

In fact, judging by two entries in May's Diaries, the management of the Arsenal does seem to have had a somewhat ambivalent attitude towards theft. In October 1941 the Superintendent met Chief Inspector Crawley of the Factory Security Police about a charge (against someone mysteriously identified, unusually for the Diary, just by initial letters) of larceny of a towel from the Arsenal. Crawley must have asked that the case be dropped, because May writes that 'I declined to be a party not to proceed with charges.' Two days later May met the Factory Superintendent, Len Corbett, to discuss prosecutions for crimes committed in the Arsenal. According to May, Corbett was 'anxious to avoid friction with workers.' Presumably the Factory manager was keen to avert possible strikes and disruption to production for the sake of minor indiscretions – such as the theft of a towel – or perhaps the enigmatic thief was a member of the management team. In any case May refused to be a party to such a policy. Instead he 'took a strong and definite tone that where clear evidence proved offence the law should not be sabotaged.' 'Treat all alike without distinction' was his watchword. Apparently Corbett was persuaded by the force of the Police Superintendent's argument: May's last entry for that day was a succinct 'he agreed.' Interestingly, three cases of theft of a towel in October 1941 were brought to the Bridgend Magistrates court against women working in the Arsenal. Two cases were dismissed, but the third lady, from Blaengarw, whose initials fit those in the Diary, was found guilty. The chairman said 'it was a serious offence, and the bench could not accept her plea that she did not know that the towel was in her possession.' The sentence was a fine of £2, or a month in prison. Justice had been done.

Workers at the Arsenal could be inventive. One worker in textiles tells how the girls would 'lock the door between two o'clock and four o'clock' on the night shift 'because there were no bosses around then.' They would cut out skirts, using the soft woollen material they were making uniforms with,

> tack them together, put them on, and pass through security without difficulty. Needless to say, we would wear the skirts out on Saturday night!

Another worker got stolen goods out of the Arsenal in a novel way. A colleague had won a chicken in a Christmas raffle in one of the canteens. The worker asked for the head and legs of the chicken, and put together a bundle of tools with the head sticking out from the top and the legs sticking out from the bottom. He was waved through security at the gate with congratulations on his good luck, and exhortations to enjoy his Christmas dinner.

Rowena Harris describes how some workers tried to get silk out of the Arsenal:

> You wouldn't believe it, but there were a lot of people who carried out parachute silk by the yard and they used to wrap it round their bodies. And then they could make blouses or shirts. A lot of people were caught, actually.

All this was small beer compared with a theft that came to court in November 1941. A painter from Cardiff was working in the Arsenal, and he took a bale containing 9 rolls of parachute silk, worth £227. A rash grocer of Caerau had acquired four of the rolls and had begun to sell lengths of silk to local women. Their dreams of new clothes were frustrated, as the court report stated that the lengths had been recovered and identified. Another man involved in the plot was caught 'red-chested' – when he was arrested he was wearing a silk shirt made of 'fabric identical to silk at the Factory.'

Matters were not made easier for the authorities when the very people who were supposed to prevent theft indulged in it themselves. In January 1942 a War Department constable from Tondu was sent down for a month for stealing 118 packets of cigarettes, worth £4.5.6d, from a canteen at the Arsenal, and for possessing cigarettes while in the danger area. The *Advertiser* made much of the event: 'Tragedy,' mourned the reporter,

> the tragedy of a career nipped in the bud was written all over his face when he heard the clerk read out the charge, while his old chief was a sorrowful onlooker.

The accused admitted that he was suddenly tempted, and he fell: 'I have lost something that I did not know how valuable it was,' he declared, 'my character, and I want everybody to know it was just a mad mistake.' The disgrace of the constable does not seem to have deterred other thieves. There was a much more serious theft of cigarettes in October 1942, when 170,000, worth £750, disappeared – presumably from a canteen storeroom.

Some people defiantly tried to justify their actions. In January 1945 Factory property worth £188 was found in the house of a worker from Blaengarw. The haul included 60 pairs of 'magazine' footwear, as well as coats, trousers, jackets, dungarees, tools, blankets and 51 towels: the police needed a lorry to take all the articles away. Security at the Arsenal could not have been very efficient. When arrested, the miscreant declared

> I do not think that I have done anything wrong, because the Government is spending my money at the rate of millions a day. This is only a bit of my income tax back.

At the same time a War Department policeman from Laleston was charged with stealing an hydraulic jack and towels from the Factory. His justification is revealing: 'What I have done is nothing to what some of the others have been doing,' he claimed. The magistrates were not impressed with the excuses, and committed both men to the Assizes.

Betting

The desire to supplement their incomes with a little illegal activity got some other Arsenal workers into trouble. In July 1939 two men were convicted of dealing in betting slips. One had obviously been watching British crime films, because when challenged by the constable he had responded in the approved way: 'the game is up. You have got to do your duty.' Evidence that the police had a sense of humour is shown when another defendant claimed that he was just walking along after the constable appeared; the police witness said 'you raced away.' (Or was this use of phrase just a happy accident?)

It appears there was a great deal of gambling going on amongst the workers building the Arsenal, because Superintendent May told the Magistrates that 'there is so much time taken up with this sort of thing that it is interfering with work.' The Chairman of the Bridgend Magistrates, Llewellyn Jones, took the opportunity to denounce the men's betting activities for squandering taxpayers hard-earned money: 'It does seem an alarming state of affairs at the Arsenal,' he pontificated from the bench, 'with people of your type wasting time at the expense of the taxpayers instead of doing your job.' Indeed according to Jones it seems that these bookie's runners were responsible for undermining the entire British economy, and destroying the Chancellor of the Exchequer's careful Budget calculations, because the magistrate concluded, 'No wonder Sir John Simon has difficulty in meeting his bills.' Obviously the bench considered gambling a very serious offence – the combined fines for the two men totalled £27.7s. 6d.

Fraudulent Clocking On.

Once the Factory was up and running a major and continuing problem and expense for the Arsenal was fraudulent clocking on. All Factory employees were allocated a time card. When they arrived at and left their place of work they had to insert the card into a machine that registered the time. This then indicated the attendance of the operative, the hours that they had been at the Factory, and therefore the wages to which they were entitled. There were two ways to defraud the Arsenal: the card could be clocked in and out by someone else, allowing the worker to be absent for the shift, or the employee could walk out having clocked on, and then return to clock out. In either eventuality, the wage for that time was effectively being stolen from the Factory. There was a way of checking the clocking on process: each workshop had a register that would indicate whether the worker was present. But the process seems to have been very lax; the registers were available to all, marked in pencil and could easily be altered. When a Magistrate asked 'Would anyone have access to the register?' the reply was 'It is generally lying about.' Unsurprisingly a solicitor commented that 'the whole system admits of all possible sorts of fraud.' In any case there does not seem to have been a consistent system for checking the time cards against the register.

The local newspapers report case after case brought before the Magistrates. The initial occasion seems to have been in April 1941, when the Chairman of the Magistrates is quoted in the *Gazette* as saying that 'these are the first cases of this kind to come before us.' Ten workers from the Arsenal were prosecuted under the Larceny Act (False Pretences). One example will show the sort of amounts involved. A lady from Swansea clocked on an absent fellow worker on two successive days, gaining her friend 8s. 10d. on each occasion. Additionally, on the second day she clocked in another missing employee, gaining that lady 9s. 9d. to which she was not entitled. The fine and costs for these offences amounted to £5 18s. – a week's wages. And of course the operatives involved would be dismissed from their jobs.

At the end of the trial the Chair of the Magistrates, Llewellyn Jones, denounced the employees, but he also gave a sideswipe at the ineffective systems operated by the Factory management.

> We are not only surprised, but astounded by the evidence given here this morning. The slackness of the Government in dealing with these matters is no excuse for what you have done.... It is extraordinary that girls employed like this should be able to spend afternoons off at Porthcawl and elsewhere without any check on their actions.

Warming to his theme he continued,

> It is astounding that this sort of thing can be allowed in this country in the 20th century.

He then turned his attention to the undesirable effect of the workers actions on the long-suffering taxpayer; not the first time that Jones had felt impelled to leap to the defence of that beleaguered group of citizens.

> The country is groaning under taxation, and yet people like you are robbing the country right and left. If the same thing applies to other factories, no wonder we are spending £14 million a day.

He ended by appealing to the Factory bureaucracy to improve their systems:

> We hope the management will adopt a better method of checking and controlling the records of when employees start and finish their work.

Apparently little had changed over the following few months. In June a worker from Ferndale was fined £5 for clocking in her sister-in-law, who had gone to Pontypridd for the day instead of labouring in the Arsenal. 'This is too prevalent,' mused the magistrate, and in another implied criticism of the authorities he suggested 'it may be too easy.' Inspired by Henry Newbolt, he denounced the defendants because they 'had not played the game with their country.'

The local public houses seem to have been an attraction too great for some men to resist. One male worker from Tonypandy clocked on, and then disappeared. In his statement he claimed that after he had clocked on at about 2.45 he had been 'sent somewhere else to await instructions.' Seeing no one there, he admitted that he had decided to 'go to a nearby village for a drink,' and that he 'stayed there to stop-tap, and then returned to the Factory.' He must have been surprised when he was arrested as he 'did not think that they would miss [him]' – but they did, and he was fined £5. Understandably the Magistrate was concerned about the worker's ability to perform safely when he returned from the pub, and he warned that

> in future anyone who comes before us on a similar charge will not be given the option, they will be sent down.

Another male employee, from Nantymoel, left his place of work without clocking off, and stayed in a nearby hotel for two hours. Perhaps as he was 66 years old he felt that he was entitled to some extra refreshment. Unfortunately for him he was seen by a policeman – though why the constable did not pull him out of the pub straight away is not explained. The truant escaped prison, but was fined £7 10s.

There does seem to have been some collusion with middle management. One of our male interviewees from the Rhondda tells how on the afternoon 2 – 10 shift on a Thursday (pay day) he would get a pass from the foreman at 6 o'clock and go off to the local pubs –

> the Prince and the White Horse in Coychurch, the Star in Treoes, the Six Bells at Coity, the Pelican, the Coach and the Fives. There were not many pubs in Bridgend that we didn't do!

One Arsenal overlooker obviously had other things on his mind. In June 1943 the *Gazette* reported the case of a man from Trealaw who had clocked in but then left the Factory, gaining 7s 4d. without working. Two girls from the Factory gave evidence that at the times involved 'he was out walking with them – one on each occasion.' Perhaps it was the fact that he had not restricted his attention to one lady that had impelled them to testify against him. The magistrate took a dim view of all this.

> You are an overlooker at the Factory, and supposed to see that other people are at work, instead of which you spend your time walking out with girls.

The matter was considered to be very serious, because the overseer was fined £20 – an unusually high figure.

Absenteeism

Some workers on the Arsenal roll did not bother with the deception of false clocking on; instead frequently they simply did not turn up for work, and so their attendance at the Factory was erratic. In fact, throughout the war one of the most persistent problems in Royal Ordnance factories across Britain was high levels of absenteeism. The Select Committee on National Expenditure raised the issue in a report to the Commons in July 1941, and again in another report a year later. In August 1942 the Minister of Supply, Andrew Duncan[1], confessed to the House that 'absence from work is still a serious problem in ROFs, and especially on the filling side.' In the same debate the chairman of the Select Committee, Lewis Silkin, claimed that 'Absenteeism in some places amounts to 20 or 25 percent,' and he went on to point out that 'It is women whose absenteeism rises to these astronomical figures.' The government insisted that there had been an improvement over the previous six months, and that casual (i.e. not for valid reasons) absence in filling factories like Bridgend had fallen for men from 12% to 4.5%, and for women from 23.5% to 13%.

This improvement was not maintained. These are the total absentee percentages for workers in all filling factories in Britain for the first five months of 1943[2]. The change in absenteeism apparent over this period was probably caused by seasonal

1943	Men	Women
January	11.1	23.1
February	10.0	21.1
March	9.5	19.5
April	8.2	18.4
May	8.0	17.7

factors; reducing levels of illness as the summer approached:

The situation at Bridgend was at least as bad as these national averages would suggest. At a conference held at the Arsenal in November 1941, the Superintendent, Len Corbett, revealed that at times absenteeism at his Factory amounted to as much as 26%. This means that on any one day nearly a quarter of the workforce of ROF53 was not in work, and naturally this would have a considerable negative effect on production.

These figures[3] show the position at Bridgend in the month of January 1942:

Cause of Absence	Male %	Female %
Injury	0	0
Sickness	1.9	3.4
Approved leave	0.4	0.8
Unapproved leave	7	24

Quite clearly, women workers at Bridgend were more liable than men to lose time because of sickness, but they were more than three times as likely to miss work for no officially approved reason. This caused serious problems at the Arsenal, where 70% of all workers were female. A minute of a Ministry of Supply meeting in July 1942 reveals that there were 'daily absences of over 5,000 persons at Bridgend[4].'

That August an article about the Brackla installations published in the Factory Newsletter shows that absenteeism was still a problem. The writer (identified only as JJB) starts by commenting on the 'happy community' and 'the wonderful spirit' at Brackla. It is then revealed that all is not well there: 'absenteeism is the canker that is upsetting [Brackla's] chances of becoming perfect.' The remainder of the article uses a form of moral haranguing to shame workers into full attendance.

> The lads who are relying on us may… find they have not sufficient ammunition to carry on the fight. Those who have thoughtlessly taken a day or two off work… have endangered the lives of those nearest and dearest to them.

The piece climaxes with a clarion call:

> See to it that you fail not in your duty to the lads who are fighting; fighting that you may live in peace. Go to it you workers of Brackla.

Finally, in a postscript, JJB indicates that these problems are common to the whole of the Factory, as the conclusion testily rebukes; 'not only does this apply to Brackla, but to the whole of the ROF.'

Figures for absenteeism at Bridgend in December 1942 seem to show that the problem was still considerable, but not quite as bad as in 1941. The figures also show major differences between the sections at the Factory[5].

Percentage absenteeism by section at Bridgend: December 1942

Pellets	24.7	40mm	17.7	Cordite	14.8
Detonators	19.6	Fuze HE	17.6	Stores I	14.6
Smoke	18.8	Pyro	16.9	Fuze T+P	13.2
Primers	18.4	Brackla S	15.5	Textile	9.2
Stores F	18.0	B East	14.9	Brackla A	8.7

What were the reasons for these high absentee rates at ROF 53? During the November 1941 conference the Bridgend Labour Officer identified three factors: the 'failure, or alleged failure, of transport, illness, and domestic troubles.' The Officer, presumably Mrs Shields, went on to denounce single girls and contrasted their commitment unfavourably with that of

> the middle-aged woman, who has carried out the arduous task of bringing up a family, [and] can stick it better than a younger person.[6]

Other factors were suggested by delegates at the meeting. The MP for Neath, William Jenkins claimed that 'that part of the country was not "factory minded,"' and so not accustomed to the discipline of the workbench. Another MP, Ness Edwards of Caerphilly, suggested that there was 'slackness at the Factory – that women went there and that there was nothing for them to do' – the implication being that there was little point in turning up conscientiously for work every day.

An additional cause was suggested in an article printed in the *Glamorgan Advertiser* during the same month as the conference. Apparently the Ministry of Labour's Wales Regional Board, considered that absenteeism was 'largely due to the clashing of their working hours with those during which their food shops are open.' The Board went on to ask shopkeepers to take this into account when deciding on closing times, and appealed to their loyalty by declaring that

> by doing so they will not only suit the convenience of customers who are patriotically engaged in war work, but they will also be making a valuable contribution towards the war effort.

Of course shopping in wartime required a great deal of troublesome organisation, the unwelcome juggling of rations, and much thankless time spent in long queues for scarce commodities. Sometimes the only way a housewife could be sure of obtaining essential supplies was to take time off work, since otherwise the articles they required would be sold out long before they could reach the shops.

In a video interview a worker at Bridgend, Margaret Plummer, described a very different type of absenteeism in which she was involved. She went up to London with her sister and two friends to stay with an aunt for a weekend. They explored Petticoat Lane 'to get bargains for the bottom drawer.' But 'when it came to Sunday we didn't feel like coming back, we were enjoying ourselves too much.' and instead they remained in the capital for a week. Margaret's final comment seems to justify the remarks of the Factory Labour Officer about single girls:

> in those days we lived from day to day – we didn't know if we would be alive the next morning. We just did things as we wanted to.

Peggy Inman gives the official view of the causes of absenteeism in the volume she wrote on Labour in the History of the War. She cites: relatively high earnings – meaning that a shift could be missed by a worker without hardship; lack of experience of the discipline of factory work; illness, accidents and fear of injury; transport problems; long hours and the inconvenience of shifts; the need to shop for food and care for members of the family; resentment among those directed into the factories;

absence of individual responsibility in such large organisations; initial lack of proper welfare and systems to deal with the problem. Support for this last reason comes from a contribution to the debate in the house by Irene Ward, Conservative MP for Wallsend. She blamed the lack of proper welfare provision in ROFs on 'a Woolwich mentality, which has been accepted by the government as standard.' She went on to aver that

> Those of us who are progressive in our views on the handling of labour are not much impressed by this 'Woolwich mentality."

Doubtless all these factors identified by Inman applied to members of the workforce at Bridgend. In fact as a result of the debate in the Commons in August 1942 the Minister of Supply asked the Industrial Health Research Board to research the main causes of absenteeism by talking to a representative selection of workers at ROF 53. This report concluded that 'the main causes of absenteeism do not recur regularly,' and so, 'There is a need for personal study of causes of absenteeism and an individual method of treatment.' In other words it was not possible to generalise on the causes of absenteeism, and each individual case had to be looked at on its merits. There does in general seem to have been a thoughtful response by the authorities to the problem. In the debate in Parliament in 1942 the Minister said that

> in view of the domestic and family responsibilities of the women, one has to be tolerant and patient. Large numbers of people have been rooted up from their normal environment and ordinary habits.

This seems a commendably relaxed view for a member of the government to take in the middle of the war.

During 1942 and 1943, and partly as a result of the criticisms made by the Select Committee, a coordinated system was set up in filling factories to deal with absenteeism. Returning workers were interviewed to find out the reasons for absence, and to try to avoid future instances. Workers absent for more than three days were sent letters. If no satisfactory response was forthcoming then the District Visitor would call. District Visitors were workers appointed and trained to interview long-term absentees in their houses. Margaret Plummer recalls a rather more drastic tactic;

after she had stayed in London for a week she received a telegram from her mother telling her that the police had knocked on the door, and demanded to know where Margaret was, and why she was absent from work. When she returned to work she was interviewed, and

> told not to do it again, we need you, your place is in the Factory. Without you we can't do this and we can't do that.

Finally a more flexible attitude was taken to the granting of leave, so that workers felt they could give warning of absences for legitimate reasons. This also made it easier for workshops to allocate their resources appropriately, and so to cope more effectively with absences.

Those who were persistently absent without explanation were given a series of graduated warnings. Eventually they would have to appear before a Factory Absentee Committee, which included representatives of both workers and management. Indeed Duncan paid tribute to the work of trade union officials who had supported the campaign against absenteeism by addressing meetings of workers in the canteens. If all else failed recalcitrant employees would be prosecuted in the local magistrates' court. Being absent from essential war work without good reason was a criminal offence, but the management of the Arsenal was clearly making efforts to deal with the problem in other ways. The *Gazette* records that the magistrates at Bridgend heard with approval of the systems at the Arsenal. The chief labour officer explained that if a person was persistently late or absent, they were given a list of the complaints against them. If this failed to excite an improvement, then they had to appear before the Absentee Committee where they were given every opportunity to explain their problems, or provide a reasonable excuse. Only after this process was a prosecution initiated. The secretary of the Absentee Committee at the Arsenal, John Clarke, was usually present at such cases, several of which are described in the *Gazette*.

In October 1942 four young women appeared before the Bridgend Magistrates. The prosecuting solicitor announced that the cases had been brought because 'the question of absenteeism was getting very serious,' so these workers were obviously being tried in order to encourage others. Certainly the records of these particular workers were not good.

The first, whose attendance was 53%, explained that she stayed away 'because she wanted to go to work nearer her home.' The magistrates could not have thought much of this defence since the girl lived at Pencoed, just a couple of miles from the Arsenal.

The second girl also lived in Pencoed. Her attendance rate was 48%, and her justification for her poor record that she wanted to leave the Arsenal and join the A.T.S.

The third girl lived in Morfa Street in Bridgend. She accounted for her attendance rate of 41% by explaining that both she and her mother had been ill – though she did confess to being late on one occasion because she had been to the pictures.

The fourth employee lived in the same street in Bridgend, and she had the appalling attendance rate of just 24%. No explanation was forthcoming for her absences.

In mitigation for the four girls Clarke indicated that their attendance had improved since they had been brought in front of the Factory Absentee Committee. This did not impress the Magistrate, who fined them £3 each and reproached them that 'if Hitler came here they would not have the opportunity of choosing their jobs.' Presumably the Bench thought that the spectre of the Führer finally finding his ideal role in life, and running the Bridgend Employment Exchange would be enough to force the women back to full time working.

A male worker from Brynmenyn who came before the Bench in January 1943 was treated much more severely. He had missed 137 shifts out of 160, so his attendance rate was a lamentable 15% – a performance which the Ministry of Labour solicitor described as 'the worst case of absenteeism ever recorded at a certain factory' (i.e. the Arsenal). Brought before the Absentee Committee he claimed that he had been turned down by the Army and

> the work here is not active enough for me; it is too light, and I can't settle down at all... The job I had in the Factory was a very easy job, more or less, and my health is pretty good.

In court he told a rather different story. Alarmingly he claimed that he had had dysentery for the month of August, and that he had been to jail twice for failing to fulfil a paternity order. The Bench were unmoved by this tale of woe, and showed their condemnation of his attendance record by sending the recalcitrant worker to prison for 14 days.

Contraband

Theft, persistent absenteeism and illegal clocking on were serious, but breaking the strict regulations covering the Danger Areas in the Factory might be fatal. Regularly the *Gazette* and The *Advertiser* published lists of the names and addresses of those brought before the Magistrates Court for carrying prohibited articles into the clean side. Obviously the intention of the authorities was to shame those who had ignored the rules – presumably in the hope of deterring others. Clearly this was a considerable problem. In June 1940, the *Gazette* reported that several workmen had been fined £2 each for having live matches or cigarettes in their possession, and the Chair of the bench was moved to refer to 'the frequency with which these cases were now occurring.'

Week after week the local newspapers carried many reports of a similar nature. One example from December 1940 is typical. Headlined simply 'Contraband,' it states that that week a total of 9 people – 8 women and just one man – were each fined £1 'for being in possession of forbidden articles in a factory.' In a society where smoking cigarettes was not believed to be unhealthy, indeed considered to be necessary to cope with the stresses of war time, the authorities were having difficulties in ensuring compliance with essential safety regulations.

Drink

The return of prosperity through the wages earned by many as a result of construction work and employment at the Arsenal was blamed for an increase in cases of drunkenness in the Bridgend Division. Superintendent May's report of March 1939 recorded a total of 133 cases before the courts in the year under review. An example of Arsenal workers with money to spend was described in June 1938 in the *Gazette* under the headline:

BRIDGEND STREET SCENE

The report began with a group of eight men causing a shocking disturbance outside the public conveniences in Derwen Road at 11.30 on a Tuesday night – singing, shouting, and drinking beer from flagons[7]. When approached by Police Officers, two of the men became aggressive. One declared that 'I am not going home for you or anyone else', and started kicking out at the police. Then the other attacked them from behind, shouting 'you are not going to ★★★★-well take him.' It took five police officers to eventually subdue the two men, who spent the night in the cells at the Police Station, a few yards away along Derwen Road. In the Court the men told the Magistrate that they could not remember anything. Not unreasonably the Magistrates' Clerk commented that they must have been very drunk. What is interesting is that both men were Arsenal workers, and obviously well paid. One earned £4.3s. a week, and the other, a foreman, earned £4.10s. They would both have been able to pay the £1.10s. fine without too much difficulty – it seems that assaulting the police was considered to be a far less serious offence than gambling in the Arsenal.

The pages of old *Gazettes* are not the only place to find evidence of the effects of the construction of the Arsenal on the streets of Bridgend. David Power recalls:

> a tremendous amount of Irish labour came in to build the Arsenal – southern Irish. The famous pub for them was the Tennis Court, where Boots the Chemist is today. Quite often when you went down town of an evening, someone would come sailing through the window – or like a cowboy film, out through the doors!

Roy Davies described another alcoholic incident:

> One evening I met my friend, he was on leave from the army, so we went for a drink in the Tennis Court. We were in there drinking, a rough pub it was, and I was on nights, so I walked up to the Arsenal and through the gate, and we were as drunk as coots, so the police had us, they said, "Come on boys," so we had a night in a cell. Cup of tea in the morning to sober up. I had to go to court for coming to work drunk.

Once the Arsenal buildings were completed during the course of

1940 labourers employed on the project moved away. In his report to the Licensing Magistrates in February 1941, Superintendent of Police May was able to celebrate soberly a considerable reduction (of 45 cases) in the number of prosecutions for drunkenness during the previous year. He attributed this satisfactory decrease to the reduction in the employment of casual labour at the Factory. Reflecting the social judgements of the time he reported that

> The class of labour at those works has now changed, and although more people are employed, their habits of life are somewhat different, and are reflected in the decreased amount of drunkenness.

But May's satisfaction was short lived: a new social phenomenon, driven by changes at the Arsenal, began to disturb him. Once the Arsenal began to employ large numbers of women as process workers, complaints began to emerge about their drinking habits. In his report on the division for the next year, 1941, a shocked Superintendent May warned that 'a marked increase had been observed of drinking among young women,' who were mostly around 20 years of age. In comments which seem to anticipate concerns about ladettes and binge drinking in the next century, he denounced these females because

> they often became under the influence to such an extent as to be quite irrational and irresponsible ... the increase in this undesirable and discreditable habit among young women appears to be one of the inevitable consequences of the war.

The Chairman of the Magistrates on the Licensing Bench was more direct when he explained that young women 'have more money to spend on drink, smoking and films' – presumably from their employment in the Arsenal. Mair Davies of Nantymoel, who worked at the Factory, confirms that there was a change in the behaviour of some. 'You didn't see women in pubs before the war – it started when they were working.' A member of Mass Observation's panel of observers gave a similar picture about girls who were living in the Factory's Pencoed Hostel. He reported that the pubs of the little town were full of young women who were 'not local girls...but girls imported to work at the Factory.'

Gloomily Superintendent May predicted 'the creation of a most serious post-war social problem.' The Chairman of the Bench seems to have disagreed with this prognosis, because in February 1943, after commenting adversely on the ability of young women to drink 'as freely as any man of mature age,' he predicted that when the war was over, and the 'high wages [paid at the Arsenal] have been reduced, they will amend their ways.'

In his report on the year 1944, May was even more forthright in his condemnation of the disagreeable effects of women drinking. 'It is not uncommon to see women sitting in public bars with the men, consuming beer.' He observed, with obvious distaste.

> The mixing of the sexes draws a certain class of custom, and there is a danger of reducing public houses ... to haunts and hunting grounds of sharks and loose women, whose business consists of exploiting the follies and weaknesses of the unsuspecting.

Interestingly the drinking habits of these poor naïve unsuspecting males do not seem to have attracted the same opprobrium.

Perhaps it was cases like the following, recorded in the *Advertiser* in June 1941, that May had in mind when he composed his reports. A 41-year-old Arsenal worker from Dowlais, who had been drinking that evening in the pubs of Bridgend, was seen by a constable to bump into the window of London House, a shop in Dunraven Place. The officer asked the woman for her identity card, which she first produced, and then tore into pieces. 'It will take a better **** man than you to take me in,' she boasted – though apparently this claim was without foundation as she was arrested by the officer, and taken to the Police Station. In his summing up, the magistrate expressed his displeasure with the behaviour of some female Arsenal workers because

> instead of going home after they have finished work, women stayed around the hotels. It was getting very serious in Bridgend, with people getting drunk about the place.

The lady from Dowlais was required to pay a £2 fine for her disruptive behaviour.

'Immoral' Behaviour

It is apparent from some of the entries in Superintendent May's Diaries that it was not only the drinking habits of Arsenal workers that was causing concern in the community and among the authorities. In June 1941 he refers to 'a person summonsed for committing an indecent act at Cowbridge Road,' and goes on to comment on 'the general complaint of immoral conduct on the part of Factory employees,' On 17th June he was dealing 'with reports relating to alleged indecency in Bridgend arising out of factory girls and troops.' He goes on to add cryptically, 'the most extraordinary part is that only two soldiers are involved in cases found.' What does this mean? It seems to imply that two men were responsible for a great deal of immorality!

Perhaps there is a clue to understanding May's enigmatic comments in the fact that on the same day that he wrote these remarks Bridgend Council had received a report from its Medical Officer of Health expressing concern at the prevalence of VD in the town. Councillors urged that immediate steps be taken to safeguard the troops stationed in Bridgend and its vicinity – no one urged measures to protect factory girls from the troops! The Council decided to call a conference on the issue with representatives from various military units and camps, the Police and the Arsenal. These groups duly met in July, and nine recommendations were made – which frustratingly are not recorded in the minutes of the Bridgend Council.

There is a reference to the Bridgend Arsenal in a short story by Dylan Thomas entitled 'Just Like Little Dogs'. Three men are whiling away an evening by chatting near the docks in Swansea. Tom says, "I knew a chap once who lives in the country near Bridgend, and they had a munitions works there in the War and it spoiled all the birds. The chap I know says you can always tell a cuckoo from Bridgend, it goes "Cuckbloodyoo! Cuckbloodyoo!"

What does Thomas mean by this? There is no clue in the story because the remark is inconsequential. Very many people went from Swansea to work at the Arsenal in Bridgend. One interpretation is that that the workers at the Arsenal were well known in Swansea for their swearing. Of course the cuckoo is a symbol of the cuckold[8] – perhaps spoiled birds refers to the virtue of girls who worked in the Factory, rather than the song of the feathered kind!

In an article in 1957 in the *Empire News* Richard Rees, who had been a worker at the Arsenal, made some dramatic assertions:

> Thousands of girls working so hard; too few eligible men; husbands overseas – trouble was inevitable. Moral standards were cracked in the pubs and bars, and pitched overboard in other places. Illegitimacy rates soared as social workers tried desperately to stem the disastrous flood which threatened to smash countless homes in the Welsh valleys.

Redwood maintained that

> there was quite a lot of fun down there one way or another. Quite a few marriages that were broken down there, and quite a few were married from there. It was a community during wartime, and during wartime Anything Goes.[9]

We found little evidence in interviews or the newspapers of 'immoral' behaviour specifically linked to the Arsenal. There was one report in the *Rhondda Leader* of the consequences of a liaison involving two ROF workers who had presumably met at the Arsenal. A single girl from Trealaw had had a relationship with a man from Ogmore Vale. According to her, she had

> been going out with him regularly on Saturday nights. They had been together to the pictures, and to Cardiff and Porthcawl.

It was not until 'she was in trouble' that she found out that he was married. When she told him of her condition the man said that he would 'take rooms' for her, an offer which she had declined. Now she was appealing to the court for an order to make him support their child.

In one sad note in his Diary, May refers to the finding of a foetus in an air raid shelter at the Arsenal. One other case of' 'immorality' was reported in the *Gazette* in July 1941 under the headline:

INDECENT SHOW AT FACTORY

According to the evidence, Dorothy Nicholl from Ogmore-by-Sea, an assistant forewoman at the Arsenal, came across a cluster of eight or nine girls gathered together in a workshop. She went up to the group to tell them to get on with their work, when she noticed one woman slip 'something in the leg of her stocking.' On investigation this 'something' proved to be a bunch of indecent photographs. There is no hint in the article as to exactly what the photos showed, and perhaps today they might not be seen to be very shocking. In the context of the 1940s, however, the pictures were taken very seriously indeed. The view of the Factory management was expressed to the court by Mrs Shields, described as a welfare worker at the Arsenal. According to Mrs Shields,

> officials were very concerned because such incidents did not contribute to discipline, and it upset the girls. [The management] felt a certain responsibility for the young girls who were employed there, and would like to feel that after the war they could send the young girls back to their homes not worse, but all the better for being there.

Two women from the Cynon Valley were held to be responsible for the incident: one was 22 years old, and from Abercwmboi, the other 30, and from Ynysboeth. Both had husbands in the army, but this had not saved them from being sacked by the Arsenal.

They were both found guilty of 'exhibiting an indecent show' at the Factory. The Chairman of the magistrates showed his intense disapproval of the women's actions by regretting that he did not have the power to send the two to prison. Bathetically they were actually fined just £5 each.

So much wickedness! Writing in the *Western Mail* in 1949, J Alun Jones sternly declared that the arrival of tens of thousands of workers into the area every day had 'a terrific impact on the social structure, and standards were seriously threatened.' According to Jones, 'Bridgend never really recovered its tone after that experience.' Strange how a previous time is always looked back on as a Golden Age.

Security

Factory security was managed by the War Department Constabulary (in association with the local Police), and the local Home Guard, which was drawn from the staff of the Arsenal. All the entrances were controlled by police posts where the passes of workers and visitors were checked. Adjacent search rooms facilitated checking on illicit contraband. Unsurprisingly in the atmosphere of a struggle for the survival of the nation there was a constant fear of terrorism and conspiracy, though this fear was to prove totally unjustified at Bridgend[10]. As Wayne Cocroft comments in *Dangerous Energy*:

> Fifth Columnists were also regarded as a very real danger, although in practice this threat never materialised.

Nevertheless, it was a concern at the time. As we have seen, during the building of the Arsenal in February 1939, a trade union official warned that workers brought in from overseas and from Ireland might 'give information to potential enemies and create sabotage,' though his principal concern at that time was actually to ensure the employment of local men rather than the security of the realm. In fact the police did have genuine worries about possible infiltration by the IRA amongst the Irish members of the Arsenal workforce. The IRA presented a very real terrorist threat in Britain at that time: in January and February 1939 they had detonated bombs in four English cities, and several people were killed. However, it is doubtful that the authorities took seriously the claims of Joseph Ryan of Limerick, a bricklayer at the Arsenal. When arrested for being drunk and disorderly in July 1939, he warned the constables 'I might belong to the IRA for all you know. There are a lot of people that do.' What the police did to him is not recorded.

Also in February 1939 a fire in the printing and photograph department at the Arsenal was, according to *The Times*, at first suspected to be sabotage – plans and blueprints were destroyed, and this might have delayed the completion of the Factory. It turned out that the actual cause was nothing more sinister than a carelessly discarded cigarette end!

Concern increased as war approached. On 26th August 1939 Superintendent May was consulting with the commander of the armed forces guarding the Arsenal about the potential for 'sabotage, and other treasonable or subversive activities.'

Once hostilities had actually begun, the possibility of treasonable activities became even more real. It will be recalled that on January 9th 1940 May received a warning from the Ministry of

Supply that 'sabotage is suspected by a foreign power.' The following day he met with Brigade Major White, and Brigadier Alson and 'discussed the question of protecting the Factory.' Obviously neither the police nor the army had sufficient manpower, as 'the Brigadier was only prepared to supply guards for the vulnerable points between the fences,' and May was prepared to offer

> assistance by reconnoitring the whole site, but could not provide fixed numbers for fixed points.

Securing the perimeter was one thing, but there was obviously also concern about the enemy within, and the loyalty of some employees. May reports in his Diary that on 12th June he met with Superintendent Edmonds, the Factory manager, and 'discussed defence measures, and the employment of certain persons.' The concerns about these people were such that in July Glyn John of the Security Branch of Woolwich Arsenal arrived at Bridgend to meet May and Chief Inspector Crawley of the Royal Ordnance Factory Security Force. The three 'discussed the activities of political extremists.' Frustratingly this is the only information we have on this matter, so we have no idea who the suspects were, and what their extremism amounted to, fascism or communism?

May took the warnings about sabotage very seriously, and several entries in his Diary criticise others for being less than rigorous. In May 1941 a Mr Nicklaus of the Ministry of Home Security arrived at the police station, asking for transport and 6 inch maps of the area – apparently his job was to make a survey of the Arsenal. Because May had not received the proper prior notification, he not unreasonably refused to grant these requests. The visitor phoned his London headquarters, and got someone there to talk to May, but quite properly the uncompromising Superintendent continued to resist cooperation until proper written authority was forthcoming.

In February 1942 the German-born Dr Werenski was admitted to the Arsenal without the necessary papers of indemnity laid down in the Aliens Order. May was having none of that. Werenski was taken into open custody until the papers or a specific authority arrived. The Superintendent ends his entry for that day with the acerbic criticism: 'most lax methods of the Ministry of Supply.'

There are just two references to possible sabotage in May's Diary. On 18th September 1942 he was contacted by the Superintendent of the Arsenal, Corbett, and told that 'he had a case of suspected sabotage.' Apparently the worm of a mortar-filling machine had been damaged. When the apparatus was taken apart, two loose brass screws each about an inch and a half long and a quarter of an inch thick had been found in the workings. These screws were normally used to secure the powder boxes containing the material used to fill the mortars. The suspicion was that the screws had been put in the machine deliberately; the more likely explanation was that the screws had been carelessly swept up with surplus powder, and tipped into the machine by accident – though May confided to his Diary that 'Investigation is continuing.'

Then in May 1943 there was another report of alleged sabotage. May was told that a railway fishplate had been inserted in a rail in such a way that it caused an obstruction on one of the railway sidings at the Arsenal. Since May makes no further reference to this, we must assume that in this case, as the other, the cause was accident, rather than deliberate sabotage.

A court case that apparently did involve a treasonable action is mentioned in May's Diary in April 1941. It appears that a Mrs Morse had had the temerity to take a shell fuze out of the Arsenal, but the Diary is silent as to what happened to her. Since the subsequent court case would have taken place in camera there is no report of the outcome in the newspapers and so we shall never know what possessed her to take the fuze to her home.

We have evidence of the outcome of another case of sedition, though it seems not to have gone to court. On 10th March 1942 May notes that he received an Arsenal worker from Porthcawl who had caused 'despondency by making the false statement that he knew Singapore would fall some days before it actually did.' May did not form a very high opinion of the man: 'he seemed a wretched and miserable type of subject.' It appears that the spreader of defeatism got off relatively lightly, as May writes that he 'administered a stern warning.'

A case of subversion that did go to court involved the landlord of the Wyndham Hotel in Bridgend, who rejoiced in the name of Hippolite Meredic Malhomme. In October 1942 he was brought before the magistrates meeting in camera, and fined a total of £31 on two charges of careless talk while on a train journey between Bridgend and Cardiff. The accused seems to have been in possession of a great deal of secret information about the Arsenal, presumably heard across the bar in the Wyndham, and to have had the discretion of a sieve. According to May, Malhomme

> disclosed information of the personnel employed at the Arsenal being over 30,000. Number of train loads of shells and bombs filled and manufactured. Where the powder factory was and the situation of magazines.

He also shared with others in his compartment information on the RAF bases at Stormy Down, St Athan and Llandow. Although £31 was a great deal of money at that time, it is perhaps surprising that he got away without a custodial sentence.

In May 1943 *ROF 53 News* published an anonymous poet's parody of a well-known children's rhyme. The verses of 'Ten Little Process Girls' describe some of the indiscretions committed by workers at the Factory:

> Ten little Process girls, feeling rather fine;
> One had a transfer – so then there were nine.
> Nine little process girls, one was always late;
> NSO said 'certainly' – and then there were eight.
> Eight little process workers, innocents from heaven;
> One thought she'd go back home – and then there were seven.
> Seven little process girls went to see the flicks;
> One stayed fast asleep, and then there were six.
> Six little process workers, one said she could drive
> A big green bus to Admin. gate – and then there were five.
> Five little process workers helping with the war;
> One helped herself as well – and then there were four.
> Four little process workers all learned their GSD;
> One called it a waste of time – and then there were three
> Three little process workers had their share to do;
> One missed too many shifts – and then there were two.
> Two little process workers, when their work was done
> Went to meet the same boy friend – and then there was one.
> One little process girl thought she'd earned some fun;
> So married her shop manager – and then there was none.

Notes

1. Sir Andrew Rae Duncan, MP for City of London, Director of Bank of England, and of ICI. Chairman of British Iron and Steel Federation. Minister of Supply for most of the War.
2. Based on figures in Inman *Labour in the Munitions Industry.*
3. Based on statistics at Kew (LAB 26/131)
4. Kew (AVIA22/704)
5. Based on information in Industrial Health Research Board: *A Case Study into Absenteeism at Bridgend.*
6. This flattering opinion of married women does not seem to have been shared by most authorities who studied the high rates of absenteeism amongst women in filling factories. Hay's opinion is more typical: 'Some small domestic upheaval or emergency might keep a married woman fast bound to her own fireside for a matter of days.'
7. There is perhaps something strangely reassuring for us in the 21st century to discover that drunken behaviour in the streets of Bridgend is not a new phenomenon!
8. 'The Cuckoo, then, on every tree, mocks married men.' – Shakespeare: *Love's Labour's Lost.*
9. 1930s musical by Cole Porter, Guy Bolton & PG Wodehouse.
10. In May 1939 Joseph Kelly, a bricklayer at Chorley pleaded guilty to selling plans of that factory to German agents for £30: He was sentenced to 10 years penal servitude.

12: Victory – and a Familiar Spectre

Fireworks and Dancing

At 2.41 am on 7th May 1945, in the red-brick Modern Technical University at Reims in France, General Alfred Jodl, the German Army's chief of staff, signed the instrument of unconditional surrender which ended the war in western Europe.

Back in Wales, May 8th was VE day. Mair Davies was at work in the Arsenal, and she still

> remembers the excitement when VE Day was announced. It came over the loudspeakers, and everyone was so happy.

The workers at ROF 53 would have been even happier with the three days off with pay allowed by the management. In all the communities from which workers travelled each day to the armaments Factory at Bridgend there were joyful celebrations. Streets, houses, shops and offices were festooned with flags and buntings. Bonfires, some topped with effigies of Hitler, blazed in every district. Church bells rang out, and churches and chapels were open for services. Every street in all the valleys seemed to have a street party, entertainment and sports for the children – and the grown ups. The *Glamorgan Gazette* reported that in Bridgend itself 'the town took on a gay appearance,' and that 'crowds thronged the streets, singing and dancing in Dunraven Place till the early hours of the morning.' One Factory worker, Peggy Hawkins, remembers,

> We celebrated; everyone was dancing in the streets, waving flags. My brother took my family from Llangeinor into town, and it was full. Everyone stood in the centre of Bridgend rejoicing that Britain had won the war.

At the Arsenal it was decided to commemorate the event with a bang. Still constrained by wartime restrictions the *Gazette* recorded that 'a firework display was given from' what it coyly described as 'a nearby factory.' The young David Lazell was 'a little disappointed by the show.' Along with most of the other inhabitants of the Arsenal's Abergarw Estate, he had trekked up the hill through Bryncethin to the water meter house at Cefn Hirgoed Common to watch the display organized down below at the Brackla site. To David the pyrotechnics he was able to see compared unfavourably with the weekly Brock displays he had observed before the war in the grounds of the Crystal Palace back in his native London. Presumably the locals found the show exciting, less accustomed as they were to metropolitan splendour.

Perhaps the Factory management thought that this firework display was a good way of using up surplus products in the stores. For General Jodl's signature marked not only the end of the war in western Europe, it also signalled the end for armaments production at ROF 53. In June there were allegations in the *Daily Express* that there was so little work for those employed at the Bridgend Factory, that they spent their time entertaining themselves with piano playing and dancing. The article in the *Express*, written by Roy Nash, was headlined: 'Arms workers dance to fill in time, but they draw full pay.' The description of affairs at Bridgend suggested that only half the workforce was actually needed 'for the drastically reduced production programme,' so many workers had nothing constructive to do. Nash began the article:

> Today they clocked in at 6.45 am as usual, and spent their time cutting the factory grass, scraping black-out paint off windows, and cleaning the canteens.

And then,

> When even the oddest of odd jobs are scarce, pianos are wheeled into the workshops, and men and women kill time by dancing between the benches.

The journalist quoted an employee as claiming that

> This Factory is just like a Marx Brothers' film now. Everybody is fed up with wasting time when there is so much work to be done getting the country back to normal.

Wittily, the journalist concluded that 'Instead of filling in shells, many of the workers are filling in time.'

The Factory management announced that 'an inquiry had been made into the allegations,' but that unsurprisingly 'it had not been possible to trace any of the particular incidents referred to.' It certainly seems unlikely that anyone would go to the trouble of hauling pianos into workshops when music was routinely broadcast about the site. The workers at the Arsenal were passionately defended by Sergeant AE Jones of Blaengwynfi, a winner of the Military Medal, who wrote to The *Advertiser* to complain that

> so much attention is being drawn to the supposed dancing and entertainments now being held in the ROF at Bridgend. Memory is short, as it is only a little while ago that young girls, elderly women and men were being carried out on stretchers maimed for life… Surely if there is at the moment some leisure time, through no fault of the workers, who are more entitled to enjoy it than these people.

A Ministry of Labour official is quoted by Nash as demanding to know 'What do you expect us to do? Throw people out on the streets?' The local MP, Ted Williams, also denounced the criticism: 'The talk about persons jigging about is sheer political nonsense,' he said. He went on to claim that the accusations were designed to 'discredit Mr Bevin, the Minister of Labour,' who had decreed that workers 'should be retained in Industry in systematic order until the Japanese war is over.' This was probably a correct analysis. The General Election was only a fortnight away; the Beaverbrook press was running a frantic campaign in support of the Conservative party, and was eager to denounce anything that smacked of the wasteful continuation of 'central control.' Nash himself characterised his article as 'the story of many thousands of men and women trussed up in the essential Work Order, and the multitude of Ministry of Labour regulations.' And Bridgend was not the only target. For several days the *Express* ran stories of idle workers in other factories eager to return to their pre-war employment, but frustrated by red tape.

In fact the fighting in the Far East continued to August. Richard Rees described the joy at the Arsenal when the end came.

> Green Shift was on nights again when an announcement blared over the loudspeaker: 'Will all workers assemble in their canteen at midnight.' There was an excited buzz of conversation. It could only mean one thing – it was all over. In a dozen canteens a mighty roar hit the ceiling. Then we sang Welsh hymns, fervently, emotionally. Tears glistened in the eyes of many women.

Rowena Harris (nee Greenslade), who worked in the Arsenal canteen, remembers that

> on VJ Day we danced round the Square in Pontycymer, and then we went to the Conservative Club on the hill.

The celebrations in Bridgend included a parade through the town, and a thanksgiving service at the Baths Field in the Recreation Grounds. The report in the *Gazette* suggests that the huge contribution of the workers at the Arsenal to the war effort was recognized, as employees from the Factory took part in the march and service, and the superintendent of ROF 53, Len Corbett, had a place of honour on the dais set up for dignitaries.

Despite Bevin's initial diktat, employees were laid off in their thousands. By the time of the VJ celebrations there were only 9,000 people left at the Arsenal. Most of those remaining had been laid off by the New Year. What was to happen to the Factory, and to those who worked there? And what would be the long-term legacy of the huge wartime effort at Bridgend?

The Fate of Government Factories

Since the many armaments factories built across Britain after 1935, including that at Bridgend, had been constructed to provide weapons for a war against Germany, it was inevitable that most of them would be closed down when that war ended. But the Labour Government elected in July 1945 decided that, in order to exercise a world role as one of the Great Powers, it was essential to have substantial well trained and well equipped armed forces able to react quickly to future emergencies.[1] To this end some armaments installations would have to be retained – even if these factories had to pay their way in time of peace in part by producing civilian products for civilian markets. As a consequence of this decision the fates of the different ROFs were not the same.

A number of munitions factories across Britain were selected to have post-war military functions. In south Wales, Pembrey continued to produce TNT and Tetryl (as well as Ammonium Nitrate for the agricultural industry) until 1964. The Royal Navy Propellant Factory at Caerwent continued production till 1967, and then was maintained as a storage facility till 1993. The ROF engineering factory at Cardiff was retained, and eventually worked on Britain's nuclear programme: it was not closed till 1997. Glascoed was kept permanently, initially filling naval ammunition. For a time a quarter of its production was non-military equipment, such as concrete railway sleepers, Airey houses[2] and jerry cans. But in the late 1950s it took over the munitions work of Thorp Arch and Swynnerton, when they were closed, and concentrated on producing a high standard of modern ammunition. Glascoed is still in operation today.

As far as filling factories like Bridgend were concerned, the government decided to retain just three[3] – Glascoed, Swynnerton (near Stoke-on-Trent), and Chorley. The retention of Chorley was a gesture which did not save the parliamentary seat for the Conservatives: Labour took the constituency in the election of 1945. Like Glascoed, Chorley was at first partly used to produce non-military equipment, including housing, specialist packaging, railway sleepers and clothing for the services and work. But its main function for several years was in breaking down and making safe or destroying surplus ammunition – including stores from Bridgend. Chorley functioned as an armaments factory until 2007.

Swynnerton rather than Bridgend was selected by the Ministry of Supply to continue to operate as a filling factory after the war at least partly because it was believed that ROF 53 was more suitable for conversion into a civilian trading estate. Swynnerton had been built to much lower standards than the Factory in southern Wales: the Arsenal was begun in peacetime, while the building of Swynnerton commenced after the start of hostilities. Thus Kohan in the official book, *Works and Buildings*, describes the Staffordshire factory as being

> built hurriedly with fewer materials to chose from, without frills or refinements, and as a temporary construction. There was more timber work, walls were reduced to 4½ inches of brick, and there was no steelwork inside buildings.

The argument seems to have been that private firms could be attracted into the better quality buildings at Bridgend – though that of course would have been a justification for closing both Chorley and Glascoed! Like other retained ROFs, Swynnerton, too, took on civilian work in the form of electrical ceramics: the factory closed in 1957.

Apart from these three, all the other filling factories, including ROF 53, were surplus to requirements, and were to be closed as quickly as possible. Unsurprisingly there was a dramatic fall in the amount of filled ammunition produced in Britain – from 2500 tons in the month of April 1945, to 133 tons by December, and to 17 tons by July of 1946.

What of Bridgend? The story is not a straightforward one. The local Trades Union Council appealed to the Minister of Supply, John Wilmot, for a re-think on the decision to close the Factory. In October 1945 his secretary sent a letter[4]. which confirmed that ROF 53 would not continue to operate. 'We cannot find a place for more than three filling factories in our permanent peace establishment,' he wrote. In case the members of the Council still did not understand the certainty of his minister's decision, he added, 'We have said that we do not need Bridgend as a permanent filling factory, and are unable to go back on our word.' That seemed very much to be that. Yet despite this apparent finality, there were two areas of the Factory which continued to serve military purposes for a time – as will be seen.

Planning for the Future

Concerns about the future for the workers at Bridgend had surfaced long before the end of the fighting in Europe. During the war the demands of the national emergency meant that there was a high level of employment in the valleys of Glamorgan – a happy state of affairs to which the Arsenal at Bridgend, other munitions establishments and the demands of the armed forces had made a major contribution. But everyone was aware of the problems caused to communities during the 1920s and 1930s by high rates of unemployment and deprivation. And alarmingly, in 1944 the Advisory Council on Welsh Reconstruction report showed that between 40% and 50% of all workers in new industries were in establishments that might stop or curtail their activities after the war.

Now that the war was over, and the stimulus to employment that it had given was ended, what would happen to the economy of the area that had benefited so much from the existence of ROF 53? In an editorial of 21st June 1945 on the future of the Bridgend Factory, the *Western Mail* summed up the magnitude of the task thus:

> The eventual re-allocation of labour will not be easy to arrange. Indeed it may be said that nowhere else in Wales is the problem of comparable magnitude and difficulty.

There seems to have been a determination on all sides to ensure that the devastation caused by unemployment in the inter-war years could never be experienced again. During the war there had been a considerable amount of discussion about and planning for the future. As early as September 1943, Len Corbett, had led a discussion in Admin. Canteen on Immediate Post-War Problems. Meanwhile in London, during the November of the same year, a Ministry of Reconstruction was set up under the popular ex-Minister for Food, Lord Woolton[5]. A White Paper in 1944 pledged the Government and its successors to 'the maintenance of a high and stable level of employment after the war.' An

Advisory Council for Welsh Reconstruction, chaired by JF Rees, was appointed, and reported to Woolton. According to KO Morgan this Welsh report

> was shot through with a fierce determination that the land should not be allowed to sink into the economic decay that had paralysed it for so long.

In particular the authors of the report recommended that the overwhelming dependence in south Wales on a few heavy industries – coal and metals – should be greatly reduced by the encouragement of a much more diverse economy. The 1940 report of the Royal Commission on the location of population and industry in the whole of Britain, chaired by Anderson Montague-Barlow, had given support to this demand. It had recommended that Governments should have the powers to refuse the establishment of additional undertakings in London and the south east of England, and the powers to encourage new industries to open in deprived areas – all this to ensure a well-balanced industrial substructure in each region of Britain.

The 1945 Distribution of Industry Act and the 1947 Town and Country Planning Act were the product of these wartime deliberations. The Acts gave Government the powers to use a licensing system to deter new enterprises from setting up in already prosperous areas, to create and manage trading estates, to build advance factories in designated Development Areas such as south Wales, to provide finance for the provision of basic services (including power, lighting, and housing) and to allocate grants to industrialists to encourage them to invest in those deprived places. In fact the South Wales Development Area, created in June 1945, was virtually coterminous with the pre-war ineffective Special Area – but the ability of the Government to direct and intervene was now far greater, and far more effective. For example the authorities would use the Board of Trade's building-licence scheme vigorously to steer industry into Glamorgan.

The Spectre of Unemployment

A war command economy cannot be switched to a peacetime economy overnight, and it would be several years before the areas of south Wales which had provided the huge workforce for the Bridgend Arsenal would experience full employment in civilian enterprises.

As far back as July 1944 Maesteg Council had been in discussions with the Board of Trade about the post war employment position in the Llynfi Valley. In April 1945 councillors representing a number of affected local authorities secured a meeting[6] at the Factory with the President of the Board of Trade, Hugh Dalton.[7] He pointed out to the meeting 'what had been done in South Wales to encourage new factories and to set up new trading estates.' As far as Bridgend ROF was concerned Dalton promised that 'a great deal of the Factory would be kept on after the cessation of hostilities, and the rest could be used as a trading estate.' Like most skilled politicians, Dalton had given his audience what they wanted to hear, and they went away in large part reassured about the future.

Once the Arsenal began to reduce production, and people were released from the Factory, the local trade unions showed that they were anything but reassured by what was happening. For the two years from March 1943 the number of workers employed at Bridgend had stayed stable, at around 20,000. In March 1945, before the surrender of Germany, 19,921 were still employed there. On May 1st, a week before Jodl's appointment in Reims, the Factory management announced that Brackla A would close in six weeks with the loss of 700 jobs, and that 900 other Arsenal workers would be made redundant[8]. By June there were still 17,133 on roll, but the unions were told that the future was 'very black.' DJ Keen, representing the unions at the Arsenal, expressed the problem with a bleak sense of humour:

> There is nothing facing these people but the employment exchange – unless perhaps they obtain work as clerks at those exchanges, because that looks like being the only industry that will thrive in South Wales.

A few employees could be sanguine about their futures: key managers and workers who obtained posts in the new trading estate; specialists who were transferred to Chorley or other ROF factories which continued to operate.

In the next months thousands of workers were let loose onto the saturated labour market of Glamorgan. By September over half the workforce had been made redundant, and only 8520 remained at the Factory. But by now the unions apparently had little faith in the confidence expressed back in April by Dalton. In a resolution[9] sent to the local MP, Ted Williams, the trade unions expressed their 'very serious concerns as to the future of the ROF.' They went on to claim that

> the rate of redundancy… will have disastrous effects on the people of this area and the surrounding mining valleys.

They suggested that some munitions work should continue at the Arsenal instead of being sent to Lancashire:

> Thousands of people are being discharged with no alternative employment, yet they are taking stuff from Bridgend to Chorley to break down in spite of the fact that there was employment in these other areas. They are even bringing in people from away into the Factory to dismantle machinery when it could be done by local labour.

And they warned against an even more shocking consequence; as between the wars, 'large numbers of young people would have to leave south Wales to look for work in England.'

In October the *Gazette* reported that by October 5th

> some 14,000 people would have left the Factory, after which they would be leaving at the rate of 1,000 a month.

Presumably about 5,000 were left there at that time. The local unions could well remember the economic and employment condition of south Wales before the war – just a few years earlier – and now the demands of the conflict had ended they had very real fears that similar problems would return. It was no surprise that the chairman of the Trades Council, D Ivor Davies, wanted 'some assurance that the spectre of unemployment, poverty and want would not again become an accepted fact.'

'It's a Lovely Day Tomorrow'

Faced with these anxieties, in December the Government sent no less a person than Sir Stafford Cripps, President of the Board of

Trade, down to Bridgend to try to assuage the very real fears of the unions. Cripps' report seemed to promise a New Jerusalem in the valleys of Wales. According to him within three years there would be 6,700 jobs in new firms on the former ROF site, 3,000 of which would be available within the next 12 months. In addition part of the Arsenal (presumably the tunnels at Brackla) would be retained for storage purposes and this would provide employment for hundreds more. He promised hope for other areas, too, with new factories at Llantrisant, Maesteg and Pyle, employing 2,900 altogether. In more general terms, Cripps claimed that the government was committed to the provision of 110,000 jobs across southern Wales, and that

> the diversity of production would ensure that no large scale unemployment would ever again arise in mid Glamorgan, as happened before through relying on the basic industry of coal.

Consequently 'the fears of long term unemployment could be removed,' and all this 'would guarantee a new era for the people of Wales.' To provide jobs while the programme of new factories was being developed Cripps promised 'to encourage the provision of employment' on public works schemes such as schools, houses, hospitals, factories, and roads. Like a magician Cripps seemed to have pulled full employment out of a hat. Unsurprisingly, his words were received with great enthusiasm, and according to the *Gazette* 'many delegates expressed their complete satisfaction with the President's statement.'

That Christmas a witty card was published at the Arsenal. A photo montage of senior managers around a table included an image of the superintendent, Len Corbett, in front of a graph of production rising from nothing in 1940 to a peak in 1944, and falling away in the time honoured fashion of bankrupt firms in cartoons, right down the wall by the end of 1945. On the table is a cake decorated with fuzes and initiators. This may have been highly amusing for the management, but doubtless the unemployed of Glamorgan would have struggled to see the joke.

During the following year, 1946, the euphoria engendered by Cripps was dissipated by persistent unemployment in the south Wales valleys. In a less upbeat but more realistic speech at a confer-

ence in London in March, attended by the unions from Glamorgan, the Minister of Labour, George Isaacs, pointed out 'that there was bound to be some unemployment because of the change over from war-time to peace-time production.' Patronisingly he advised the union officials that 'they should keep calm and collected, and not get alarmed.' This was not enough for the unions, who were in turn distressed by persistent unemployment, and cheered by optimistic promises from central Government. In March D Ivor Davies was reporting to the unions[10] that a factory employing 3,000 to manufacture a mysterious new wax would be coming to the former ROF, and that with the 7,000 promised by Cripps, plus 3,000 working to turn Llandow into a civil airport, the Bridgend area could look forward to become 'the most prosperous area in Wales, and probably in Great Britain.'

But not yet. In May over 4,500 people were unemployed[11] in Bridgend and its valleys[12], and many of the 800 jobs that had just been created at the former Arsenal had been taken by girls aged under 18. By September the local unemployment figure had risen to nearly 5,000; when Neath and Port Talbot were added in there

On the table a 2″ mortar; on the cake, left and right, fuzes; at the back a primer for naval shell; at front, rocket igniter

was a total of 7,690 registered as without work from this core part of the original catchment area of ROF 53. Further afield the situation was no better; in the Rhondda in July almost 7,000 people were registered as unemployed.

As the situation worsened old rivalries and mistrusts between town and valleys resurfaced. Accusations were made that workers from the Bridgend area were being given preferential treatment at the former ROF. A representative from the Garw valley complained[13], not unreasonably, that

> if the workers of the Valleys were good enough to work at Bridgend during the war, then they are good enough to have a share of the work that is going there now.

All sides could unite in attacking perceived advantages being given to the English regions. D Ivor Davies complained[14] that

> whereas south Wales and the mining valleys in particular do not appear to be having priority in materials, you find in places like the Midlands they are so well advanced that they seem to be short of labour.

This was a shortage that Davies claimed was being made up by workers from Wales:

> Hundreds of men and women had left the Principality since the war to find work in the Midlands – a loss that Wales could not afford.

Davies, no longer as optimistic as in March, concluded with a rallying cry:

> There is a danger that south Wales is being left in the lurch… Are we to allow South Wales to go through another period of depression and unemployment, or shall we make a very strong stand?

Concern continued to the end of that year and beyond. The unions had clear policies to deal with the problem. They wanted an end to the Means Test and an increase in the unemployment benefit, termination of the transference of labour from Wales, the compulsory direction of firms to areas of high unemployment, a speedier switch over from war to peacetime production at the former Bridgend ROF, more jobs, and higher Government grants to local authorities for public works in the interim period. A mass demonstration of workers in support of these demands was held in Bridgend on November 30th, 1946. It is impossible to say how big the demonstration was: the *Gazette* report gives no numbers. It simply records that the Blaengarw Band led a procession round the town of men bearing banners and that this was followed by a meeting in the Town Hall at which there were a number of speeches. County Councillor Jenkin John spoke about the future of the Arsenal. He was insistent that the new trading estate should be publicly owned because 'It was built as a national arsenal out of public funds, and belongs to the people.' His frustration at the time it was taking to create jobs on the former filling Factory site is shown in this passage:

> We have been told that factories are coming there when the buildings have been converted, but that is not enough. We must stress that these factories be put into operation immediately, that our men shall not be thrown back on the scrap heap.

All this union effort and clamour seemed to have little effect. A year later, in November 1947, the unemployment rate in Wales was higher than any area of Scotland or England, at 5.2%, representing 44,000 people[15]. Things could only get better.

Notes

1 Such as the Korean War (1950-1953)

2 Two storey pre-cast concrete panelled and steel framed buildings designed by Edwin Airey to deal with the post-war housing crisis.

3 In addition, Burghfield (near Reading) and Thorp Arch (in Yorkshire) were both reactivated during the Korean War.

4 *Gazette* 2.11.45

5 Who gave his name to a war-time dish, the Woolton Pie, which consisted of carrots, parsnips, potatoes and turnips in oatmeal, topped with a pastry or potato crust and served with brown gravy.

6 *Advertiser* 4.5.45

7 Later to be Chancellor of the Exchequer under Attlee.

8 *Gazette* 22.6.45

9 *Gazette* 7.9.45

10 *Gazette* 5.4.46

11 *Gazette* 7.6.46

12 Bridgend 1341; Ogmore Vale 708; Garw 875; Maesteg 1633.

13 *Gazette* 5.4.46

14 *Gazette* 11.10.46

15 KO Morgan *Wales 1880-1980* Ch 11

Cast of Abergarw Estate's *Aladdin*, Christmas 1945

13: Swords into Ploughshares

The Legacy of the Bridgend Arsenal.

The process of change may have been too slow for the unions, but it was inevitable and inexorable. Post-war South Wales was in a far better position to attract willing investors because of the very considerable outcomes of the wartime experience. The demands of war had compelled the Government to enforce social changes, to invest many millions of pounds, and so to create facilities and services which would not have existed otherwise. Many of these changes endured into the post-war period, and led in due course to the creation of an entirely new economic and social structure in the catchment area of the former Arsenal. What exactly was this legacy?

In the first place the ROF at Bridgend had been part of an amazingly complex yet hugely successful pattern of supply, manufacture and transport to many other places around Britain. The integration of south Wales into this war production machine through the railway network helped to eliminate the perception of industrialists in England that the area was somehow too remote and difficult to be a location for modern industries.

As well as armaments many other new industries had been directed to Wales during the war; some remained[1], and so provided the beginnings of a more diverse economy than had existed hitherto. This in turn acted as a multiplier and offered the opportunity for other new enterprises to succeed.

By working in places like the Bridgend Arsenal tens of thousands of people in Glamorgan had acquired many new, intricate and transferable skills. Ken Morgan in *Wales 1880-1980* describes the post-war workforce as

> more adaptable to newer technology, more familiar with the handling of modern machinery, and better suited for employment in engineering and light manufacturing.

In addition a large core of experienced foremen and managers had been created which could be used in the organisation of new enterprises.

This was especially the experience of many women from ROF 53 and other armaments factories. Female workers had had the benefit of good salaries, and the advantages that had given to themselves and their families. And as Graham Humphrys writes in his book, *Industrial Britain – South Wales*,

> Familiarity also established the respectability of factory work, which was an important factor in the social context of the region.

Many of the women of southern Wales now had a different attitude towards such employment. Here was a large and willing pool of labour for new factories. As a correspondent in the *Gazette* gushed in July 1945,

> Man has humbled himself to admit that the frivolous female can be as efficient with a drilling machine as she was with cooking pans.

The attraction of the Bridgend Arsenal had encouraged people to journey from some distance, and often at considerable inconvenience. Although people might not be so ready to travel so far in peacetime, nevertheless a culture had developed in Glamorgan in which travel to work outside one's community was accepted as normal.

Finally the physical legacy of the Factory itself was supremely important. This was a time of rapidly expanding markets and opportunities for manufacturers, but also a time when materials, labour and licenses to construct new buildings were all at a premium right across the United Kingdom. But here at Bridgend was a vast treasure trove of opportunity for entrepreneurs – a huge site of 380 acres with hundreds of empty buildings totalling 1,630,000 square feet, and suited to conversion for small or medium enterprises plus a few large firms. In addition the site was connected to the rest of Britain through extensive railway sidings, and was provided with all services except gas – a deficiency soon remedied.

At Last, Prosperity

Over the next few years this inheritance from the war, plus consumer demand and government policies brought the often promised but long delayed Utopia to the area that had supplied the vast workforce to the Arsenal. By 1949, 179 new factories had opened in South Wales of which 112 were government-assisted projects. Captain Oram, the Board of Trade controller in Wales announced that a grand total of 64,000 jobs had been created since 1945[2]. The unemployment rate then was just 2.8% – compared with over 20% just before the start of the war. This was a remarkable return to a prosperity last experienced thirty years before, at the end of the First World War. The editor of *The South Wales Industrial Review* for January 1950 was roused sufficiently to proclaim that a second industrial revolution had totally transformed the economy of south Wales.

Very many jobs were made available in the communities from which workers had travelled to Bridgend. In the Rhondda 25 factories, many of them government-assisted, had been opened by 1955. These establishments produced goods as diverse as toys, batteries, bicycles, mattresses and clothes; over 5,000 were employed in these works, about 3,000 women and 2,000 men.

The development of industrial (or trading[3]) estates was a major part of the Development area strategy, and several of these besides Bridgend would provide opportunities for former Arsenal workers. The Trefforest Trading Estate had been started before the war. By 1955 there were 80 factories based there, employing nearly 10,000 people, of which a third were women. The former small arms factory at Hirwaun was closed and converted to industrial use; by 1947 25 businesses had been set up there in the former ROF buildings. Old industries were not forgotten – employment opportunities were enhanced by the investment of nearly £32million in the collieries of the Cardiff region by 1953, including a huge new project at Nantgarw.

Spears into Pruning Hooks.

There was progress at Bridgend, too. Conversion from wartime to peacetime use began on the ROF as soon as the decision was taken not to keep the Arsenal as an armaments factory. This was quite a lengthy process as the site had first to be decontaminated because of the many chemicals that had been used at the Factory. In due course most of the land, buildings and services were transferred from the Ministry of Supply to the Board of Trade, which intended to create an industrial estate on the Waterton site under the management of Wales and Monmouthshire Industrial Estates.

Two areas of the Arsenal continued to deal with munitions for a time, so providing a link with the immediate past:

On the Brackla site the tunnels were kept for the storage of ammunition, and the fuze factory was retained, operated by the Ministry of Works (later the Ministry of Public Buildings and Works) and providing parts to the Admiralty till 1963.

At Waterton, part of the West section was railed off since it had been retained to supply munitions to the Royal Navy. David Lazell, who worked at the estate in its earliest days, remembers that

> for quite a time the black composition walkways away from the main road were busy with trolleys humming along with interesting ordnance under wraps. These displays were organized by the RNAD,[4] which also had a nice line in trucks painted a deep blue.

One part of the former Arsenal – the main administration buildings – was destined to have a grand new function. Before 1939 the Glamorgan Police authority had planned to build their new HQ near the Ewenny roundabout on a site that is today the

Bridgend Science Park, but Hitler put paid to that idea. After the war the authority bought the former Arsenal administration buildings from the Estate for £68,000, and converted them into the Glamorgan Police Headquarters. On 15th February 1947, there was a grand opening by James Chuter Ede, the Home Secretary, at which he declared to the Authority,

> You have an headquarters of which the force itself can feel proud – a home that is worthy of them.

The former Burning Ground eventually became the site of South Wales Police Sports and Social Club.

But the rest of the Waterton site became the Bridgend Trading Estate. According to a report presented to the Trades Council in September 1945, the Factory was quickly being prepared for its new life as a civilian industrial estate. The 'Board of Trade were hurrying up the clearing of certain workshops,' and machinery was being removed and sent to other factories. The plan at that time was that the east side of the Arsenal would be turned over to private firms, and the expectation was that by the start of 1946 about 6 firms employing1,600 people would be in operation. The west half was to be retained by the Admiralty, and if the plans formulated were accepted by the Ministry of Supply it would mean that work would be provided there for at least a year or two.

The people who wanted to start new businesses needed office equipment as well as buildings, and the ROF had plenty available. Mair Davies, who worked in stores, recalls that

> people who wanted to open new factories on the site used to come to buy tables, chairs and filing cabinets. I stayed on to book these out to people. I was one of the last [ROF employees] to go.

Some people had tried to acquire equipment in a less conventional way. As the Factory began to wind down, it became even more vulnerable to theft. In July 1945 the *Gazette* reported the case of a transport driver from Nantyffyllon, who had acquired a wooden table from the mess room of the garage at the Administration buildings. Apparently he had taken the table, hidden it under a hedge at the perimeter fence, and then, when going home, stopped and picked it up. His defence, that he had taken the table for a bet and had intended to return it, must have been offered more in hope than expectation – certainly it was not accepted by the magistrates. The Chairman of the Bench mused

> we cannot understand how it was possible for an article of this size to be taken away unnoticed. At this rate it would not be surprising to see the Factory taken away.

Which, in a way, in the end, it was.

At first firms began to move into the existing ex-ordnance buildings. If not necessarily entirely suitable, they were at least available. David Lazell worked in one of the first businesses to open on the Arsenal at 1.L.13. According to David,

> it was housed in a row of rather lightweight buildings, with very limited insulation properties, as we discovered in the hard winter of 1946-47; but there was room for development.

The firm of Kiefts occupied the enormous former Textile building at OM 15/16/17. Over time structures were adapted to peacetime use; for example clerestory windows were inserted into roofs to provide more natural light. At first this alterations programme was hindered by an inevitable post-war shortage of materials and specialist labour, but by April 1947 the estates company was working on 74 projects and had already completed adaptation work covering nearly 500,000 sq ft.

Changes were also made to the services on the estate. There had been no gas supply to the munitions Factory because of the danger of explosion. Industrialists needed this alternative source of energy, so an ingenious solution was found that was both cheap and avoided the disruption of laying a completely new system. There had been two separate water supplies to the Arsenal – the normal, or domestic system, and the emergency system. Engineers decided to use the former 'domestic' water piping to transport gas about the site, leaving the former emergency water pipelines to continue to carry water. The electricity power station on the estate was found to be uneconomic, so it was demolished, and the supply obtained instead from the Electricity Board. This in turn caused another problem. The steam from the power station had been used to heat the buildings of ROF 53, so the estate management had to install a coal boiler for each group of buildings – about 160 Cochran boilers in all.[5] The aboveground pipe work that had carried the steam about the site, and that was such a distinctive feature of the Arsenal was then removed. This was actually a benefit to the expense of running the estate since the value of the loss of energy through radiation from these pipes was estimated at £200,000 pa. The total cost of all these alterations to the services was £500,000, which had to be paid for by the Industrial Estates Company.

The Board of Trade retained ownership of a total of 44 ROF houses which continued to house key workers and managers. The former superintendent of the Arsenal, Len Corbett, became the manager of the new facility, thus providing a smooth transition from munitions factory to industrial estate. In October 1947 he was promoted to the management of all government estates and factories in Wales: he was replaced by Brigadier JK Jones.

On the Bridgend estate factories began to open for business, and increasing numbers of people were employed. In December 1945 Stafford Cripps was able to visit two of the newly opened factories. It was during this visit that he promised 6700 jobs at the Arsenal in the future, 3000 by the end of 1946. In fact his primary target was missed by some 600 jobs, and his long-term objective had not been achieved by 1970! Not the last time that optimistic government targets were not reached.

In May 1946 there were just 800 workers on the industrial estate. In that month a photographic essay about the new industrial estate appeared in *The Times*. Five photos show workers (mainly women) at work in former ordnance buildings – including one welding an aeroplane seat frame. Other activities pictured are the manufacture of: cushions for aircraft seats (Christie, Tyler); wallpaper trimming machines (Thomas Machine Co.); collar studs (CH Collins); men's shoes (George Webb and Sons). The journalist notes that the footwear company had brought skilled operatives from its Northampton factory to Bridgend 'to teach women who were formerly working on munitions at the ordnance Factory.'

The number employed at the site rose to 1,427 by September 1946 (when 28 firms were operating), and to 2,380 by the end of that year. Included in that figure were 74 workers at Remploy – the first factory for the disabled in Britain. In a flight of florid phrasing the Minister of Labour, George Isaacs encouraged the disabled by declaring them to be 'the flotsam and jetsam of industry and war,' who, through Remploy factories, 'would not be thrown up and left useless on the beach of life.' By the following year 74 firms were operating on the estate. The number of workers employed on the estate increased gradually – to 3250 in 1950, and to 4900 by 1955[6].

Employment at Bridgend Industrial Estate 1946 - 1970

Year	Numbers Employed
1946	2380
1950	3250
1955	4900
1965	6040
1970	6597

David Lazell's father set up one of the first businesses on the estate – a printing works – and David gives an evocative description of the area at that immediate post-war time in his book, *The Bridgend Biffy*. Security was still extant:

> To enter the embryonic trading estate in those early days, it was necessary to secure a pass, a khaki-covered folder about the size of an identity card, which bore the awesome symbol of a red dot. Waving one of these passes in the well-focused features of an ROF constable was necessary for entry.

At first the heating was still through steam pipes

> which were covered with white asbestos, itself sealed with waterproof sheeting, though some of the asbestos was clear to the naked eye. Most of these pipes hissed, some even snorted.

The Arsenal's canteens were still operating – though presumably at a much reduced level:

> Designed to lift the spirits the facilities were low cost and supervised by selfless people, like Jean, who dispensed tea by the enamel jug-full for 2d, as well as succulent doughnuts and jam tarts.

The class divisions of the Arsenal persisted at the main Canteen 1.J.1, where there was

> the basic serve yourself, the waitress service, and, if you had two shillings and sixpence to spare, the executive dining room had much the same food, but rather deeper upholstered seating.

The canteens were subsidised by the estate management at an annual cost of £1,500. David's father had a key to the original 'palatial' toilets and washroom with its circular sink, accurate sprinklers and topped-up liquid soap dispensers.

Abel Jones lists other facilities on the estate, one of which was inherited from the Arsenal:

> An industrial medical unit, consisting of a doctor and two nurses treats cases of illness and accident on the spot.

Other provision was new – an employment exchange, for workers made redundant, and banks to contain the profits of the new enterprises.

David describes the estate in its early days as 'a sort of wonderland of busy people.' A huge variety of firms were allocated space on the former ROF by August 1946. The largest allocation was 125,600 square feet to Koray Ltd to manufacture pills, powders and wax substitutes, and the smallest just 100 square feet to WR Rees for printing film.[7] Therc were firms involved with such essential products as vacuum flasks, floral wirework, dental fixative, corn solvents, toys, clockwork motors, asbestos insulation, medicines, furniture, glandular extracts, clothing, printing, plastics, food, and a huge variety of industrial products. This was the diversity that the planners of the new Wales had craved.

According to Rowena Harris, who carried on working in the canteen, there was a different atmosphere on the estate after the war:

> People started to say, that's your job, that's my job. They never did that in the war.

The estate inherited the Arsenal's rail system and two of its diesel engines, plus the one steam locomotive. Two others remained on the Admiralty factory at the Brackla site. The rest were disposed of. Geoffrey Percival, in his history of Welsh industrial estates, dismisses these inherited shunting engines as 'costly toys.' The annual loss to the management of running the rail system at Waterton was £3,000 a year. David remembers 'these placid and immaculate locomotives in their green and black livery.' Usually they were stationary, and he 'gained the impression that the driver was waiting for something to happen.' Within ten years the other steam engine was sold, and in 1960 the Factory system was shut down – much to the relief of the estates management. The passenger railway station at Tremains, that had been so busy during the war, was also closed in the early 1960s: thus both businesses and workers were left to rely on road transport.

By 1965 6,040 people were employed on the former ROF. At that time an advertisement for the estate optimistically proclaimed that: –

> The estate breathes a general atmosphere of progressive efficiency that betokens a lively future for its tenants

despite the fact that 'in some areas the mounded buildings and narrow clean ways still betray its origins.' But not for much longer. In the late 60s the Admiralty finally vacated its land in the west of the estate, which added some 250,000sq ft to the total available for civilian use. In 1966 John Hick was appointed manager of the estate; in 1968 it was decided that the site could no longer continue to be simply an adapted ordnance factory, and a major programme of modernisation began. As an article published in the *Gazette* in September proclaimed,

> The time has come to face the fact that many of the original buildings should be replaced. They are ugly, inadequate, expensive to maintain: they are also so widely spaced that the land on which they stand is not being utilised to the best advantage. This involves moving thousands of tons of earth and rubble, but the work must be done if we are ever to see a modern, properly designed estate to house the industry of the second half of the twentieth century.

Geoffrey Percival put the project into a wider context thus:

> Bridgend was now to be attacked, not simply from the point of view of the removal of eye-sores, but as an integral part of the long-term industrial structure of South Wales.

The decision was the death knell of most of the physical remains of ROF 53. By 1972, 850 of the original 1000 or so Arsenal buildings had been demolished, and modern purpose-built factories erected in their stead. The existing potholed, weed-infested streets were replaced with a new internal road system. The industrial estate now covered 310 acres, on which 80 firms occupied 1,650,000sq ft of factory space. Total employment there reached 6,597 by 1970 – the equivalent of just one shift at the old Arsenal. About 70% of workers in the various factories were male, and 30% female – the reverse ratio to that of ROF 53.

At the same time as the main estate at Waterton was being modernised, the government finally relinquished control of most of the storage area and magazines at the Brackla site. The land was taken over by the local authority, which began to develop it as another smaller estate, named Brackla Industrial Estate. By September 1968 thirty firms were based on this part of the former Arsenal, and they employed nearly a thousand people.

A Woman's Place

What of the many thousands of women who had worked in the Arsenal?[8] Over 70% of employees at the Factory were female by 1941, and although that percentage had reduced as the war went on, there was still a majority of women in May 1945. This means that over 10,000 females were made redundant from the Factory between May and December that year. Some were able to go back to the employment they had followed before hostilities. Myra Evans recalls that

> I was quite pleased to go back into shop work, at Stradlings the Grocers. And I was lucky because I was taken on to manage, and I got the same money as I was getting in the Arsenal.

Of course by no means all ex-Arsenal women sought previous or alternative jobs. Many had been directed into the Factory in the first place, saw the whole thing as a necessary but temporary inconvenience, and were anxious to return to their former roles at home as wives and mothers. This is the conventional attitude summed up by a female correspondent (rejoicing in the byline of 'Eugene') writing in the *Glamorgan Gazette* in July 1945:

> Some of you may have difficulty in settling down to the normal routine of life at home again, but [there is a] flood of overwhelming relief that at last your time is your own. No more day and night shifts...your energy and attention can once more be focused on working for the welfare of home and children.

The expectation of many men, and of workers' organizations, was that women would return without fuss to their 'proper' place in the kitchen. Most of the post-war concerns of the unions and other organisations in the former ROF catchment area were about male unemployment – real jobs. A suggestion from the TUC in London that the local Trades Council should consider setting up a women's section brought the acerbic warning that 'there would be much ill-feeling regarding the employment of women in the forthcoming reorganization of industry in Bridgend'. At a conference of mid-Glamorgan councillors and trade unionists in September 1946 the priority was clear – the increase of industry 'to absorb adult and particularly male labour.' Councillor Mordecai, speaking at a meeting of the Maesteg Council, expressed the feeling that employers preferred women because they were cheaper. At the same meeting Councillor Mel Thomas denounced 'such factories as are now being given to the area' as 'mere sweatshops in which girls are expected to work for low wages.' In Bridgend D Ivor Davies agreed with these judgements – he dismissed the first jobs on the former ROF as 'largely consisting of juvenile and female labour,' which 'did not meet the needs of the Mid-Glamorgan area in the slightest degree.'

But there were very many women who had been changed by the opportunity provided by the Arsenal. They had become accustomed to travelling to work, to the regulations of factory life, to the camaraderie, to the excellent wage, and to the standard of living and the social freedom which that allowed. One contributor to the BBC radio programme expressed this change vividly:

> You went back to where you had left years before, but you had a different outlook on life, different expectancy. Before I wouldn't say 'Boo' to a goose. But when I went into the Factory, I questioned, because you were taught by association with the other girls, well, they're not putting up with it so why should I? Life was never the same afterwards.

The genie had been let loose from its bottle. These women did not want to return to their pre-war state, but actively sought work, and had to be registered as unemployed if they could not find it.

More evidence of a changed attitude comes from an association of unemployed former Arsenal workers in the Garw valley who demanded that the Bridgend Trades Council allow them to push for work in the new businesses on the new industrial estate. As their spokesperson explained, 'We want to take our place in industry with our men folk on an equal footing.' An indication of the size of the problem in finding alternative work is that the number of women recorded as unemployed in Wales as a whole rose from 7,000 in July 1945 to 30,000 in July 1946. More specifically, in September of that year there were 3,208 females noted as seeking work in mid-Glamorgan (compared with 4,482 males).

One solution to the problem caused considerable disquiet in Wales. Government organizations sent thousands of surplus women to areas of England that were short of labour, such as the Midlands and the southeast.[9] According to Mari Williams, using the records of Undeb Cymru Fydd,

> The vast majority of those sent to Birmingham hailed from the Bridgend/Maesteg areas, and almost all were former employees of Bridgend ROF.

Other female ROF employees who had been on the register for 6 months were dispatched to pack tomatoes in Jersey.

Nevertheless, many former female employees of the Factory did find work locally. By June 1946 women filled 46% of all positions in redundant ROF factories in South Wales. In September 680 women (out of 1427) were employed on the Bridgend site. One of these was Sally Evans: she recalls,

> When the Factory was closing, there was a Mr Vincent working in the Arsenal. He was my boss in Time Fuze, and later I used to wait on him in the canteen. He was going to open a factory making buttons, so he came and asked me to be manageress for him, so that's where I ended up.

Eunice Jones worked in the Time and Motion section during the war; she had impressed one manager so much that when he transferred to Miles Laboratories he declared: 'I want that lady there,' and paid her an increased salary. New factories on new sites provided many work opportunities for women. The Polikoff[10] clothing factory at Ynyswen in the Rhondda was employing 1000 females by 1949. As the whole of Glamorgan entered a prosperous era in the early 1950s, so female unemployment rates fell, and those from the Arsenal who wanted to work in paid employment were able to do so.

A revealing exercise is to compare the percentage of females in paid work in Glamorgan before the war, in 1931, with that in 1951.

Percentage of Women in Full-Time Employment

Local Authority	1931	1951
Aberdare	14	22
Bridgend	28	26
Maesteg	12	21
Mountain Ash	12	24
Neath	20	27
Ogmore & Garw	11	20
Pontypridd	17	28
Rhondda	11	24

This table[11] clearly reveals the extent of the changes brought about by the wartime experience to the women of the area that had served ROF 53. In all the coal mining valley communities the percentage of females in paid employment had increased considerably.[12] In terms of the numbers employed in south Wales, there were 105,000 women in paid employment in 1948, almost double the 55,000 in 1938. Other evidence shows that the type of work had changed significantly as well. The numbers of women in domestic service had dropped dramatically, and there were increases in clerks, typists, and manufacturing. In addition, a much higher percentage of the female workforce consisted of married women – another change that had its origins in the experiences gained at armaments factories like the Bridgend Arsenal. In fact by 1951 32% of all women workers in Wales were married.

One feature of work at the Arsenal which had caused much discontent among the male workforce did not continue into peacetime. Women's wages were no longer relatively high: the average wage of a Welsh woman in 1948 at £3.18s a week was half that of a man at £7.3s

A New War

It would seem, then, that the world had at last moved on, and that the Factory built for the war against Hitler was, in the second half of the twentieth century, simply the location of many different types of peaceful production. But the war functions of the Arsenal had not yet completely disappeared. There was, after all, a new potential enemy, the Soviet Union, and there were new and much more terrible weapons to be guarded against. The old Arsenal still had a part to play in this new Cold War, and on both the Brackla site, and the Waterton site.

'Revealed; secret H-bomb bunker at Brackla,' proclaimed the *Glamorgan Gazette* headline for 8th October 1981. The article explained that members of the Campaign for Nuclear Disarmament had alerted the *Gazette* to the existence of a nuclear bomb fallout shelter near Bridgend. This shelter had been constructed using two of the Arsenal's original magazine stores built at Brackla in the Thirties under the direction of Temple-Richards. The bunker was designed to operate as the seat of government for the whole of South and Mid Wales, should control of Britain from the centre be rendered impossible in the wake of a nuclear attack. A start had been made on adapting the tunnels in the 1970s. In 1979 the Conservatives came to power: Prime Minister Thatcher was determined to spend on upgrading civil defence facilities for use in the event of an attack by the Soviet Union, and so the Bridgend site was extensively re-fitted.

The *Gazette* reporters contacted the Home Office, and a representative told them teasingly that

> We do not confirm or deny where [the nuclear bunkers] are...but there will be one in the South Wales area.

He went on to declare that

> there is nothing particularly sinister about them. One of the reasons we do not reveal locations is the problem of vandalism.

Perhaps the Home Office thought the bunker was more susceptible to damage by Welsh hooligans than by the might of the Soviet Union.

Obviously the bunker was not as secret as the headline appeared to suggest. Within a few days the Home Office had sent three officials down from London, to give *Gazette* reporters a guided tour. The edition of November 5th 1981, printed their report, and included 12 photographs of the amenities provided inside. The site was unrecognizable from the time of its function as storage for explosives. At the entrance the opening for the entry of railway wagons had been reduced and replaced with steel blast-proof doors. There was a decontamination unit for those trips outside. A filtration system meant that uncontaminated air could be pumped throughout the shelter. A 169 bhp 6-cylinder diesel generator provided power, and tanks held fuel and 60,000 gallons of clean water. The two magazines between them provided 25,000 square feet of what the *Gazette* reporter described as

> Brightly-lit and centrally-heated office and living space for 380 privileged civil servants.

Facilities included dormitories with bunk beds and lockers for men and women; showers, sinks and toilets; a fully equipped kitchen and dining rooms with tables and chairs; a communica-

Group 7 Filled-store Building, that was to have been used as Mid Glamorgan Emergency HQ. Note CND Cymru daffodil painted on the wall

tions room (linked to other Regional HQs) with teleprinters; a 200-line telephone exchange. A radio studio ensured that the Regional Commissioner[11] could broadcast to the unfortunates outside on every-day matters such as radiation levels and how to bury the dead. The walls were painted a bright yellow (reminiscent of sunshine), and decorated with pictures and mirrors. The tidy civil servants would appreciate the waste-paper bins, the clock-watchers' timepieces in every room, and the sleepy ones the provision of a coffee machine.

Fitting out a Regional Seat of Government was not the only preparation for a post-nuclear world on the territory of the former munitions Factory. Someone had to execute the orders coming out of the Regional HQ. Thus the scheme of government required that every county in Britain had its own shelter from whence county officials and workers could carry out the will of the Regional Commissioner. Mid Glamorgan County Council had an existing civil emergencies building on the Bridgend Industrial Estate – the Waterton site of the old Arsenal. The facility was based in an old Group 7 filled store building – a reinforced and earthed store for completed components, now bizarrely situated on the central reservation of the main dual carriageway through the estate. This provision was insufficient for the government's demands – it would not have withstood a nuclear attack, nor been able to protect its inmates from the ensuing radiation. In January 1982 the County council signed a £400,000 contract with Fairclough Engineering and work on upgrading the centre began soon after. But many in South Wales had a similar attitude towards any preparation for a nuclear Holocaust that people had expressed fifty years before in opposition to the building of the original Arsenal. On 25th January CND Cymru started a campaign to prevent the completion of the enhanced facility. This began with a peace camp and demonstrations based around a borrowed caravan parked at the site. The work proceeded apace, and the contractors had completed the shuttering for the blast proof walls by the beginning of March. It was at this point that the demonstrators started direct action; in particular they climbed onto the shuttering to prevent the pouring of concrete. It was impossible for the work to proceed, and within a week, on March

15th, the county councillors held an emergency meeting to discuss the issues. At the end councillors voted overwhelmingly by 63 votes to 4 to abandon the project. Anti-war protesters of the 1980s had proved to be far more organised and effective than their predecessors who had protested against the building of the Arsenal in the 1930s.

That left the Regional HQ at Brackla. At the end of the journalists' tour there in 1981 a Home Office official had said that 'We sincerely hope that this shelter is going to lie dormant for the next 20 to 30 years.'

In fact the life of the facility as a nuclear shelter was much shorter than that. The Cold War had ended by the close of the decade, and in 1995 the bunker was sold for peaceful storage purposes. The last connection to military activity had finally been broken at ROF 53, the Royal Ordnance Filling Factory, Bridgend.

Notes

1 E.g. at Kenfig: British Industrial Solvents (calcium carbide for the plastics industry).

2 KO Morgan *Wales 1880-1980* Ch 11.

3 The first really successful industrial estate was that at Slough. It was initially called a 'trading estate', because originally it had been a military depot from which huge quantities of surplus equipment were sold – or traded – after 1918. The title 'Trading' stuck, and was used for future industrial estates till the 1950s. Thus the original name at Bridgend was the Bridgend Trading Estate. It became the Bridgend Industrial Estate in 1957.

4 Royal Navy Armaments Department.

5 So that a rather specialised claim to fame of the Estate was that it boasted the greatest concentration of Cochran Boilers in the world!

6 Based on figures in AJ Griffiths and in the *Gazette*

7 Two of the original companies on the estate, Groom and Llewellyn, and Kieft, worked together to build a racing car in 1949 driven successfully by Stirling Moss.

8 For a detailed discussion of Welsh women war factory workers after 1945, see Mari Williams Ch 5

9 Aug 1945-July 1946 2112 sent through the ministry of Labour: April-July 1946 1346 sent through the Voluntary Temporary Transference scheme. This scheme was not so voluntary – girls who refused to go had their benefit stopped.

10 Later owned by Burberry. And closed by that company in 2007.

11 Based on tables in Mari Williams *A Forgotten Army*.

12 Though interestingly in the Bridgend UDC area, over a quarter of women had been working in 1931, and the percentage did in fact fall slightly by 1951.

8x Magazines in the 1980s. Opposite: loading platform in the Magazine. Top: railtracks leading to the Magazine. Bottom: entrance to the Magazine

Appendix A

SHUNTING LOCOMOTIVES

AT BRIDGEND ROF 53 1939 – 1946

Engine Designation	Type	Manufacturer	Maker's Number	Date of Manufacture	Origin	Destiny
ROF Bridgend No1	0-4-0 Diesel Mechanical Transmission	John Fowler Leeds	22882	1939	New	Shell Ltd Stanlow Cheshire 1946
ROF Bridgend No2	0-4-0 Diesel Mechanical Transmission	John Fowler Leeds	22888	1940	New	Colvilles, Clyde Ironworks Glasgow
ROF Bridgend No3	0-4-0 Diesel Mechanical Transmission	John Fowler Leeds	22891	1940	New	Bridgend Industrial Estate
ROF Bridgend No4	0-4-0 Diesel Mechanical Transmission	John Fowler Leeds	22896	1940	New	ROF Glascoed 1946 Woolwich 1958
ROF Bridgend No5	0-4-0 Diesel Mechanical Transmission	John Fowler Leeds	22915	1940	New	Brackla MOW Factory
ROF Bridgend No6	0-4-0 Diesel Mechanical Transmission	John Fowler Leeds	22917	1940	New	English Clays Plymouth 1948
ROF Bridgend No7	0-4-0 Diesel Mechanical Transmission	John Fowler Leeds	22933	1941	New	Bridgend Industrial Estate
ROF Bridgend No8	0-4-0 Steam Outside Cylinders	Peckett & Sons Bristol	2040	1943	New	Bridgend Industrial Estate
9	0-4-0 Diesel Mechanical Transmission	John Fowler Leeds	22950	1941	ROF Elstow by Oct 43	Brackla MOW Factory
-	0-4-0 Diesel Mechanical Transmission	John Fowler Leeds	22999	1943	New	ROF Eastriggs Dumfries 6/43

Appendix A

AT BRIDGEND INDUSTRIAL ESTATE 1946 - 1961

Engine Designation	Type	Manufacturer	Maker's Number	Date of Manufacture	Origin	Destiny
3	0-4-0 Diesel Mechanical Transmission	John Fowler Leeds	22891	1940	ROF Bridgend	Hirwaun Trading Estate 1952
7	0-4-0 Diesel Mechanical Transmission	John Fowler Leeds	22933	1941	ROF Bridgend	RS Hayes Bridgend 5/61 (Scrap)
8	0-4-0 Steam Outside Cylinders	Peckett & Sons Bristol	2040	1943	ROF Bridgend	Unknown
-	0-4-0 Steam Outside Cylinders	Peckett & Sons Bristol	2025	1942	Hirwaun ROF c 1946	Abelson & Co Birmingham 3/53 Later Llanelly Steelworks
ROF 9 No 7	0-4-0 Steam Outside Cylinders	Peckett & Sons Bristol	2016	1941	North East Trading Estates by 8/48	Sold for Scrap

AT BRACKLA FACTORY, MOW 1946 - 1962

5	0-4-0 Diesel Mechanical Transmission	John Fowler Leeds	22915	1940	ROF Bridgend	A. King & Sons Norwich 1962
MOW No9	0-4-0 Diesel Mechanical Transmission	John Fowler Leeds	22950	1940	ROF Bridgend	Steel Supply Co Jersey Marine 1962

Based on information in G Hill: *Industrial Locomotives in Mid and South Glamorgan*

Appendix B

REPORTED BOMBING INCIDENTS WITHIN A 5 MILE RADIUS OF THE ARSENAL

DATE	LOCATION	MFA*	NOTES
3/7/40	Tyla Farm, Nr Broadlands	2	13 craters in fields
15/7/40	RAF Llandow	5	
1/8/40	Monknash	5	
6/8/40	RAF Llandow	5	
10/8/40	Southerndown	4	
17/8/40	Llysworney	4	
19/8/40	Marcross	5	
20/8/40	Kenfig, Nr Carbide works	5	4 bombs, craters 25ft deep
21/8/40	RAF Stormy Down Mouth of River Ogmore	4 4	12 bombs, 2 killed
2/9/40	Heol-y-Cyw	2½	
17/9/40	New Inn Bridge, Merthyr Mawr Wick	1½ 4	
27/9/40	Newton nr Porthcawl	5	Incendiary
28/9/40	Marcross and Wick	5, 4	
19/10/40	North Cornelly Bettws	5 3½	UXB Incendiaries
17/11/40	Sea off Ogmore and Nash Point	5	
23/11/40	RAF Llandow	5	
4/1/41	Norton, nr Ogmore-by-Sea St Brides Major	3½ 3	
5/1/41	Waterton Cross	¼	UXB
19/2/41	Brynna Gwynion	3½	People killed, 70 houses damaged
12/3/41	Litchard Abercynffig	½ 2½	
15/3/41	Penyfai Common	2	
17/3/41	Blackmill	3½	UXB

Appendix B

12/4/41	Treoes	1	Land Mines – Shock broke shop window in Bridgend, and damaged Ewenny Priory Church
22/4/41	Llangan	2	
29/4/41	Wick	4	24 bomb craters
	Coedymwstwr Woods	1	Incendiaries
	and Pencoed	2	
30/4/41	Coity	¼	12 Incendiaries and Flares
	Flare over the Arsenal		
	Tondu	2½	UXB
3/5/41	St Brides Major	3	32 bombs
4/5/41	St Brides Major	3	
	Wick	4	
5/5/41	Tondu	2½	Nr the Navigation Colliery
	Kenfig Hill	4½	7 bombs (1 UXB) – St Theodore's Church damaged, plus over 200 other properties
6/5/41	Wick	4	
	RAF Llandow	5	UXB
12/5/41	RAF Llandow	5	
2/7/42	Nr Schwyll Water Works, Ogmore Castle	2	Merthyr Mawr Church damaged by Blast
	St Brides	3	
	Wick	4	
	Ewenny	1	
	Litchard	½	
16/2/43	NE of Coity Fields	¼	String of 4 red balls

MFA – Approximate miles from the Arsenal

Based on information in R Williams: *Bridgend Report and Control Centre* and RE Cottrell: *Hostile Sky*

Appendix C

BRIDGEND ROF – TOTAL WAR OUTPUT: 1940 TO 1945

From: *Construction of Filling Factories* – Ministry of Supply unpublished narrative.

All figures in thousands

ARMY			
Type of Ammunition	Type of Store	Separate Shell	Loading Cartridge
Gun Medium	HE Shrapnel		690
Gun Medium	Smoke and practice	2300	
Gun Heavy	HE		520
Type of Store:			
Mines, Demolition charges, Grenades HE		1100	
Trench Mortar – High Explosive		10000	
Trench Mortar – Smoke		2500	
Rocket heads		290	
Rocket tails		4500	
Fuzes With Time ring		8000	
Fuzes Without Time rings		75000	
Tracers and Igniters		30000	
Primers and Tubes		48000	
Detonators and Caps		140000	
AIR FORCE			
Type of Ammunition	Type of Store		
Aircraft Bombs	Small	154	
Detonators		3600	

Appendix C

NAVY (40% of Bridgend's production was destined for the Admiralty)			
Type of Ammunition	Type of Store	Separate Shell	Fixed Ammunition
Gun Light	Prac. Smoke Star		1500
Gun Medium	Prac. Smoke Star		1400
Gun Heavy	Prac. Smoke Star	27.1	
Type of Store:	Fuzes (all types)	36000	
	Tracers and Igniters	4000	
	Detonators and Caps	53000	
	Underwater components	2800	
Pyrotechnics	Flares	3000	
	Signals	1400	
	Target Indicator Bombs	62	
	Thunderflashes	2000	
Other miscellaneous		2000	

Based on statistics in Ministry of Supply – Construction of Filling Factories (AVIA 46/178)

Appendix D

What was actually made at ROF 53

The list of what was manufactured at the Bridgend Factory for the Army, the Navy and the RAF during the war shows that many millions of individual items were made there. Some were themselves complete rounds of ammunition, but many of the components filled were sent on to other ROFs for insertion into the finished article. Only chemists and the military can understand exactly what went on. For the rest of us the list is shrouded in a mist of alchemy, sorcery, and the dark arts. This appendix is an attempt to explain in simple terms what was manufactured

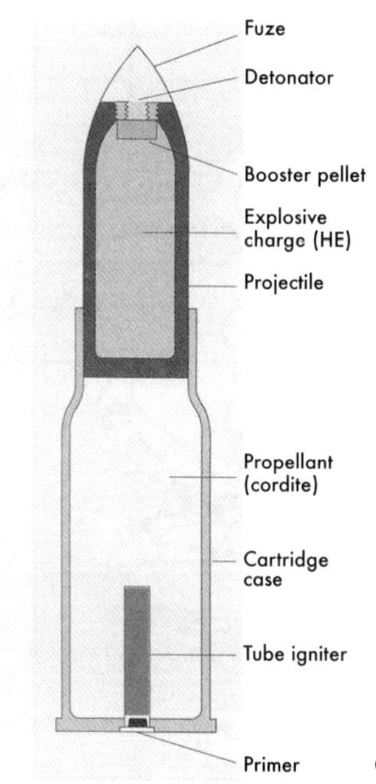

Components in a round of ammunition

there. It does not pretend to be comprehensive, or even particularly accurate. Before we examine terms used in the Factory, and explain the items that were manufactured there, we must understand the processes that take place in a projectile when it is fired.

Delivery and Explosion

Every projectile consists of two explosive systems, each of which requires an independent triggering process.

The first system propels the weapon towards the intended target. In the Second World War, Cordite was the material usually used to achieve this. (Bombs dropped from aircraft usually do not need this first system – they simply use gravity to arrive at the target!)

The second system causes the munition to explode at or in the vicinity of the target. This system usually consists of a fuze incorporating a detonator and a booster, which finally initiates the main High Explosive charge.

The Triggering Sequence

Each of these two systems requires a triggering sequence – a series of explosive events that results in the firing of the difficult-to-ignite main charge. An analogy that may help to explain this process is that of a coal fire in a grate. It would be useless to hold a match to a lump of coal – burnt fingers would be the only result. Instead a fire is started by a triggering sequence: a match is lit by friction; the match flame lights paper; the burning paper sets light to the wood; the burning wood ignites the coal. Of course all this

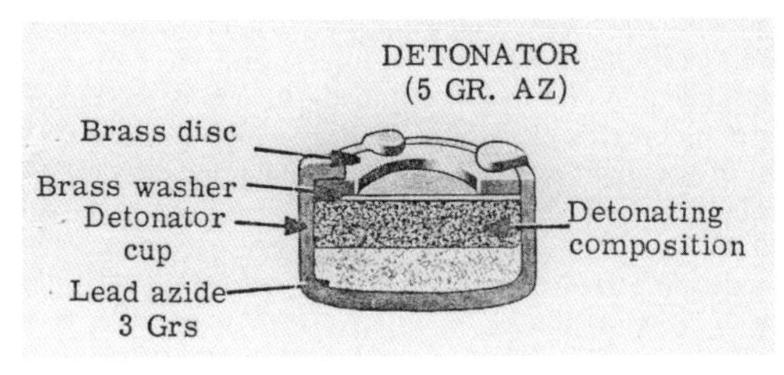

takes several minutes. In essence, and with different materials, the same process happens in igniting ammunition, though it takes place almost instantaneously.

This is the usual triggering process: –

1) A physical or electrical shock sets off the highly sensitive initiator, detonator, cap or tube.

2) This in turn sets off the slightly less sensitive booster, or pellet, which creates a shock wave.

3) Finally the least sensitive material – the Cordite, or the High Explosive is detonated by the shock wave.

Directory of Terms

Explosives and components

Cordite. A mixture of nitro-cellulose and nitro-glycerine made up in the form of cords or sticks. This was the 'low explosive' propellant used to send projectiles to the target. Most of the Cordite processed at Bridgend came from RNOF Caerwent. At ROF 53 Cordite bags were made in Textiles, and the Cordite inserted into the bags in Group 5 of the factory. Cordite is safe to handle.

Detonator or Cap. Also called the Primer. These were the very small copper shells used to initiate the triggering process. Initiation was usually by percussion using a firing pin, which would be sufficient to ignite the detonator. These components were filled by hand with highly sensitive and dangerous materials such as lead azide, or fulminate of mercury. These materials were liable to cause injuries to hands, fingers and faces in the filling process. Filled in Group 1, the Initiator Group of the factory.

Fuze. A complex piece of machinery which controls the detonation of the main charge. It would usually include a detonator and a booster. Two main types of fuzes were used in the Second World War:

Percussion Fuze – Initiated by the impact of the missile at the target.

Time Fuze – Also called Mechanical Time Fuze. The timing is

achieved by the burning of a length of gunpowder inside the housing of the fuze. In some fuzes this time was set, in others it could be adjusted using time rings just before firing. One early use was in anti-aircraft shells, so that they could be timed to explode when they had reached the height of the target aircraft.

At ROF 53 there was a fuze section, Group B, where fuzes were manufactured, and Group 3, the Fuze group, where a huge variety of fuzes were filled.

Gunpowder. An explosive made from a nitrate (usually saltpetre) plus sulphur, plus charcoal, (from willow, alder or buckthorn). At Bridgend gunpowder was used in the manufacture of time fuzes. On the Brackla site there was a small factory producing powder (presumably fine grain gunpowder) for fuzes. The gunpowder had to be produced to a very high specification to ensure a consistent burning rate. On the main site at Waterton was Group 4, the Gunpowder Group.

High Explosive. This was the main charge – the material used to explode the projectile at the target. It was relatively safe to handle because it needed the shock wave produced by a booster to detonate. At Bridgend the usual HE chemical was TNT (Tri-nitro-toluene) which mostly came from ROF Pembrey. The TNT was used in two Brackla sections: in Group A to fill 2-inch and 3-inch mortars, and in Group S to fill 40mm shells for Bofors anti-aircraft guns.

Pellet. The intermediate feature, a booster, that assisted in the ignition of HE projectiles. Filled with a Composition Explosive, usually Tetryl: (2,4,6-trinitrophenyl-N-methylnitramine) which came to Bridgend from Pembrey. This was the infamous yellow powder which affected the skin of those who worked in Group 2, the Pellet Group. The filling in the pellets had to be pressed at approximately three tons per square inch by a hydraulic press. Tetryl is sensitive, and caused several serious accidents at ROF 53.

Tube. A type of primer used with larger projectiles or shells. It was used to ignite the propellant charge, usually Cordite, which was contained in textile bags. The tube itself was placed into an aperture at the back of the gun breech, and it was detonated by a mechanical firing pin, or more usually by an electrical impulse. Presumably tubes were filled in Group 1.

Munitions and weapons:

Demolition charge. Packets of explosives designed to destroy buildings, bridges etc.

Grenade. Small missile fitted with a time fuze, and filled with High Explosive. Designed to be thrown by soldiers in close combat.

Mine. Weapon containing a detonator and High Explosive, and usually buried under the surface of the ground. Designed to cause injury to enemy troops, or damage to enemy vehicles.

Pyrotechnics. Items not intended to harm the enemy – essentially military fireworks. Many different kinds were filled at ROF 53:

Thunder flashes were used during training to simulate battlefield conditions.

Smoke shells were used to conceal troops from the enemy.

Flare shells indicated targets to bombers.

Illuminating or Star shells lit up the battlefield at night.

Signal shells used different colours to communicate instructions to troops: red – strontium, green – barium plus potassium, yellow – sodium.

Although these stores were not intended to kill, they were still explosives, and did cause serious accidents in Group 6, the Pyrotechnics Group.

Rockets. The tails contained the propellant, presumably Cordite, filled in Group 5: the heads contained the HE. Unguided rockets were developed during the war in great secrecy, initially for anti-aircraft use. These were launched from Z-gun batteries, with 16 or 30 tube loading systems, projecting large numbers of 2-inch and 3-inch diameter missiles in the general direction of enemy bombers. An infantry version, named the Mattress, was used in the last months of the war during the invasion of Germany itself. This had a range of some 8,000 yards. A rocket range was marked on the plans for ROF 53, located next to the burning ground, on the site of the South Wales Police sports area at Waterton Cross. It is possible that this area was used for testing the components of the new weapon, though there is no evidence to support this.

Shrapnel Cartridge. This Cartridge was the propellant part of a munition that contained metal pellets or spherical bullets which exploded before impact, and could cause heavy casualties and considerable damage to equipment. The propellant was Cordite, and the Cartridges were filled in Group 5, the Cordite Group.

Target Indicator (TI) Bombs. These were dropped by pathfinder planes to enable following bombers to target more accurately. TI bombs were first used during an attack on Berlin in January 1943. These munitions fell like ordinary bombs until they reached a predetermined height – usually 3000 feet – where they explosively ejected 60 brilliantly coloured pyrotechnic candles. The candles spread out during their fall to form a distinctive pool of fire some 300 yards in diameter on the ground. The candles from the normal target indicator burned on the ground for about three minutes. At the Arsenal TI bombs were filled in Group 6.

Tracers. These were slow-burning units fitted to the rear of projectiles to allow their flight path to be observed to improve accuracy. The composition used was usually magnesium plus strontium nitrate, which gives off a red coloured trail. Tracers were filled in Group 6.

Trench Mortar. A 2 or 3-inch missile fired from a muzzle loading, portable, smoothbore weapon at a high trajectory over relatively short distance. A complete round consists of fuze, propellant and the main HE charge. At ROF 53 these were filled at the Group A section on the Brackla site.

Underwater Components. Presumably parts of torpedoes and naval mines.

Appendix E

NUMBERS EMPLOYED AT THE ARSENAL: SEPTEMBER 1939–SEPTEMBER 1945

Date		Male	Female	Total
1939	Sept-Dec			28
1940	March			312
	April	700	250	950
	May	1200	1150	2350
	June	1471	2071	3542
	Sept	2064	3884	5948
	Oct	2418	4946	7364
	Nov	2835	6005	8840
	Dec	3327	6810	10137
1941	Jan	3999	7374	11373
	Feb	4614	8559	13173
	March	5225	10613	15838
	April	7283	15913	23196
	May	7642	16432	24074
	June	8265	17569	25834
	July	8338	18792	27130
	Aug	8384	19943	28327
	Nov	8581	23465	32046

Appendix E

Date		Total
1942	March - Gross*	32577
	March - Net*	28707
	June	27180
	Sept	25238
	Dec	23853
1943	March	20620
	June	19537
	Sept	20281
	Dec	19928
1944	March	19982
	June	19856
	Sept	19928
	Dec	19798
1945	March	19921
	June	17133
	Sept	8520

* In March 1942 the figure of workers employed was changed to represent those actually in work i. e. to exclude absentees.

Based on statistics in AVIA 46/277 and LAB 12/82 (monthly report on the Labour Supply position - Wales)

Numbers employed at the Arsenal: September 1939 - September 1945

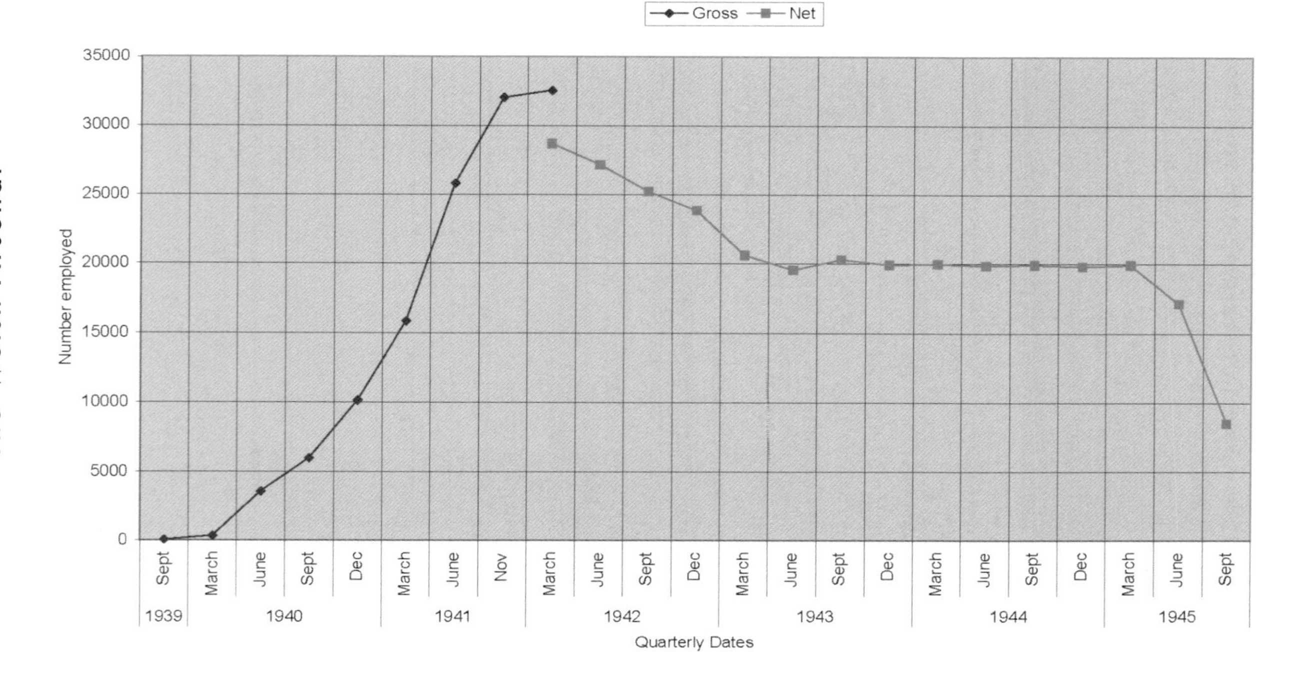

Appendix F

FATALITIES IN ROYAL FILLING FACTORIES

1 January 1941 to 31 July 1945

ROF	Men	Women	Total
Chorley	3	4	7
Bridgend	11	6	17
Glascoed	2	-	2
Hereford	8	-	8
Swynnerton	10	3	13
Risley	4	1	5
Kirkby	5	13	18
Thorpe Arch	1	2	3
Aycliffe	7	10	17
Total	51	39	90

Analysis by year

Year	Men	Women	Total
1941	10	8	18
1942	11	14	25
1943	9	4	13
1944	8	10	18
1945	13	3	16

Based on statistics in AVIA 44/289

Bibliography

Printed sources

All Clear (Bridgend Writers Circle 1995)

Bomber Command (Royal Air Force Museum)

Coychurch Chronicle (Parish of Llangrallo November 1991)

House of Commons Debates Vol 382 (HMSO 1942)

Official Opening of Glamorgan Police Headquarters (Glamorgan Constabulary 1947)

Post-war Reconstruction in Wales (Ministry of Reconstruction 1944)

Rules of the Danger Area – Royal Ordnance Factory Bridgend (HMSO 1941)

Symposium on Wartime Engineering Problems (Institution of Civil Engineers 1948)

HE Bates *The Tinkers of Elstow* (Lyons & Co 1946)

WD Cocroft *Dangerous Energy* (English Heritage 2000)

RE Cottrell *Hostile Sky* (Unpublished typescript)

M Davies (Ed) *The Valleys Autobiography* (Cwm a Bro)

G Dow *It Can Now Be Revealed* (British Railways1945)

C Ducker *Rugby Bristol Fashion* (BRFC 1988)

J Grenfell-Hill *Growing Up in Wales* (Gomer 1996)

AJ Griffiths *The Industrial Estate at Bridgend* (Unpublished Thesis 1975)

MJ Haslam *The Chilwell Story* (RAOC Corps Gazette 1982)

I Hay *R.O.F.* (HMSO 1949)

G Hill *Industrial Locomotives of Mid & South Glamorgan* (Industrial Railway Society 2007)

W Hornby *Factories and Plant* (HMSO & Longmans 1958)

G Humphrys *Industrial Britain – South Wales* (David and Charles 1972)

P Inman *Labour in the Munitions Industry* (HMSO/Longmans1957)

A John & G Williams (Ed) *Glamorgan County History* Vol V (Glamorgan History Trust 1980)

A Jones *The Story of Glamorgan* (Christopher Davies 1955)

CM Kohan *Works & Buildings* (HMSO/Longmans 1952)

D Lazell *The Bridgend Biffy* (Cwm a Bro 1995)

Lloyd & Jackson *South Wales Outline Plan* (HMSO 1949)

AS MacNalty (Ed) *The Civilian Health and Medical Services* (HMSO 1953)

P Massey *Industrial South Wales* (Gollancz 1940)

PE Masters *Safety in Royal Filling Factories* (HMSO 1950)

WC May *War Diaries* (Unpublished typescript)

H Menai *The Simple Vision* (Chapman & Hall 1945)

Bibliography

KO Morgan *Wales 1880-1980* (OUP/UWP 1981)

Nevell, Roberts, Smith *Royal Ordnance Factory, Chorley* (Carnegie 1999)

G Percival *The Government's Industrial Estates in Wales 1936 – 1975* (Welsh Development Agency 1978)

MM Postan *British War Production* (HMSO 1952)

GJ Rees *Tondu House* (Gwilym J Rees 1997)

T Simpson *No Bunkers Here* (Mid Glamorgan CND 1982)

D Mack Smith *Bridgend* (Unpublished Typescript1945)

P Summerfield *Women Workers in the Second World War* (Croom Helm 1984)

P Tapper, S Hawthorne *Wales and the Second World War* (Mid Glamorgan CC 1991)

AJP Taylor *English (sic) History, 1914-1945* (OUP 1965)

RA Webb *Sirens Over the Valley* (Alun Books 1988)

MA Williams *The Forgotten Army* (UWP 2002)

R Williams *Bridgend Report and Control Centre* (Unpublished typescript 1945)

Newspapers/Periodicals

Aberdare Leader; Glamorgan Advertiser; Daily Express; Rhondda Leader; Empire News; South Wales Echo; The Times; Glamorgan Gazette; Western Mail; ROF53 News

Certificates of Births, Marriages and Deaths, from the Office of National Statistics

Minutes of Local Councils held at the Glamorgan Record Office

Bridgend, Penybont, Maesteg, Ogmore & Garw, and Porthcawl

Minutes of the National Union of General and Municipal Workers held at the National Library of Wales, Aberystwyth

Audio–Visual Sources

Radio Programme: *The Girls Who Made the Thing-ummy-bobs* (BBC Wales 1989)

Recordings of Interviews by Mari Williams.

Video interview with Margaret Plummer *Back of the Front Line* (Swansea Women's History Group)

Film: *Danger Area* (Ministry of Information/ Imperial War Museum)

Acknowledgements

In the first place I would like to pay tribute to my father, Alan Clubb, for instilling in me an interest in History when I was young; I hope he would have been pleased with this volume.

Many texts were consulted in the writing of the book, and all were useful: they are listed in the bibliography. However I must mention three in particular. During the War Dennis Mack Smith worked in the Cabinet Office at Downing Street. When peace came he was asked to write the story of the decision making and planning behind the construction of twenty-two of the weapons factories built across Britain, including ROF 53; his research remains in manuscript, and gives an invaluable insight into the processes by which the Bridgend Factory came into being. Mari Williams investigated the story of the women who served in War factories across southern Wales, and published the results of her research in *A Forgotten Army* (2002): the archive of her interviews of workers, many from Bridgend, is in St Fagan's. A huge debt is owed to both writers, as their works provided a great deal of information, and a plethora of leads and references.

I was privileged to bc able to read the wartime Diaries of Bridgend's Superintendent of Police, William May. These give a fascinating insight into the social impact of the Arsenal and its workers on the local area, as well as information on the Factory itself. Very many thanks are due to May's son-in-law and daughter, Mr and Mrs Frank Knights, for allowing me access to the unpublished typescript.

All researchers into the past are indebted to the many librarians and archivists who so willingly help. My thanks, then, are due to the staff of these libraries: Aberdare, Pontypridd, Treorci, Cardiff Central, The National Library of Wales Aberystwyth, and especially Bridgend Park Street; and of these institutions: The Glamorgan Record Office, The Imperial War Museum, The Industrial Railway Society, The National Archive at Kew, The National History Museum at St Fagan's, NCAHMW at Aberystwyth, English Heritage's National Monuments Record at

Swindon and The Classic Buses Website. Special thanks are due to Carol Richards of The Institute of Civil Engineers, Jeremy Glen of South Wales Police, Philip Davies of Bridgend, RE Pearson of Royal Ordnance, Simon Villis of Bridgend Industrial Estate, and Steve Preece of Welsh Water. I am particularly indebted to the kindness of Glen Chapelle of BAE Systems Archive at Glascoed, and Mary Lewis of the Bridgend Register Office.

The photographs in this book are formally acknowledged elsewhere, but I must thank all the many people and institutions that have given permission to reproduce the images. At the time of writing none of these has charged me for using these illustrations except for the National Archive in Kew, which demanded £70 to use the 12 images at the end of chapter 2. I am touched by the generosity of all the other institutions which waived their normal fees.

In the end the facts detailed and the opinions expressed in this book were decided by me, but I had the inestimable benefit of advice from many wise people. Brian and Lyn Lewis translated the German on the Luftwaffe reconnaissance photographs. Lacking a military or scientific background, I had no comprehension of what was actually manufactured at ROF 53: Eric Happe, a munitions expert, and Glen Chapelle both helped me to have some understanding of the bewildering variety of items produced at the Welsh Arsenal. I was fortunate that the entire manuscript was read through by Cary Archard, Gareth Clubb, Andy Croll, and Phil Tapper, and all four have proffered valuable advice, and saved me from embarrassing errors which I had not noticed.

Philip in particular has worked with me, acting as an editor, planning, making suggestions, pointing out mistakes, researching, establishing contacts and leads, obtaining documents and photographs: his knowledge of the Second World War is encyclopaedic. My wife, Catherine has been involved in research and in site visits, and has contributed essential technical expertise to an IT idiot; but more importantly she has given me advice, support and encouragement throughout the twenty years that this project has been in development.

The form of the book is entirely the result of the work of Simon Hicks, my graphic designer, and I can only wonder at his ability to magically improve poor quality images, and at the enormous well of patience he has.

It is, of course the memories of the people who worked at the Factory, and their relatives which adds colour and life to statistics and facts. Every grateful thanks and respect is due to these who told their stories, whether in face to face interviews, on video or audio tapes, or in written accounts, who lent documents and photographs, and who served me with welcome cups of tea. These are their names:

Teresa Barnett (née Hann), Edna Barber (née Bevan), David Bugler, Christmas Davies, Mair Davies, Roy Davies, Gwyn Davis, Betty Edwards (née Cartlidge), Harry Fletcher, Will Francis, Rowena Harris (née Greenslade), Joan Hunt (née Chuckley), Myra Jenkins (née Evans), Megan Jones, David Lazell, Etta Lewis, Peggy Little (née Thomas), Gwen Lloyd, Jack Loveday, Sally Loveday (née Evans), Stan Martin, Betty Nettle (née Reynolds), Margaret Plummer, David Power, Catherine Radford (née Williams), R Redwood, Richard Rees, Peggy Rowlands (née Hawkins), R Gwyn Thomas, Jim Westrop, Vera White, Rosina Williams (née Davies), Les Wills, George Wood.

These, of course, are only a few, a very few, of the tens of thousands who worked at ROF 53 from 1940 to 1945. We all have a particular debt of gratitude to those men and women of Glamorgan who contributed to the defeat of Nazism by labouring at Wales' own Arsenal. And especially to those who made the ultimate sacrifice. Rhaid eu cofio.

Additional Fatality

After the first publication of this book, we discovered one more death caused by an explosion at the Arsenal. Thomas Millward was born into a mining family in Treorchy in 1893. He died on the Burning Grounds on 6th May, 1945, less than 24 hours before the German surrender. Friends of the family report that a controlled explosion did not go off immediately, that Tom eventually stood up to peer over the protective embankment, and that his head was blown off in the delayed blast.

Image Acknowledgements

Numbers refer to pages in the book. Where there are two images from different sources on the same page, U stand for the upper image and L for the lower image. Every effort has been made to contact copyright holders. If any have been overlooked, the publisher will be pleased to make the necessary arrangements.

Alan Ballinger (157L, 170, 183); Edna Barber (224, 226); Blaengwawr Comprehensive School (125L); Bristol United Press (88); David Bugler (223); Coed Park Library (148, 241); © Crown Copyright, NMR, Swindon (13); © Crown Copyright, Royal Commission on the Ancient and Historical Monuments of Wales, Aberystwyth: Aerofilms collection (8, 68, 192); *Glamorgan Gazette*: Media Wales Ltd (47, 102, 103, 104); Glascoed Archive BAE (83, 99, 121, 124, 125U, 178, 181, 182, 195, 196, 216); Mark Hoskins (86); Simon Hicks (67, 69); Institution of Civil Engineering (33, 35); Ron Meadows (65); Keith Morgan (144, 146); National Archive, Kew (54, 55, 56, 57, 58, 59); National Railway Museum, York (140, 141); Police Museum, Bridgend (70U, 186); David Power (80, 150); Megan Randall-Hall (167); *Rhondda Leader*: Media Wales Ltd (166, 236); *ROF53 News* (164, 177, 213, 255); *South Wales Echo*: Media Wales Ltd (23, 25, 52, 232); Trinity Mirror[1] (228, 234); Trustees of the Imperial War Museum, London[2] (126, 127, 153, 155, 157, 169); USA National Archive, Washington (243); *Western Mail*: Media Wales Ltd (20): Vera White (81, 112, 297).

Photographs on these pages were taken by myself: 70L, 75, 79, 191, 313, 316, 317.

1 Although these photos appeared in the Empire News originally, and the images are therefore now owned by Trinity Mirror, I obtained the photographs from a copy of the paper held at Y Llyfergell Genedlaethol Cymru / the National Library of Wales in Aberystwyth, so I acknowledge that permission.

2 It is a condition of a permission to use Imperial War Museum images that the negative numbers are noted. These are: D-006214, D-006249, D-006247, D-006330, D-006359, D-006232, D-006361, D-006350, D-006324

Index

Index

Index